LF

Perception
An Annotated Bibliography

Garland Reference Library of the Humanities (Vol. 39)

Perception
An Annotated Bibliography

Kathleen Emmett
and
Peter Machamer

Garland Publishing, Inc., New York & London

1976

Library of Congress Cataloging in Publication Data

Emmett, Kathleen.
   Perception : an annotated bibliography.

   (Garland reference library in the humanities ; vol. 39)
   Includes index.
   1. Perception--Bibliography. I. Machamer, Peter K.,
joint author. II. Title.
Z7204.P45E45   [BF311]   016.1537   75-24086
ISBN 0-8240-9966-4

Printed in the United States of America

Contents

Preface

The bibliography presented here is intended to provide a useful research tool for scholars and students of perception. The primary concentration of our efforts has been on the philosophical literature during the period of 1935-1974. We hope that the works listed in this area are reasonably complete, though we have deleted certain works that might have been listed as being too tangential, or, for some reason or another, as being unreasonable. In addition to these philosophical works on perception we have on occasion and at somewhat arbitrary discretion included works from other areas of philosophy and of other "academic" disciplines. We think that philosophers may find helpful especially those works listed in the psychology of perception. The works listed in these other areas are in no way complete. They represent our judgments as to what works have been or should be important to philosophers interested in perception.

Not all the works listed are annotated. It was felt that where the title of the article was reasonably indicative of its content, annotation was unnecessary; likewise some small notes and discussions are left uncommented upon. The annotations will seem to vary considerably in length and in the detail of description. This is primarily a function of the values and vagaries of the particular annotator at the time the annotation was made; it became clear early on that Dr. Emmett was far more assiduous than Dr. Machamer. We have attempted to keep the annotations descriptive and to some extent free from quality judgments; this was not always accomplished.

This project grew out of Machamer's large bibliography that he composed while researching for his article in the *American Philosophical Quarterly* (1970). A small unannotated part of this bibliography appeared at the end of that article. We have made use of later additions to this original work, as well as

PREFACE

bibliographical data provided us by David Sanford and James Cornman. The psychological material has been garnered from many perception seminars in the psychology department at Ohio State University and through discussions with many persons, most especially, Dean Owen. To all those mentioned above and to many other friends and colleagues we owe thanks for the help they have given.

Doing bibliographies is tedious and hard work, but it was undertaken and completed with the hope that however flawed the results turn out to be they will constitute an improvement over the present state of affairs and will be of some use to the professions that take perception as their subject matter. We would be happy to hear from anyone concerning suggestions they have about additional material.

Kathleen Emmett   University of Tennessee
Peter Machamer   The Ohio State University

ABBREVIATIONS USED:

A: Analysis

Amer Psych: American Psychologist

APQ: American Philosophical Quarterly

ASSP: Aristotelian Society Proceedings, Supplementary Volumes

BJPS: British Journal for the Philosophy of Science

Brit J Aes: British Journal of Aesthetics

I: Inquiry

IPQ: International Philosophical Quarterly

JAAC: Journal of Aesthetics and Art Criticism

Jour Exp Psych: Journal of Experimental Psychology

JP: Journal of Philosophy

J Physiol: Journal of Physiology

M: Mind

MS: Modern Schoolman

N: Nous

P: Philosophy

PAS: Proceedings of the Aristotelian Society

Phil Studies: Philosophical Studies

PPR: Philosophy and Phenomenological Research

PQ: Philosophical Quarterly

PR: Philosophical Review

PS: Philosophy of Science

Pysch Bull: Psychological Bulletin

Psych Rev: Psychological Review

R: Ratio

RIP: Revue Internationale de Philosophie

RM: Review of Metaphysics

S: Synthese

1. Aaron, R. I., "How May Phenomenalism be Refuted," PAS 39
        (1939), 167-184.
    Criticism of Braithwaite [#184].

2. _____, "The Causal Argument for Physical Objects,"
        ASSP 19 (1945), 57-76.
    Symposium with Ewing and McNabb. Gives an analysis of
    theoretical doubts concerning the existence of physical
    objects.

3. _____, "The Common Sense View of Sense-Perception,"
        PAS 58 (1958), 1-14.
    Discussion of how common-sense may be used to combat epis-
    temological dualism.

4. Aaronson, Doris, "Temporal Factors in Perception and Short-
        Term Memory," Psych Bull 67 (1967), 130-44.
    Reports studies of error in short-term memory and their
    relation to duration and presentation rate of stimulus. It
    is suggested that subjects may develop perceptual strate-
    gies to increase performance in short-term memory tasks.

5. Achinstein, Peter, "Theoretical Terms and Partial Inter-
        pretation," BJPS 14 (1964), 89-105.
    Discussion and criticism of the thesis of Partial Inter-
    pretation--a thesis held by Hempel, Carnap, Nagel, Braith-
    waite, etc., about the nature of theoretical terms and
    their difference from metaphysical terms.

6. _____, "The Problem of Theoretical Terms,"
        APQ 2 (1965), 193-203.
    Examination of theoretical/non-theoretical term distinction.
    Argues there is no unique set of criteria underlying this
    distinction.

7. Adams, E. M., "The Nature of the Sense-Datum Theory," M 67
        (1958), 216-26.
    Argues that the sense-datum theory represents an alterna-
    tive ontology, or conceptual framework, according to which
    the uncategorized "new given" is categorized differently
    than it would be on a view such as direct realism.

8. _____, "Perception and the Language of Appearing,"
        JP 55 (1958), 683-90.
    Distinguishes three types of perceptual 'seeming-' or
    'appearing-statements' and discusses the meanings of des-
    criptive terms used in each, as compared with their meanings
    in 'is-statements'.

9. _____, "Mind and the Language of Psychology," R 9
        (1967), 122-30.

10. _____, "The Inadequacy of Phenomenalism," PPR 20
    (1959), 93-102.
    Phenomenalism cannot provide a satisfactory account of what
    it is for a physical object statement to be equivalent to
    a series of sense-datum statements.

11. Adrian, E. D., The Physical Background of Sensation,
    (Oxford: Oxford University Press, 1947).

12. Agassi, Joseph, "Sensationslism," M 75 (1966), 1-24.
    Reviews and criticizes traditional arguments against the
    view that all knowledge comes to us via the senses and
    argues that recent versions of this view can also be
    refuted on updated grounds.

13. Aiken, L. S. and Brown, D. R., "A Feature utilization
    analysis of the perception of pattern class structure,"
    Perception and Psychophysics 9 (1971), 279-83.

14. Aldrich, Virgil C., "What We See With," JP 35 (1938), 253-
    63.
    Seeing is analogous to touching; sensations of color and
    texture occur where the optical organ (the eye plus physical
    illumination) touches an object. Optical organ is developed
    from infancy--in a sense we are all born blind.

15. _____, "A Note on Visual Data in Esthetic Per-
    spective," JP 39 (1942), 661-63.
    Elliptical appearance of suitably-placed round object is not
    a "given" but a constructed ("projected") shape. The shape
    is given as round. Phenomenological awareness involves
    cognitive activity.

16. _____, "What Appears?," PR 63 (1954), 232-40.
    What appears so-and-so is never a sense-datum. What
    appears is always either a physical object or an "image"
    (a kind of sensation).

17. _____, "Is An After-Image a Sense-Datum?,"
    PPR 15 (1954), 369-76.
    If after-images are sense-data then the latter are not
    present in most perceptual experiences. Both are discussed
    in terms of determinate/determinable distinction.

18. _____, "Images as Things and Things as
    Images," M 64 (1955), 261-63.
    Language of describing things held to be on a continuum
    with language of describing images. Ordinary things are
    not presented adequately enough to allow our description
    of them to count as strict observation statements.

19. _____, "Image-Mongering and Image-Management,"
    PPR 23 (1962), 51-61.
    Distinguishes several kinds of imagining and logical/

conceptual features of each. Imagining or seeing x as y
entails supposing x is not y.

20. _____, "A Point About Spaces," PPR 24 (1963),
397-401.
Discussion of contrast between seeing something as a physical object and seeing it as an aesthetic object. Not
everything appearing in physical space need appear as a
physical object--e.g., framed paintings.

21. _____, "On Seeing Bodily Movements as
Actions," APQ 4 (1967), 222-30.
Seeing walking as an action compared to hearing spoken
words as a complete speech act. Related to remarks about
intending and pretending. Seeing another's behavior as
an action involves perceiving many sub-(atomic) actions as
part of purposive activity.

22. _____, "Review of Dretske's Seeing and
Knowing," JP 67 (1970), 994-1006.

23. _____, "Sight and Light," APQ 11 (1974), 317-
22.
Offers a view of light, colors and vision that is neither
wholly physicalistic nor wholly mentalistic based on a
synthesis of fields of vision and light in the visual field
and its contents. Argues that the terms 'field of vision'
and 'field of illumination' are closely related and applies
this to Dretske's case of a man seeing colors through an
opaque wall.

24. _____, "Visual Noticing Without Believing,"
M 83 (1974), 512-33.
Discussion of Sibley's basic epistemic sense of 'see'.
Argues that focusing on something is sufficient for seeing,
and that concepts of optical focus and attending should not
be separated, nor should the physical and mental aspects of
vision. Criticizes Sibley and Dretske for confusing the
indeterminacy of belief with the indeterminacy of visual
noticing.

25. Alexander, Peter, "Theory-Construction and Theory-Testing,"
BJPS 9 (1958), 29-38.
Defends the "dictionary" view of scientific theories and
the relation between theoretical and observation-state-
ments. A reply to M. Hesse [#642].

26. _____, Sensationalism and Scientific Explanation, (London: Routledge and Kegan Paul, 1963).
An attack on a Machian form of sensationalism and a
sketchy but interesting account of explanation in science.

27. _____, "Inferences about Seeing," in Knowledge

3

and Necessity, Royal Institute of Philosophy Lectures,
Vol. 3, (London: MacMillan, 1970), 73-90.
Argues statements about simple seelings are transparent
contexts and allow inferences of the form "I see x; x is y;
therefore, I see y." There are other uses of 'see', 'saw',
etc. that do not license such inferences.

28. Allen, Diogenes, "Tactile and Non-tactile Awareness," M 78
    (1969), 567-70.
    There is a difference between tactile and other forms of
    awareness, consisting in how these awarenesses are attri-
    buted to us in a way that shows them to be mental. Assimi-
    lating other forms of awareness, like seeing, to the tac-
    tile led to the mistaken idea that awarenesses are identi-
    cal with brain states.

29. Allport, Floyd H., Theories of Perception and the Concept
    of Structure, (New York: Wiley, 1953).
    A classic review of pre-cognitive theories of perception.

30. Alston, William P., "Is a Sense-Datum Language Necessary?"
    PS 24 (1957), 41-45.
    There are no perceptual situations whose description
    requires use of a sense-datum terminology; such terminol-
    ogy is parasitic on ordinary discourse. Qualified defense
    of the theory of appearing.

31. Ames, A., Visual Perception and the Rotating Trapezoidal
    Window, (Washington: Am. Psychol. Assoc., 1951).
    A transactionalist approach to perception based on the
    account of the illusion of the trapezoidal window.

32. Anders-Stern, Guenther, "The Acoustic Stereoscope," PPR 10
    (1959), 238-43.

33. Angell, R. B., "The Geometry of Visibles," N 8 (1974), 87-
    117.
    The geometry that best accords with objects and their
    relationships in the visual field is non-Euclidean, two-
    dimensional and elliptical. Critical of Luneburg [#836].

34. Anscombe, G. E. M., "The Intentionality of Sensation: A
    Grammatical Feature" in R. J. Butler, ed., Analytical
    Philosophy, Second Series, (Oxford: Blackwell, 1965).
    Anscombe provides three criteria for intentionality and
    argues that they apply to sensation statements; this is a
    feature of the grammar of sensation statements.

35. Aqvist, Lennart, "Notes on A. J. Ayer's 'The Terminology of
    Sense-Data'," A 20 (1959), 106-11.

36. Arber, Agnes, The Mind and the Eye, (Cambridge: Cambridge
    University Press, 1954).

4

Interesting reflections on observation in science by a
biologist.

37. Ardley, Gavin, "The Nature of Perception," AJP 36 (1958),
189-200.
Argues that perception is a static situation, and that the
"signal picture" that most philosophers have used in
talking about perception is largely a heuristic device,
not to be taken literally.

38. Armstrong, D. M., "Berkeley's Puzzle about the Water that
Seems Both Hot and Cold," A 15 (1954), 44-46.
Solves the puzzle without sense-data by analyzing 'the
water seems hot to one hand and cold to the other' as 'the
water is hotter than one hand and colder than the other'.

39. _____, "Illusions of Sense," AJP 33 (1955), 88-
106.
Defends direct realism against difficulties raised by
illuminations and variations in appearance. Argues that
various sorts of illusions and hallucinations can be
analyzed in terms of false beliefs.

40. _____, Berkeley's Theory of Vision, (Melbourne:
Melbourne University Press; London and New York:
Cambridge University Press, 1960).
Valuable exegesis and analysis of Berkeley's New Theory of
Vision. Defends Berkeley's claim that we do not immediately
perceive the distance of objects by sight, which he restates
as the claim that the signs by which we judge of distance
by sight are not necessarily connected with the actual distance of the object. Includes a chapter on Hume on tastes
and smells, which he suggests is an extension of the theory
developed by Berkeley.

41. _____, Perception and the Physical World, (London: Routledge and Kegal Paul; New York: Humanities
Press, 1961).
Defends a direct realist position against representational-
ist and phenomenalist arguments. Perception said to be the
acquisition of beliefs or inclinations to believe certain
propositions about the material world. Sensory illusion is
explained in terms of inclinations to believe falsely that
some proposition is true. Distinguishes between immediate
and mediate perception; latter held to be based on a process of suggestion such that the beliefs acquired immediately produce an automatic transition to other beliefs.
Immediate perception is not incorrigible; these are immediate sensory illusions. Final chapters outline the difficulties inherent in the attempt to reconcile a Realistic
interpretation of physics with direct realism; these con-
cern the status of the secondary qualities. Gives an argument to show that it is impossible that objects should
possess only primary qualities.

5

42. _____, Bodily Sensations, (London: Routledge and
    Kegan Paul, 1962).
    Distinguishes two sorts of bodily sensations--transitive
    (warmth, pressure, motion) and intransitive (aches, pains,
    itches). The former are identified with bodily sense-
    impressions; immediate awareness of bodily states.
    Transitive bodily sensations can, unlike those that are
    intransitive, be identified with perceived sensible quali-
    ties of the body. Discusses and criticizes several
    accounts of intransitive bodily sensations. He arrives at
    an analysis of them as perceptions of disturbances in some
    portion of the body, and refines this account in order to
    meet objections. Concluding remarks deal with the implica-
    tions of such an account for a theory of secondary quali-
    ties.

43. _____, "Is Introspective Knowledge Incorrigi-
    ble?" PR 72 (1963), 417-32.
    Argues against his earlier view [#41, Ch. 4 and #42, Ch.
    9] that introspective knowledge is incorrigible, and that
    we have logically privileged access to our own mental
    states. Apprehension of a mental state must be distinct
    from the state itself; hence each can be conceived as an
    existing apart from the other. Objects of introspective
    awareness can exist when we are not aware of them.

44. _____, "A Theory of Perception," in B. B.
    Wolman ed., Scientific Psychology: Principles and
    Approaches, (New York: Basic Books, 1965), 489-505.
    Presents and defends the view that sense perception is a
    flow of knowledge or information about our environment.

45. _____, "The Secondary Qualities: An Essay in
    the Classification of Theories," AJP 46 (1968), 225-
    41.
    Distinguishes two three-fold accounts of secondary quali-
    ties. The Subjectivist, Lockean and Realist accounts are
    about the nature of such properties, while the Dualist,
    Attribute and Materialist accounts are about their loca-
    tion. There are nine possible permutations, and it is
    argued that each of the resulting views has actually been
    defended. Objections to each discussed.

46. _____, A Materialist Theory of Mind, (London:
    Routledge and Kegan Paul, 1968).
    A major attemt to account for mental concepts in such a
    way as to render central state materialism plausible. The
    basic account of perception given in [#41] remains
    unchanged; perception is the acquiring of beliefs about
    the material world. Here there is an extended discussion
    of what beliefs are, as well as an analysis of non-
    inferential (immediate) knowledge.

47.   _____, "Colour-Realism and the Argument from
            Microscopes," in Brown, R., and Rollins, C. D., eds.,
            Contemporary Philosophy in Australia, (London: Allen
            and Unwin, 1969), 119-31.
        Defense of color-realism--the view that colors exist in-
        dependently of their being perceived--against the argu-
        ments generated for color-relativity from facts about how
        colored things appear through microscopes. Argues that
        there is no logical basis for preferring "standard"
        viewing conditions to those provided by microscopes.

48.   _____, "Epistemological Foundations for a
            Materialist Theory of the Mind," PS 40 (1973), 178-93.
        Discussion and defense of materialist theory of mind. The
        most important elements of such a theory said to be that
        (1) mental processes are in fact nothing but physical pro-
        cesses in the brain and (2) phenomenal qualities are in
        fact identical with physicalistically respectable proper-
        ties.

49.   Arnheim, Rudolph, Art and Visual Perception: A Psychology
            of the Creative Eye, (Berkeley and Los Angeles:
            University of California, 1954).
        An attempt to apply a Gestalt-type theory of perception to
        problems of aesthetics and creativity.

50.   _____, Towards a Psychology of Art, (Berkeley:
            University of California Press, 1966).
        A collection of previously published essays and reviews.

51.   _____, Visual Thinking, (Berkeley: University
            of California Press, 1969).
        Claims all thinking is basically perceptual in nature and
        that the fundamental processes of vision involve mechanisms
        of reasoning. Discusses abstraction process, thinking in
        shapes and with words, and relation to art and education.

52.   _____, Entropy and Art, (Berkeley: University
            of California Press, 1971).

53.   _____, "Colors--Irrational and Rational," JAAC
            33 (1974), 149-54.
        A discussion of certain features of colors that have
        hindered a systematic theory of color-relationships.

54.   Arnoult, M. D., "Stimulus Predifferentiation: Some Gen-
            eralizations and Hypotheses," Psych Bull 54 (1957),
            339-50.
        Summary of articles and dissertations on stimulus pre-
        differentiation. Suggests what generalizations can be
        drawn from conflicting results and what evidence could be
        adduced in support of various explanatory hypotheses.
        Suggests that the consideration of additional variables
        might be of use in clarifying existing ambiguities.

7

55. Arthadeva, M., "Naive Realism and Illusions of Reflection,"
    AJP 35 (1957), 155-69.
    Analyses mirror-illusions so as to render them consistent
    with naive realism.

56. _____, "Naive Realism and Illusions: The Ellipti-
    cal Penny," P 34 (1959), 323-30.
    The penny that looks elliptical when seen from an angle is
    seen as having a shape it does not have; however, such
    cases should not be treated as illusions.

57. _____, "Naive Realism and the Illusions of Refrac-
    tion," AJP 37 (1959), 118-37.
    Naive realists cannot consistently allow a distinction
    between veridical and abnormal or delusive perceptions.
    The illusions of refraction can be explained within the
    framework of a consistent naive realism.

58. _____, "Mirror Images are Physical Objects: A
    Reply to Mr. Armstrong," AJP 38 (1960), 160-62.
    Raises doubts about Armstrong's claim that when a person
    sees a mirror-image he is mistakenly inclined to think
    they are seeing when in fact they are not.

59. _____, "Naive Realism and the Problem of Color-
    Seeing in Dim Light," PPR 21 (1960), 467-78.
    "Solves" the problem by suggesting that in the dark we do
    not see objects with altered colors because in fact we
    don't see objects. Likewise in dim light we are, to some
    degree, not seeing objects.

60. Ashby, W. R., Design for a Brain, (2nd edition; New York:
    Barnes and Noble, 1960)(1st edition; New York: John
    Wiley and Sons, Inc., 1952).
    Attempt to explain the nervous system's ability for adap-
    tive behavior. Mathematical statement of the theory in
    an appendix.

61. Attfield, R., "Berkeley and Imagination," P 45 (1970), 237-
    39.
    Reply to Woolhouse [#1450]. Berkeley was careful to dis-
    tinguish between illusions, fancy and dreams in Principles,
    paragraph 33.

62. Attneave, F., Applications of Information Theory to Psych-
    ology, (New York: Holt, Rinehart and Winston, 1959).
    An influential attempt to apply information-type talk to
    various areas of psychology including perception; math-
    ematically it does not succeed in any interesting way.

63. _____, "In Defense of Homunculi," in W. A. Rosen-
    blith, ed., Sensory Communication, (Cambridge: MIT
    Press, 1961), 772-82.

Answers to some current objections to the view that there is a perceiver--as it were a homunculus--inside the head who receives sensory input and directs the organism's responsive activity. Defends a neurophysiological model of such a homunculus.

64. _____, "Perception and Related Areas," in S. Koch, ed., Psychology: A Study of a Science, (New York: McGraw Hill, 1962), Vol. 4, 619-59.
Discussions of relationships between psychophysics and perception with special attention to work of S. S. Stevens on measurement of sensory magnitudes. New methods and results of psychophysical research discussed. Author gives a formal description of relationship between perceptual and information-processing mechanisms. Suggests that in a hierarchical representative system that includes both cognitive and perceptual functions those that are perceptual are "lower" in the hierarchy. Discussion of the extent to which perceptual functions are learned. Special attention to Osgood's behavioristic approach and to Rosenblatt's "perception" device. Includes bibliography.

65. _____, "Criteria for a Tenable Theory of Form Perception," in W. Wathen-Dunn, ed., Models for the Perception of Speech and Visual Perception, (Cambridge, Massachusetts: MIT Press, 1967), 395-408.

66. _____, "From Multistability in Perception," Sci Amer (1971), 63-71.
Visual inputs are matched to acquired or learned schemata of classes of objects. Identification consists in this process of matching; this can be used to account for ambiguous figures.

67. Atwell, John E., "Austin on Incorrigibility," PPR 27 (1966), 261-66.
Argues that incorrigibility is, contra-Austin, a function of the kind of sentence used in making a claim and that sense-datum statements are incorrigible in a slightly stronger sense than are physical-object statements.

68. Aune, Bruce, Knowledge, Mind and Nature, An Introduction to the Theory of Knowledge and the Philosophy of Mind, (New York: Random House, 1967).
Attack on foundational theories. Color is a primary concept, though science forces us ultimately to adopt a non-common-sensical theory.

69. Austeda, Franz, (trans. by A. E. Blumberg), "Phenomenalism," Encyclopedia of Philosophy, Vol. 6, p. 130.

70. _____, (trans by A. E. Blumberg), "Stoicism," Encyclopedia of Philosophy, Vol. 8, p. 21.

71. Austin, John L., "Other Minds," ASSP 20 (1946), 148-87.
       Reprinted in Philosophical Papers, (Oxford: Clarendon
       Press, 1961), 44-84.
     Distinguishes several types of answers given to the ques-
     tion "How do you know?" Important overlap with the prob-
     lem raised by Wittgenstien [#1428] concerning criteria for
     the correct application of a term--e.g., 'goldfinch'. Dis-
     cusses feasibility of empirical knowledge claims. Claims
     that while empirical judgments are predictive, certain
     outrageous future events would serve to make us revise our
     ideas about material things rather than falsify those
     judgments. Raises doubts about alleged certainty of "looks
     Ø to me" statements, and traces tendency to regard them as
     certain to use of 'know' in direct-object constructions.

72. _____, Sense and Sensibilia, (Oxford: Oxford
       University Press, 1962), reconstructed by G. J. War-
       nock.
     Lecture notes published posthumously. Attacks the sense-
     datum theory particularly as expounded by A. J. Ayer [#76].
     Defends the common-sense view of illusions and perceptual
     variations by appealing to how things look under various
     conditions. Such "looks" assimilated to actual properties
     of things rather than to extra-physical entities. Halluc-
     inations treated as a species of mental aberration. Con-
     cluding remarks deal with Warnock [#1375].

73. Avant, Lloyd L., "Vision in the Ganzfeld," Psych Bull 64
       (1965), 264-58.
     Summary of findings on experiments with exposure to struc-
     tureless visual fields. Such exposure is characterized by
     reports of "immersion in a sea of light" which distinguishes
     into figure and ground as brightness is increased. Some
     observers report complete cessation of all visual activity
     upon exposure to the ganzfeld, and this has been correlated
     with increased alpha activity in the brain.

74. Averill, Edward, "Perception and Definition," JP 55 (1958),
       690-99.
     Discusses how pains and after-images might be reconstructed
     so as to allow us to say that they are public objects.

75. Ayer, Alfred J., Language, Truth and Logic, (London: V.
       Gollancz, 1936; 2nd ed. 1946).
     In the context of classifying, revising and defending the
     principle of verifiability as a criterion for meaningful-
     ness of empirical statements Ayer sets out a reinterpre-
     tation of the problem of perception which, as he construes
     it, is the problem of giving a rule for translating sen-
     tences about a material thing into sentences about sense-
     contents. Such a rule presupposes an answer to the ques-
     tion "What is a material thing?" and this question is held
     to require a linguistic answer--a definition of 'material
     thing' in terms of which two sense-contents can be said to

10

be related to the same material thing. He holds that sense-
contents are in no way part of material things. The latter
are logical constructions out of the former and this is,
itself, a linguistic, not an empirical, claim.

76. _____, The Foundations of Empirical Knowledge,
     (London: Macmillan, 1940).
Defends a linguistic version of the sense-datum theory,
according to which talking about sense-data is conceived
as an alternative "language" to one in which the objects of
perceptual experience are material things. The occurrence
of certain sense-data is some, though never conclusive,
evidence for the existence of a material thing. There are
some empirical propositions, called "basic" or "experiental"
propositions that are indubitable descriptions of sensory
experiences. No set of such descriptions entails any
statement about the existence of a material thing because
statements about material things are never conclusively
verifiable.

77. _____, "The Terminology of Sense-data," M 54
     (1945), 289-312. Also in [#80], 66-104.
G. E. Moore's attempts to give directions for picking out
visual sense-data are inadequate, since identifying sense-
data requires prescribing rather than discovering the use
of the terms 'sense-datum' and 'directly apprehended.'
Claims about qualities of sense-data cannot be verified
empirically. Includes extensive reply to H. H. Price
[#1079]. Ayer reiterates and explains his claim that a
sense-datum language is logically prior to a physical thing
language.

78. _____, "Phenomenalism," PAS 47 (1947), 163-96.
     In [#80], 125-66.
Discussion of the role of sense-data as what, on phenomenalism, physical objects are logical constructions out of.
Includes an interesting attack on the act-object analysis
of sensation, and an attempt to show how one can talk about
sense-data in terms of "sense-fields" without presupposing
such an analysis. Rejects his former view that no physical
object statement can be conclusively verified. Were future
experiences of unexpected sorts to occur we would say the
object had been transformed or had ceased to exist, but not
that we had been wrong about it all along. Despite problems about possible sense-data, phenomenalism is basically
correct. Beliefs about physical objects should be treated
as constituting a theory to explain our sensory experiences.

79. _____, "Basic Propositions," in M. Black, ed.,
     Philosophical Analysis, (Ithaca: Cornell University
     Press, 1950), 60-74. Also in [#80], 105-124.
Discussion of what it means to say of an a priori and of
an empirical proposition that it is certain. An a priori
proposition may not be known for certain. Moore's claim

11

that an empirical proposition may be known for certain
examined, together with the reasons why philosophers find
Moore's arguments unconvincing. Ayer claims that statements describing one's immediate experience may be indubi-
table--whether any proposition is certain is a function of
the meaning-rules of the language.

80.   _____, Philosophical Essays, (London: Macmillan,
       1954).
Includes "Individuals," "The Identity of Indiscernibles,"
"Negation," "The Terminology of Sense-data," "Basic Propo-
sitions," "Phenomenalism, "Statements About the Past,"
"One's Knowledge of Other Minds," "On What There Is," "On
the Analysis of Moral Judgments," "The Principle of
Utility," and "Freedom and Necessity."

81.   _____, The Problem of Knowledge, (London: Mac-
       millan, 1956).
Discussion of perception is an elaboration and refinement
of view defended in [#76]. Emphasizes relationship between
my seeing x and its seeming to me that I see x. Ayer introduces the term 'seeming-x' to denote what is seen when it
seems to me that I see an x and defends the inference from
'it seems to me that I see x' to 'I perceive a seeming-x.'
Seeming-objects are then identified with sense-data.

82.   _____, "Perception," in C. A. Mace, ed., British
       Philosophy in Mid-Century, (London: George Allen and
       Unwin, 1957), 215-36.
Further discussion and defense of the sense-datum theory as
a linguistic recommendation. Qualified rejection of his
former defense of phenomenalism.

83.   _____, "Has Austin Refuted the Sense-Datum
       Theory?" S 17 (1967), 117-40. Reprinted in [#402].
A rejoinder to Austin.

84.   _____, "Rejoinder to Professor Forguson," in K.
       T. Fann, ed., Symposium on J. L. Austin, (New York:
       Humanities Press, 1969), 342-48.

85.   Ayers, Michael R., "Substance, Reality, and the Great, Dead
       Philosophers," APQ 7 (1970), 38-49.
Extended criticism of Jonathan Bennett [#118]. Argues
against reconstructing history of philosophy in terms of
contemporary dogmas. Extensive discussion of Locke and
Berkeley on substance and perception of primary and secondary qualities.

86.   _____, "Perception and Action," in Knowledge
       and Necessity, Royal Institute of Philosophy Lectures,
       Vol. 3, (London: Macmillan, 1970), 91-106.
Argues that perception is active and that this shows how
Locke, Berkeley and Strawson are wrong.

87. Bach, Kent, "A Criterion for Toothache?" Phil Studies 19
      (1968), 49-55.
      Argues against criterial views: there is only a contingent
      connection between characteristic toothache-behavior and
      toothaches, and the former is not a criterion for the
      latter.

88. Baird, John C., Psychophysical Analysis of Visual Space,
      (Oxford: Pergamon, 1970).

89. Bakan, Paul, ed., Attention: An Enduring Problem in
      Psychology, (New Jersey: Van Nostrand, 1966).
      An anthology including articles on various aspects of
      attention by William James, Titchener, Vernon, Gardner;
      Broadbent, Maltzman and Raskin; Bakan, Belton and Toth;
      Silverman; Hernandes-Péon; Deutsch and Deutsch.

90. Baker, M. J., "Perceptual Claims and Certainties," A 11
      (1950), 108-13.
      Discussion of the relationship between indubitable claims
      made in sincere first-person statements and physical ob-
      jects statements.

91. _____, "Perceiving, Imagining, and Being Mistaken,"
      PPR 14 (1953), 520-35.
      Discusses cases in which imagining can be mistaken for per-
      ceiving, and why we do not confuse modes of perception
      (e.g., seeing for hearing) except in rare cases when
      imagination is involved.

92. _____, "Seeing," PPR 15 (1953), 377-85.
      Analysis of the nature of the mistake involved in believing
      one sees something yellow and shortly thereafter realizing
      that one in fact sees something orange.

93. Balowitz, Victor H., "Persons as Subjects of Perception,"
      Personalist 53 (1972), 102-03.
      Imaginary situations do not succeed in showing that a non-
      Cartesian subject of visual experience can have more than
      one body. Where S sees from must be part of a body.

94. Bannan, John F., "Philosophical Reflection and the Pheno-
      menology of Merleau-Ponty," RM 8 (1954), 418-42.

95. Barker, S. F., "Appearing and Appearances in Kant," Monist
      51 (1967), 426-41.

96. Barnes, Winston H. F., "The Myth of Sense-Data," PAS 45
      (1944-45), 89-117. Also in [#1292].
      Criticism of sense-datum theories as defended by Broad and
      Price. Criteria for identity and individuation of sense-
      data are arbitrary. Rejects argument from variation in
      appearance. Sketches an alternative to the sense-datum
      theory along the lines of a multiple-relation theory of

appearance.

97. _____, "Talking About Sensations," PAS 54
        (1953-54), 261-78.
    Distinguishes several senses of 'feel', some of which are
    found to be related to perceiving, others to sensing. Dis-
    cusses the "privacy" of sensations, whether it is possible
    to observe sensations, whether sensations are "in the
    mind," and whether they exist when not perceived. Many
    interesting distinctions--the whole discussion is carried
    on with an eye to its relevance to the mind-body problem.

98. _____, "On Seeing and Hearing," in H. D.
        Lewis, ed., Contemporary British Philosophy III, (Lon-
        don: George Allen and Unwin Ltd., 1956), 63-81.
    Seeing and hearing are experiences a person has, and this
    in turn implies that seeing and hearing are private and
    immaterial. Argues against Ryle that 'see' is not primar-
    ily an achievement verb. Note made of the similarities and
    differences between seeing as an experience one has and the
    having (experiencing) of a sensation. Seeing and hearing
    are not physiological or mental states; they are "states of
    consciousness."

99. Bartlett, F. C., Remembering, (Cambridge: Cambridge Uni-
        versity Press, 1932).
    A classic book on memory which includes a widely accepted
    experimental paradigm for perceptual studies.

100. _____, "Some Problems in the Psychology of Tem-
        poral Perception," P 12 (1937), 457-65.

101. Bartley, S. H., Principles of Perception, 2nd edition,
        (New York: Harper and Row, 1969).
    Perception is the immediate discriminatory response of the
    organism to energy-activating sense organs. Perception is
    essentially constructive; there is a "symbolic" relation
    between the perceiver and what triggers the perceiving.

102. Baylis, Charles A., "The Given and Perceptual Knowledge,"
        in Philosophical Thought in France and the United
        States, (Buffalo, New York: University of Buffalo,
        1950).

103. _____, "Professor Chisholm on Perceiving," JP
        56 (1959), 773-91.

104. _____, "A Criticism of Lovejoy's Case for
        Epistemological Dualism," PPR 23 (1962), 527-37.

105. _____, "Perception and Sensations as Presen-
        tational," in F. C. Domneyer, ed., Current Philosophi-
        cal Issues, Essays in Honor of Curt Ducasse, (Spring-
        field, Illinois: C. L. Thomas, 1966).

14

106. _____, "Foundations for a Presentative
        Theory of Perception and Sensation," <u>PAS 66</u> (1966),
        41-54.
        Argues for direct realism.

107. Beardsley, D. C., and M. Wertheimer, eds., <u>Readings in
        Perception</u>, (New York: Van Nostrand, 1958).
        Anthology, works by: Clifford T. Morgan, Abram Hoffer,
        Ira J. Hirsh, Julian E. Hochberg, William Triebel, and
        Gideon Seaman, Kurt Koffka, D. Katz, George A. Miller,
        M. Wertheimer, J. M. Bobbitt, D. M. Michael, M. H. Mowatt,
        E. Mcalister, E. Rubin, D. E. P. Smith and W. H. Mikesell,
        M. Bentley, Hans Wallach, H. Helson, J. S. Bruner, L.
        Postman and J. Rodrigues, F. J. Langdon, A. H. Risen, R.
        Melzack and W. R. Thompson, W. H. Bexton, W. Heron, and
        T. H. Scott, W. Kohler, A. Michotte, H. Hoagland, L. L.
        LeShan, E. H. Hess, J. J. Gibson, W. H. Ittelson, and
        F. P. Kilpatrick, A. I. Hollowell and E. G. Boring, W. W.
        Lambert, R. L. Solomon, and P. D. Watson, S. S. Stevens,
        S. Wapner, Cheves W. Perky, U. Neisser.

108. Beardsley, M. C., "Problems of Aesthetics," <u>Encyclopedia
        of Philosophy</u>, Vol. 1, p. 36.

109. Beck, Lewis White, "Construction and Inferred Entities,"
        <u>PS 17</u> (1950), 74-86.

110. _____, "Psychology and the Norms of Knowledge,"
        <u>PPR 14</u> (1953), 494-506.
        Proposes a hierarchical model for briding the gap between
        the distinct concerns of the epistemologist and the
        psychologist in giving a causal theory of knowledge.

111. Bedford, E., "Seeing Paintings," <u>ASSP 40</u> (1966), 47-62.
        Symposium with R. Meager.
        Problem of seeing what paintings are "of".

112. Begbie, G. Hugh, <u>Seeing and the Eye</u>, (Garden City, New
        York: Anchor Books, 1973).
        An introductory discussion of the physics, physiology and
        psychology of the eye and vision.

113. Belaval, Yvon, "Le probleme de la perception chez
        Leibniz," <u>Dialogue</u> (Canada) <u>8</u> (1969-1970), 386-416.

114. Beloff, John, <u>The Existence of Mind</u>, (London: MacGibbon
        and Kee, 1962).

115. Benardete, José A., "Sense Perception and the <u>A Priori</u>,"
        <u>M 78</u> (1969), 161-77.

116. Benjamin, A. Cornelius, ."The Essential Problem of Empiri-
        cism," <u>PS 10</u> (1943), 13-17.
        Distinguishes two versions of empiricism according to which
        the experiencer is passive or active. Defends an active

version and suggests that such a theory requires an investigation of various types of mental operations.

117. Bennett, Jonathan, "Berkeley and God," P 40 (1965), 207-21.
An examination of Berkeley's two arguments for the existence of God.

118. _____, "Substance, Reality and Primary Qualities," APQ 2 (1965), 1-17.
Argues that Berkeley and most English-speaking philosophers since Berkeley have tended to conflate three distinct theories: (1) an account of what it is for a quality to be instantiated, (2) an account of the distinction between appearance and reality, and (3) an account of primary and secondary qualities.

119. Bentley, Arthur F., "Sights-Seen as Materials of Knowledge," JP 36 (1939), 169-81.
Introduces the term 'sight-seen' as a way of collapsing subject-object distinction.

120. _____, "The Fiction of the 'Retinal Image'," in S. Ratner, ed., Inquiry into Inquirers, (Boston: Beacon Press, 1954).

121. Bergmann, Gustav and Spence, Kenneth M., "The Logic of Psychophysical Measurement," Psych Rev 51 (1944).
A scientific empiricist (positivist) view of measurement, arguing that attributes should be defined by means of discriminatory responses to physical events or objects.

122. Bergmann, Gustav, "Sense Data, Linguistic Conventions, and Existence," PS 14 (1947), 152-63.
Discussion of Ayer's notion of a sense-datum terminology, with consideration given to the question what is involved in choosing a language or defining set of linguistic conventions in doing philosophy.

123. _____, "Professor Ayer's Analysis of Knowing," A 9 (1949), 98-106.
Defense of non-dispositional, non-relational account of the existence of mental acts.

124. _____, "Some Remarks on the Philosophy of Malebranche," RM 10 (1956), 207-26.
An ontological assay of Malebranche's accounts of perception and substance.

125. Berleant, Arnold, The Aesthetic Field: A Phenomenology of Aesthetic Experience, (Springfield: Thomas, 1970).

126. Berlin, Isiah, "Empirical Propositions and Hypothetical

Statements," M 59 (1950), 289-312.
Attack on phenomenalism in its recent linguistic versions.
Phenomenalism is not even plausible, even as a theory
about the translatability of material-object claims into
sense-datum statements.

127. Berlyne, Daniel, Structure and Direction in Thinking,
        (New York: Wiley, 1965).
     A psychological study of thought process in which curios-
     ity and subsequent attempts to satisfy it assume a role
     as the basis motivating factor in all thinking.

128. Bernstein, Richard J., "Sellars' Vision of Man-in-the
        Universe," RM 20 (1966), 113-43 and 290-316.
     Helpful exposition of the views of Wilfrid Sellars.

129. _____, "The Challenge of Scientific
        Materialism," IPQ 8 (1968), 252-75.
     Criticizes eliminative materialism.

130. Bertalanffy, L. von, "An Essay on the Relativity of Cate-
        gories," PS 22 (1955), 243-63.
     Asks to what extent the categories of our thinking depend
     on biological and cultural factors. Discusses Whorfian
     hypothesis and offers qualified defense of the possibility
     of absolute knowledge.

131. Bertocci, Peter A., "The Nature of Cognition: Minimum
        Requirements for a Personalistic Epistemology," RM 8
        (1954), 49-60.

132. Best, A. E., "Misleading Questions and Irrelevant Answers
        in Berkeley's Theory of Vision," P 43 (1968), 138-51.
     Much of the obscurity in Berkeley's New Theory of Vision
     is a consequence of his having relied implicitly on
     assumptions he sought to reject; and of his attempting to
     answer certain questions which legitimately arise only in
     the context of previous unacceptable theories.

133. Bird, Graham, "Subliminal Perception," PAS 73 (1973), 217-
        32.
     Certain cases of subliminal perception should be described
     as perception without awareness.

134. Birren, Faber, Color in Your World, (New York: Collier,
        (1972).
     A popular book.

135. _____, Color, Form and Space, (New York: Reinhold
        Publishing Company, 1961).

136. _____, Color Psychology and Color Therapy: A
        Factual Study of the Influence of Color on Human

Life, (New Hyde Park, New York: University Books, 1961).

137.   , Creative Color, (New York: Reinhold
         Publishing Company, 1961).

138.   , Light, Color and Environment: A Thorough
         Presentation of Facts on the Biological and Psycho-
         logical Effects of Color, (New York: Van Nostrand
         Reinhold Company, 1969).

139. Black, Max, "Comments on a Recent Version of Phenomen-
         alism," A 7 (1939), 1-12.
     Comment on Braithwaite [#184].

140.   , "The Language of Sense-Data," ("Phenomenal-
         ism"), in Science, Language and Human Rights,.
         (Philadelphia: University of Pennsylvania Press,
         1952). Symposium with R. Firth. (Reprinted in
         [#141].)

141.   , Philosophical Analysis (Ithaca, New York:
         Cornell University Press, 1954).
     Includes Chisholm's "Theory of Appearing" and Marhenke's
     "Phenomenalism" among other essays.

142.   , "How Do Pictures Represent?" in Gombrich,
         Hochberg and Black, Art, Perception and Reality,
         (Baltimore: Johns Hopkins University Press, 1972),
         95-130.

143. Blake, A. G. E., "Thinking," Systematics 9 (1971), 113-
         51.
     Comparison of thinking and perceiving.

144. Blake, R. R., and G. V. Ramsey, eds., Perception: An
         Approach to Personality, (New York: Ronald, 1951).
     Anthology, works by: Robert R. Blake, Clifford T. Mor-
     gan, Frank A. Beach, Ernest R. Hilgard, Jerome S. Bruner,
     Wayne Dennis, Alfred Korzybski, Urie Bronfenbrenner,
     James G. Miller, Norman Cameron, Carl R. Rogers, George
     S. Klein, Else Frenkel-Brunswik.

145. Blakemore, Colin and Cooper, Grahame F., "Development of
         the Brain Depends upon the Visual Environment,"
         Nature 228 (1970), 477-78.
     Kittens raised in environments that have only vertical or
     horizontal stripes are able to see only those stripes
     corresponding to the environments in which they were
     raised. The neurons of the visual cortex seem to adjust
     to the nature of the visual environment.

146. Blakemore, Colin and Mitchell, Donald E., "Environmental
         Modification of the Visual Cortex and the Neural

Basis of Learning and Memory," Nature 241 (1973), 467-68.
Details concerning the modifications of the visual cortex of kittens raised in differing visual environments.

147. Blanche, R., La Notion de fait Psychique: Essai sur les rapports da physique et du mental, (Paris: Alcan, 1935).

148. Blanshard, Brand, The Nature of Thought, (London: Allen and Unwin, 1939).
A classic idealist statement on the problems of mind.

149. _____ and Skinner, B. F., "The Problem of Con-sciousness--A Debate," PPR 27 (1966), 317-37.
An interesting debate between a humanistic philosopher and the arch-behaviorist.

150. _____, "Review of Nature, Mind and Modern Science," PQ 5 (1955), 166-74.

151. Blau, J. L., "Idealism," Encyclopedia of Philosophy, Vol. 4, 116.

152. Block, Irving, "Truth, and Error in Aristotle's Theory of Sense Perception," PQ 11 (1961), 1-9.

153. _____, "On the 'Commonness' of the Common Sen-sibles," AJP 43 (1965), 189-95.

154. Blocker, Harry, "Physiognomic Perception," PPR 29 (1969), 337-90.
A discussion of a type of perception in which expressive qualities are seen as belonging to "faces" of natural objects.   Related to work of Arnheim and Werner.

155. Blomberg, Jaako, "Psychophysics, Sensation and Informa-tion," Ajatus 33 (1971), 106-37.
Information-flow account of perception.

156. Blumfeld, David C., "On Not Seeing Double," PQ 9 (1959), 264-66.

157. Blyth, John W., "A Discussion of Mr. Price's 'Perception'," M 44 (1935), 58-67.

158. Boas, George, "The Perceptual Element in Cognition," PPR 12 (1951), 486-94.
Discusses the nature and degree of information conveyed by a simple sentence like "I am seeing a yellow patch." Attempts to raise doubts concerning the feasibility of the empiricist contention that all knowledge is based on per-ceptual experience.

19

159. Boden, Margaret A., "Machine Perception," PQ 19 (1969), 33-45.
There is no conceptual impossibility in supposing that finite-state (Turing) machines could be capable of the tasks we associate with perceiving. Machine-behavior may be characterized both mechanically and intentionally.

160. _____, Purposive Explanation in Psychology, (Cambridge, Massachusetts: Harvard University Press, 1972).
Presents a teleological model for psychological explanations (based on McDougall) that purports to reconcile hierarchist explanatory patterns with purposive patterns. Perception is often used as an example.

161. Bohm, D., The Special Theory of Relativity, (New York: Benjamin, 1965), Appendix: "Physics and Perception."

162. Bohnen, Alfred, "On the Critique of Modern Empiricism: Observational Language, Observational Facts and Theories," R 11 (1969), 38-57. (Translated from the German.)
Discussion of the empiricist position on the foundations of knowledge with special attention to current developments in psychology of perception.

163. Bohr, Niels, Atomic Theory and the Description of Nature, (Cambridge: Cambridge University Press, 1961, originally, 1935).
A collection of articles and addresses. Most are popular discussions of problems of observation and description with quantum theory; includes his article on Einstein.

164. _____, "Discussion with Einstein on Epistemological Problems in Atomic Physics," in P. Schilpp, ed., Albert Einstein, (Evanston, Illinois: Northwestern University Press, 1949).
On observation problems connected with quantum theory; a very clear discussion with a reply by Einstein in the same volume.

165. Boring, Edwin G., The Physical Dimensions of Consciousness, (New York: Century, 1933).
A famous statement on the physiological process involved in perception.

166. _____, Sensation and Perception in the History of Experimental Psychology, (New York: Appleton-Century-Crofts, 1942).
The most famous history of perception; a mine of information.

167. _____, "The Relation of the Attributes of

Sensation to the Dimension of the Stimulus," PS 2
(1935), 236-45.
Attacks the view that the four classical attributes of
sensation (quality, intensity, extensity and portensity)
are to be correlated with four aspects of a stimulus.

168. Borst, C. V., "Perception and Intentionality," M 79
(1970), 115-121.
Attack on Anscombe [#34]. Borst rejects thesis that perceptual verbs are intentional. Defends an Austinian
approach according to which only in exceptional cases do
such verbs take objects that may not exist.

169. Bouman, Jan C., The Figure-Ground Phenomenon in Experimental and Phenomenological Psychology, (Stockholm:
Fallmarks Boktryckeri, 1968).
Includes a description of phenomenological psychology and
its methodological differences from physical psychology.
Author presents findings of many subsequent researchers
in the figure-ground phenomenon, arguing that not much
significant has been added to work by Edgar Rubin. Proposes phenomenological analysis of the figure-ground
phenomenon. References to experimental research in
English, German, French and Swedish.

170. Bouwsma, O. K., "Moore's Theory of Sense-Data," in T.
Schilpp, ed., The Philosophy of G. E. Moore,
(Evanston, Illinois: Northwestern University Press,
1942), 203-21.
Critical analysis of Moore's definition of 'sense-data'.
Bouwsma suggests Moore's instructions for picking our
sense-data are ill-conceived; this point expanded into
critique of Moore's conception of the sense-datum controversy.

171. _____, "Descartes' Skepticism of the Senses," M
54 (1945), 313-22.
Characteristically delightful and inciteful discussion of
the dream argument.

172. _____. "Reflections on Moore's Recent Book," PR
64 (1955), 248-63.
Review of G. E. Moore's Some Main Problems of Philosophy.

173. Bower, T. G. R., Development in Infancy, (San Francisco:
W. H. Freeman, 1974).
A general text on developmental psychology, with an
exceptionally good chapter (V) on object perception.

174. _____, "Slant Perception and Shape Constancy in
Infants," Science 151 (1966), 832-33.
Infants of 50 and 60 days old possess some capacity for
shape constancy. Constancy results from invariants in
the environment.

175. _____, "The Visual World of Infants," Sci Amer
215 (1966), 80-92.
Experiments measuring infant responses to stimuli of various shapes and sizes suggest that infants register most
of the information that an adult does, but can handle less
of it. This conflicts with the traditional theory that
infants receive only fragmentary information that is used
in constructive processes to produce an ordered perceptual world.

176. Boyne, Chris, "Vagueness and Colour Predicates," M 81
(1972), 576-77.
If x is F (a color somewhere between red and orange), the
author thinks 'x is red' will always be true and this will
not entail 'x is not orange'.

177. Boynton, R. M., "Some Temporal Factors in Vision," in
S. A. Rosenblith, ed., Sensory Communication,
(Cambridge: MIT Press, 1961), 739-56.
Report of three psychophysical experiments involving temporal relations in vision. High-intensity short flashes
can look brighter than longer flashes of the same intensity, thus reinforcing the classical Broca-Sulzer effect.
Discrimination may vary depending on whether the eye has
just been exposed to an increased level of stimulation or
whether it has been allowed to adapt to it. The third
involves measuring the test-flash thresholds in the presence of a 30-cps flickering stimulus. Includes bibliography.

178. _____, "The Visual System: Environmental Infor-
mation," in Edward C. Carterette and Morton P.
Friedman, eds., Handbook of Perception, Vol. 1 (New
York: Academic Press, 1974), 285-307. Reply by
Gibson, 309-12.
Gibson's use of a stationary convergence point does not
fit with the requirements for an optical device with
decent sensitivity and resolving power.

179 Bradley, R. D., "Avowals of Immediate Experience," M 73
(1964), 186-203.
Argues against the unfalsifiability or incorrigibility
of first-person avowals of experience.

180. Brain, W. Russell, "The Neurological Approach to the
Problem of Perception," P 21 (1946), 133-46.
Neurological account of the causation of sense-data and
discussion of how this is to be reconciled with the
phenomenon of immediacy of sense-data.

181. _____, Mind, Perception and Science, (Springfield, Illinois: C. H. Thomas, 1951)

182. _____, The Nature of Experience, (Oxford

University Press, 1959).
The author is a neurologist who attempts to bring his
scientific knowledge to bear on philosophical problems,
often with interesting results.

183. _____, "Space and Sense-Data," BJPS 11 (1960),
177-91.
Argues that neurophysiological findings necessitate some
sort of sense-datum theory but that such a theory can be
held without postulating a multiplicity of private spaces
to account for hallucinations.

184. Braithwaite, R. B., "Propositions About Material Objects,"
PAS 38 (1938), 269-90.
Sentences expressing propositions about material objects
are defined by a verificationist method; it is then
argued that such propositions are weakly verifiable.

185. Brandt, Herman F., The Psychology of Seeing, (New York:
Philosophical Library, 1945).

186. Braunstein, M. L., "The Perception of Depth Through
Motion," Psych Bull 59 (1962), 422-33.

187. Breton, Stanislas, "Rationalite, Oaverture, Experience,"
RIP 24 (1970, fasc. 3, 4).

188. Brink, Lars, "Experience, Reality and Conditions for Description," I 11 (1968), 85-100.
Description and analysis of Peter Zinkernagel's Omverdens-
problemet.

189. Brittan, Jordon J., Jr., "Measurability, Commonsensibility,
and Primary Qualities," AJP 47 (1969), 15-24.
Primary qualities are (but secondary goals are not)
measurable and/or perceived by more than one sense.

190. Britton, Karl, "On Public Objects and Private Objects,"
Monist 46 (1936), 190-210.

191. _____, "Seeming," ASSP 26 (1952), 195-214.
Symposium with Price and Quinton.

192. Broad, C. D., An Examination of McTaggert's Philosophy,
(Cambridge, Cambridge University Press, 1939).
See especially, Volume II, section VII.

193. _____, "Professor Marc-Wogau's Theorie Der Sinnes-
data," M 56 (1947), 1-30 and 97-131.

194. _____, "The Relevance of Psychical Research to
Philosophy," P 24 (1949), 291-309.
Argues that psychical research is highly relevant to
philosophy since the results of such research seem to

23

conflict with the basic limiting principles that are provided by ordinary experience and scientific theories.

195. _____, "Some Elementary Reflexions on Sense-
          Perception," P 27 (1952), 3-17.
      Phenomenological account of seeing, hearing and feeling
      contrasted with the epistemological role played by such
      experiences.

196. _____, "Reply to My Critics," in P. Schilpp, ed.,
          The Philosophy of C. D. Broad, (New York: Tudor,
          1959).

197. Broadbent, D. E., Perception and Communication, (London
          and New York: Pergamon, 1958).
      Pioneering work on uses of information and communication
      theory in psychology. An information theory of perception
      is developed.

198. _____, "Attention and the Perception of Speech,"
          Sci Amer 206 (April, 1962), 143-51.
      When two voice messages are simultaneously presented to a
      listener only one of the messages is understood. This is
      taken to show that the brain contains a mechanism for
      attending to and selecting desired information.

199. _____, Decision and Stress, (New York: Academic
          Press, 1971).

200. Broadley, M. C., "A Note on a Circularity Argument," AJP
          42 (1966), 91-94.
      Criticizes D. M. Armstrong's argument [#41] for the claim
      that it is logically impossible for a physical body to
      have only primary qualities.

201. Brody, B. A., "On the Ontological Priority of Physical
          Objects," N.5 (1971), 139-55.
      Criticizes Strawson's arguments [#1286] for the ontolog-
      ical priority of physical objects and offers alternative
      supporting arguments for such a view.

202. _____, "Reid and Hamilton on Perception," Monist 55
          (1971), 423-41.

203. Bronaugh, Richard N., "The Argument from the Elliptical
          Penny," PQ 14 (1964), 151-57.
      This typical argument used in support of sense-data is
      seen to involve a mistaken inference. The distinction
      between sensation and perception is likened by the author
      to that between seeing and seeing as.

204. Brotherston, Bruce W., "Sensuous and Non-sensuous Percep-
          tion in Empirical Philosophy," JP 40 (1943), 589-97.
      Discussion of Dewey and the function of "non-sensuous"
      perception.

205. Brown, Harold, "Perception and Meaning," _APQ Monograph
     Series_, No. 6, (1972), 1-9.
     The primary purpose of perception is to provide us with
     information about the world. Different individuals obtain
     different information in a given perceptual situation
     depending on their needs and previous knowledge. To
     identify an object is to be aware of a meaning, and so
     the object of any significant perceptual experience is a
     meaning.

206. Brown, Norman, "Sense-data and Material Objects, _M 66_
     (1957), 173-94.
     Once representationalism is rejected the sense-datum
     theory can be shown to play an important role in empiri-
     cist philosophy.

207. Brown, S. C., ed., _Philosophy of Psychology_, (New York:
     Harper and Row, 1974).
     A collection of papers presented at a conference on the
     Philosophy of Psychology at the University of Kent in 1971
     (sponsored by the Royal Institute of Philosophy).
     Included in a section on Perception are the following:
     Gregory, R. L., "Perceptions as Hypotheses," 195-210.
     Anscombe, G. E. M., "Comments on Professor Gregory's
     Paper," 211-20. Vesey, G. N. A., "Chairman's Remarks,"
     221-30.

208. Browning, Lorin, "On Seeing Everything Upside Down," _A 34_
     (1973), 48-49.
     Reply to N. G. E. Harris [#602]. The claim that someone
     else sees everything upside down is not a testable claim
     since there is no external standard by which objects in
     one's visual field could be located.

209. Bruner, Jerome S. and Goodman, Cecile C., "Value and Need
     as Organizing Factors in Perception," _J. Abnormal
     and Social Psych 42_ (1947), 33-44.
     Claims that what an organism sees represents a compromise
     between what is presented and motivational factors. Coins,
     socially valued objects, were judged by subjects to be
     larger in size than gray discs and the greater the value
     of the coin the greater is the deviation of apparent size
     from actual size.

210. Bruner, Jerome S. and Postman, Leo, "On the Perception of
     Incongruity: A Paradigm," _J. Pers 18_ (1949), 206-23.
     An organism will fail to perceive the unexpected or incon-
     gruous as long as possible. Uses an experiment involving
     trick cards to establish compromise reactions of per-
     ceivers to elements that fail to fit their expectations or
     set.

211. Bruner, Jerome S., and D. Krech, eds., _Perception and
     Personality_, (Greenwood Press, Publishers: New York,

1968 (originally, 1959)).
Anthology, works by: J. S. Bruner and D. Krech, Karl
Zener, Heinz Werner, Hans Wallach, Leo Postman, George S.
Klein and Herbert Schlesinger, Edward C. Tolman, G.
Murphy, Egon Brunswik, Seymour Wapner, Else Frenkel, H. A.
Witkin, Robert A. McCleary and Richard S. Lazarus, Julian
E. Hochberg and Henry Gleitman, Jane W. Torrey, Elliott
McGinnies and Warren Bowles, D. C. McClelland and Alvin
M. Liberman, James M. Vanderplas and Robert R. Blake.

212.   Bruner, Jerome S., "On Perceptual Readiness," Psych Rev
       64 (1957), 123-52.
       Perception involves categorization. Veridical perception
       is adequate categorization, where adequacy is shown by
       trial and error actions based upon the categorization.
       Perceptual readiness is specified by the level of acces-
       sibility of a given category.

213.   _____, "The Course of Cognitive Growth," Amer
       Psych 19 (1964), 1-15.
       Concerned with the transition from iconic to symbolic
       representation.

214.   _____, Beyond the Information Given: Studies
       in the Psychology of Knowing, (edited by Jeremy M.
       Anglini) (New York: W. W. Norton, 1973).
       A collection of Bruner's classic papers; Section 1 is on
       perception.

215.   Brunswick, Egon, "Psychology as a Science of Objective
       Relations," PS 4 (1937), 227-60.
       A famous psychologist's statement of creed. Very worth-
       while.

216.   _____, Perception and the Representative Design
       of Psychological Experiments, (Berkeley and Los
       Angeles: University of California, 1949).
       A classic statement of the author's probabalistic theory
       of perception (i.e., the probability of occurrences of
       kinds of events in the perceiver's environment). Includes
       an important statement on experimental design.

217.   _____, The Conceptual Framework of Psychology,
       in O. Neurath, et. al., International Encyclopedia of
       Unified Science, (Chicago: University of Chicago
       Press, 1952), Vol. 1, 1-102. (Also printed separ-
       ately.)
       Argues that novel kinds of research designs are needed to
       make psychology "objective" but that these are not incom-
       patible with the unity of all sciences. A review of many
       theories with an attempt at constructive criticism; all
       things tend toward functionalism.

218.   _____, "Scope and Aspects of the Cognitive

Problem," in Contemporary Approaches to Cognition, (Cambridge, Massachusetts: Harvard University Press, 1957), 5-31.

219. Brunton, J. A., "Berkeley and the External World," P 28 (1953), 325-41.
Discussion of Berkeley's claim that the absolute existence of unthinking things involves a logical contradiction.

220. Bucklew, John, "The Subjective Tradition in Phenomenological Psychology," PS 22 (1955), 289-99.

221. Buchler, Justice, "On the Class of Basic Sentences," M 48 (1939), 484-90.

222. Bunge, Mario, "New Dialogues Between Hylas and Philonous," PPR 15 (1954), 192-99.

223. Burgener, R. J. C., "Price's Theory of the Concept," RM 11 (1957), 143-59.

224. Burlingame, C. E., "After-Images," M 81 (1972), 443-44.
Argues that after-images are sensations, rather than perceived objects.

225. Butter, C. M., Neuropsychology: The Study of Brain and Behavior, (Belmont: Brooks/Cole, 1968).
A useful textbook with a good discussion of the work on vision and the visual cortex by Hubel and Wiesel.

226. Cahn, S. M., "Change," Encyclopedia of Philosophy, Vol. 2, p. 77.

227. Cain, W. S., and Marks, L. E., ed., Stimulus and Sensation: Readings in Sensory Psychology, (Boston: Little, Brown and Co., 1971).
Articles by Stevens, Miller, James, Cattell, Woodworth, Blough, Thurstone, Garner and others.

228. Calhoun, Edward, "Human Likeness and the Formation of Empirical Concepts," RM 13 (1959), 383-95.
Discusses concept-formation in terms of the perception of the likeness of an experiencer to himself.

229. Campbell, C. A., "Sense-Data and Judgment in Sensory Cognition," M 56 (1957), 289-316.
Sensation analyzed in terms of a judgment evoled by sense-datum.

230. Campbell, Donald T., "Methodological Suggestions From a Comparative Psychology of Knowledge Processes," I 2 (1959), 152-82.
Comparative psychology of knowledge can provide insights into problems in the social sciences.

231.   _____, "Pattern Matching as Essential in Dis-
        tal Knowing," in K. R. Hammond, ed., The Psychology
        of Egon Brunswick, (New York: Holt, Rinehart and
        Winston, 1966), 81-106.

232.   _____, "Evolutionary Epistemology," in P.
        Schilpp, ed., The Philosophy of Karl Popper,
        (LaSalle, Illinois: Open Court, 1974).

233.   Campbell, F. W. and Kulikowski, J. J., "Orientational
        Selectivity of the Human Visual System," J Physiol
        187 (1966), 437-45.

234.   Campbell, Keith, "Colours," in R. Brown and C. D. Rollins,
        eds., Contemporary Philosophy in Australia, (London:
        Allen and Unwin, 1969), 132-57.
        Colors are not, strictly speaking, properties of what is
        seen; rather they are powers to bring about effects in
        observers.

235.   Cantril, H., ed., The Morning Notes of Adelbert Ames,
        (includes correspondence with John Dewey), (New
        Jersey: Rutgers University Press, 1960).
        Discussion of the original Ames' experiments and their
        implications.

236.   Capek, Milec, "The Development of Reichenbach's Epistem-
        ology," RM 11 (1957), 42-67.
        Critique of Reichenbach's philosophy of science.

237.   Caplan, David, "A Note on the Abstract Readings of Verbs
        of Perception," Cognition 2 (1973), 269-77.

238.   Care, Norman S. and Grimm, Robert H., eds., Perception
        and Personal Identity (Proceedings of the 1967
        Oberlin Colloquium in Philosophy), (Cleveland: Case
        Western Reserve Press, 1969).
        Contains: Popkin, Richard H., "The Sceptical Origins of
        the Modern Problem of Knowledge." Fogelin, Robert J.,
        "Thinking and Doing." Dretske, Fred I., "Seeing and
        Justification." Hugh, Philip, "Comments on Dretske."
        Chisholm, Roderick M., "The Loose and Popular and the
        Strict and Philosophical Senses of Identity." Shoemaker,
        Sydney S., "Comments on Chisholm." Hintikka, Jaakko, "On
        the Logic of Perception." Clark, Romane, "Comments on
        Hintikka."

239.   Carnap, Rudolph, "Testability and Meaning," PS 3 and 4
        (1936-7), 420-71 and 2-40.
        Classic article in positivistic philosophy of science;
        argues that observations are unproblematic.

240.   Carrier, David, "Three Kinds of Imagination," JP 70 (1973),
        819-31.

There is no need for a division in the unity of self
generated by the requirement that one can both do something and imagine doing it.

241. Carrier, L. P., "Immediate and Mediate Perception," JP 66
       (1969), 391-402.
       The distinction between immediate and mediate perception
       can be drawn along purely grammatical lines. Once drawn
       it leads to no conclusions regarding the status of sense-
       impressions.

242. _____, "The Time-Gap Argument," AJP 47 (1969),
       263-72.
       The premises of the time-gap argument are true, though the
       conclusion may be rejected. What we see in the case of
       exploded stars is light--hence not something non-physical.

243. _____, "Time-Gap Myopia," AJP 50 (1972), 55-57.
       A reply to Charles B. Daniels [#320]. Carrier reasserts
       his original conclusion that light is perceived when what
       one "sees" is a non-existent star.

244. Carsetti, A., "Visual Perception and Systems of Pattern
       Recognition," Scientia 107 (1972), 477-93.
       Survey of significant studies in field of neurophysiology
       of vision, pattern recognition and simulation of percep-
       tual processes by automata. Author proposes guidelines
       for an advanced situation of the recognition of complex
       forms of a conceptual nature and of the simulation of
       this type of recognition by artificial intelligence.

245. Carter, William R., "Locke on Feeling Another's Pain,"
       PS 23 (1972), 280-85.
       Argues that Don Locke's distinction between "having
       (owning) a pain" and "feeling a pain" cannot be sustained.

246. Carterette, Edward C. and Friedman, Morton P., eds.,
       Handbook of Perception: Vol I: Historical and
       Philosophical Roots of Perception, (New York:
       Academic Press, 1974).
       Philosophical articles by Firth, Yost, Harman, Deutscher.
       Historical articles by Werthrimer, Earhard, Metzger,
       Berlyne, Royce. Contemporary approaches discussed by
       Hochberg, Rozeboom, Dowling and Roberts, Gregory, Boynton,
       Gibson, Hater, Suppes and Rottmayer, Vurpillot,
       Føllesdall, and Dallet.
       Vol. II: Psychophysical Judgment and Measurement.
       Articles by Jones, Garner, Galanter, Sandusky, Parducci,
       Upshaw, Holman and Marley, Anderson, Luce and Green,
       Stevens, Carroll and Wish, Indow.
       Vol. III: Biology of Perceptual Systems.
       Articles by Roberts, Stevens, Horridge, Kruger and Stein,
       Tretarthen, Schleidt, Thomas, Sutherland, Wenzel, Burgess,
       Taylor, Lederman and Gibson, Howard, Hensel, Abramov and

Gordon, Maserton and Diamond, Webster.

247. Cassirer, Ernst, "The Concept of Group and the Theory of
     Perception," PPR 5 (1944), 1-3 (originally 1938 in
     German).

248. _____, Das Erkenntnisproblem, (Berlin: B.
     Cassirer, 1907; English translation, Yale University
     Press, 1950).

249. _____, Philosophie der Symbolische Formen, 3
     vols., (Berlin: B. Cassirer, 1923-31; English trans-
     lation, Yale University Press, 1953-7).
     A particular·Cassirer version of neo-Kantian categorical
     theory of perception. See volume 3, Phenomenology of
     Experience.

250. Chandler, J. H., "Incorrigibility and Classification,"
     AJP 48 (1970), 101-06.
     We cannot have incorrigible knowledge of our own current
     mental states because any description of such states
     involves classification which, in turn, relies on (fal-
     lible) memory. Argues that memory is involved in
     identifying a property (e.g., crimson) that is being
     currently observed, and thus that we have no incorrigible
     awareness of such properties.

251. Chapman, H. Wallis, "Colour," P 12 (1937), 443-56.
     Given that colours are not qualities of objects (since
     they vary with conditions of observation) author attempts
     to explain the meanings of colour-terms.

252. Chari, C. T. K., "On the 'Space' and 'Time' of Hallucina-
     tions," BJPS 8 (1957), 302-06.
     We have no criteria or measurements for determining the
     geometry of hallucinatory spaces or hallucinated figures.

253. Chessick, Richard D., "The Application of Neurological
     Studies in an Approach to some Philosophical Prob-
     lems," PS 20 (1953), 300-12.
     Application of neurophysiology to problems of aesthetics
     and cosmology.

254. Child, Arthur, "Projection," P 42 (1967), 20-36.
     The title refers to the subject's act of adding something
     to his experience of objects which he mistakes for some-
     thing belonging to the objects. This notion used to dis-
     cuss theories of perception.

255. Chisholm, Roderick M., "The Problem of the Speckled Hen,"
     M 51 (1942), 368-73.
     One's immediate experience of a visual datum of a speckled
     hen does not provide an answer to the question how many
     speckles the datum comprises.

256. _____, "Russell on the Foundations of
     Empirical Knowledge," in Schilpp, ed., The Philosophy
     of Bertrand Russell, (Evanston, Illinois: North-
     western University Press, 1944).

257. _____, "The Problem of Empiricism," JP 45
     (1948), 512-17.
     A critique of C. I. Lewis [#811]. Chisholm argues against
     the thesis that thing-statements analytically entail sense-
     datum statements, and that the former are translatable into
     the latter.

258. _____, "The Theory of Appearing," in Max
     Black, ed., Philosophical Analysis, (Ithaca: Cornell
     University Press, 1950), 102-18.
     Proposes an alternative to sense-datum terminology. It is
     maintained that although we can say anything we wish to
     about perception without explicit reference to sense-data
     we cannot avoid talking about the sorts of facts to which
     sense-datum theorists refer, and that talking instead about
     how objects appear to us does eliminate multiplication of
     entities. There are further metaphysical puzzles involved
     in the theory of appearing, however; e.g., that nothing
     appears when there are no perceivers.

259. _____, "Reichenbach on Observing and
     Perceiving," PS 2 (1951), 45-48.
     Criticism of Reichenbach's suggestion that perceiving an
     object is to be understood as being in a certain bodily
     state which is physically necessary for observing that
     object. Chisholm suggests that the requisite bodily state
     must be characterized in greater detail.

260. _____, "Verification and Perception,"
     RIP 5 (1951), 251-67.
     Perceiving may invite three sorts of mistakes: mistakes
     about the existence of physical things; mistakes about
     characteristics of an appearance; and mistakes about
     whether one is being appeared to at all (as in madness
     and hallucinations).

261. _____, "Ducasse's Theory of Properties
     and Qualities," PPR 13 (1952), 42-56.

262. _____, "Sellars' Critical Realism," PPR
     15 (1954), 33-47.
     A qualified defense of Roy Wood Sellars' view concerning
     the role of appearances in perception.

263. _____, "'Appear', 'Take', and 'Evident',"
     JP 53 (1956), 722-39. Reprinted in [#1292].
     Analyzes 'There is something such that S perceives that it
     is f' in terms of there being something that S takes to be
     f, S having adequate evidence for the proposition or

hypothesis that the thing is f, and the thing being f. Attempts to define the notions of 'taking' and 'adequate evidence' without employing 'see', 'hear' and 'perceive'.

264. _____, "Epistemic Statements and the Ethics of Belief," PPR 16 (1956), 447-60.

Defines epistemic terms (including 'know', 'certain', 'evident') in terms of the undefined notion 'S ought to refrain from accepting h.' Suggests that 'S sees x' is to be defined in terms of 'S knows that ...' rather than 'S is certain that ...'.

265. _____, Perceiving: A Philosophical Study, (Ithaca: Cornell University Press, 1957).
Part One treats epistemic uses of terms 'perceive', 'know', and 'evident'. Part Two attempts to give necessary and sufficient conditions for having adequate evidence for the truth of a proposition in wholly non-epistemic terms. Part Three contains discussions of epistemic and non-epistemic uses of perceptual terms and relations of these to the terminology of appearing. Includes criticism of behavioral theories of belief.

266. _____, "Intentionality and the Mental," in Feigl, Scriven and Maxwell, eds., Minnesota Studies in the Philosophy of Science, II, (Minneapolis: University of Minnesota Press, 1958).
Correspondence with Wilfrid Sellars concerning the intentional character of mental events. Starts with Chisholm's reactions to Sellars' "Empiricism and the Philosophy of Mind." Chisholm argues intentionality is an essential characteristic of mental acts.

267. _____, "Evidence as Justification," JP 58 (1961), 739-48.
Attempt to formulate an ethical definition of 'evident' and to generate rules of evidence for empirical statements. Suggests that statements of the form 'I see that a is F' do not provide ultimate stopping-points in the request for evidential supports; i.e., such perceptual states as these are not "self-presenting."

268. _____, "The Principles of Epistemic Appraisal," in F. C. Donmeyer, ed., Current Philosophical Issues: Essays in Honor of Curt John Ducasse, (Springfield, Illinois: C. C. Thomas, 1966).

269. _____, Theory of Knowledge, (Englewood Cliffs, New Jersey: Prentice-Hall, 1966).
Discusses difference between knowledge and true belief and the role of evidence in the distinction. Concept of evidence related to ethical concepts. The notion of "self-presenting" states is introduced; such states are directly evident, and are related to things that are known (which

are indirectly evident) by "rules of evidence" which are
neither deductive nor inductive rules of inference. Much
attention given to the role of perception in justification
o knowledge-claims. Defends the theory of appearing as
an alternative to sense-datum theories. In this context
Chisholm criticizes the fundamental inference of a sense-
datum theory: viz., that from 'something appears F' to
'something presents an appearance that is F'.

270. _____, "On Some Psychological Concepts and
     'Logic of Intentionality'" in H. Casteneda, ed.,
     Intention, Mind and Perception, (Detroit: Wayne
     State University Press, 1967). Comments by R. Sleigh.
Compares intentional to alethic contexts; offers criteria
for intentional contexts.

271. _____, "On The Observability of the Self,"
     PPR 30 (1969-70), 7-21.
Criticizes Hume's arguments concerning the unobservabil-
ity of the self. Argues that perceiving oneself differs
from perceiving (visually or non-visually) external
objects.

272. Chomsky, Noam, "Perception and Language," in M. Wartofsky,
     ed., Boston Studies in the Philosophy of Science, I,
     (Dordrecht-Holland: Reidel, 1963).
A brief summary of the paper originally read.

273. Choudhury, Prabas Jean, "The Problem of Form and Content
     in Physical Science," PPR 10 (1949), 229-47.

274. Clark, Michael, "Knowledge and Grounds," A 24 (1963), 123-
     31.

275. _____, "Intentional Objects," A 25 (1964), 123-31.

276. Clark, Romane, "Sensuous Judgments," N 7 (1973), 45-56.
Criticizes view held by Aune, Geach and Sellars that sense
impressions have no cognitive or conceptual status. Sense
impressions are conceptual constituents of perceptual judgments because they give perceptual judgments their reference, and must therefore have conceptual status in much the
same way as demonstrative expressions have conceptual
status in assertions.

277. Clarke, Thompson, "Seeing Surfaces and Physical Objects,"
     in Max Black, ed., Philosophy in America, (Ithaca,
     New York: Cornell University Press, 1965), 98-114.
An ingenious and delightful examination of the claim that
since all we can see of objects are their surfaces we can't
really be said to see (or have perceptual knowledge of)
the objects. Argues that if a portion of an object is seen
it is neither true nor false of the object that it is seen.

278. Clement, W. C., "Seeing and Hearing," BJPS 6 (1955), 61-
      63.
      Discussion of the physical and physiological conditions of
      seeing and hearing. Suggests that it is only a contingent
      fact that we do not hear the surfaces of objects.

279. _____, "Quality Orders," M 65 (1956), 184-99.
      Argues against the construction of quality-orders (series
      of qualities that are determined by the natures of the
      qualities themselves) as proposed by W. E. Johnson, M.
      Schick and N. Goodman.

280. Cleobury, F. H., "The Bearing of Relativity on the Contro-
      versy between Realism and Idealism," PQ 4 (1954),
      302-09.

281. Clifford, Paul R., "Knowledge as Trans-sensational," RM 17
      (1963), 361-71.

282. Coady, C. A. J., "The Senses of Martians," PR 83 (1974),
      107-25.
      Coady argues that there are problems in Grice's proposed
      criteria for distinguishing having a new sense from having
      an extended range or ability in the use of an old sense.

283. Cobb, William S., Jr., "Whitehead's Twofold Analysis of
      Experience," MS 47 (1970), 321-30.

284. Cohen, A., "On Methods in the Analysis of Speech Percep-
      tion," S 17 (1967), 331-43.

285. Collins, Arthur, "The Epistemological Status of the Con-
      cept of Perception," PR 76 (1967), 436-59.
      Argues that perception is not the acquisition of know-
      ledge, nor does it consist in forming judgments or beliefs.

286. Conway, David A., "Sensations and Bodily Position: A Con-
      clusive Argument?" PS 24 (1973), 353-55.
      Argues against Anscombe's claim that we do not know what
      position our body is in in the basis of kinaesthetic
      sensations.

287. Cook, John W., "Hume's Scepticism with Regard to the
      Senses," APQ 5 (1968), 1-17.

288. Cooper, D. E., "Materialism and Perception," PQ 20 (1970),
      334-46.
      Criticism of materialist accounts of perception, espec-
      ially D. M. Armstrong's. Argues that the only satisfac-
      tory criteria for distinguishing between the senses are
      introspective criteria, and that a materialist cannot,
      given his account of introspection, appeal to such cri-
      teria.

289.   Copleston, F. C., "On Seeing and Noticing," P 29 (1954),
        152-57.
        Asks whether metaphysicians see or notice things that
        non-metaphysicians do not--in particular whether they can
        be said to have "an intuition of being."

290.   Corcoran, D. W. J., Pattern Recognition, (Baltimore: Pen-
        guin Books, 1971).
        On computer pattern recognition.

291.   Cornman, James W., "On the Elimination of Sensations and
        'Sensations'," RM 22 (1968), 15-35.
        Contrasts three versions of materialism with respect to
        the reference of sensation-terms. Concludes that unless
        sensation-terms can be eliminated the eliminative mater-
        ialist may be forced to abandon his view in favor of
        reductive materialism.

292.   _____, "Mental Terms, Theoretical Terms, and
        Materialism," PS 35 (1968), 45-63.
        Includes a definition of 'observational term' and uses
        that concept to analyze materialist theories.

293.   _____, "Sellars, Scientific Realism, and
        Sensa," RM 23 (1970), 417-51.
        Examines Sellars' theory of sensa and argues that his
        rejection of materialism is unfounded.

294.   _____, "Observing and What It Entails," PS 38
        (1971), 415-17.
        Reply to Machamer [#865].

295.   _____, Materialism and Sensations, (New Haven:
        Yale University Press, 1971).
        Examines and critically rejects three versions of mater-
        ialism: reductive materialism, eliminative materialism
        and adverbial materialism. Argues that it is reasonable
        to reject the concept of sensa. Suggests that an adver-
        bial view of sensations is compatible with an adverbial
        view of materialism.

296.   _____, "On Direct Perception," RM 26 (1972),
        38-56.
        Critically discusses different senses of 'direct' in per-
        ceptual sentences.

297.   _____, "Theoretical Phenomenalism," N 7 (1973),
        120-38.
        The author criticizes Sellars' attack on theoretical
        phenomenalism--the view that physical objects are
        "theoretical constructions" out of sense-data or ideas.

298.   Cornsweet, T. N., Visual Perception, (New York: Academic
        Press, 1970).

299. Corso, J. F., "A Theoretic-Historical Review of the
     Threshold Concept," Psych Bull 60 (1963), 356-70.
     Traces the concept of a threshold from its origins in
     1824 to the present. Problems stemming from this concept
     are discussed. It is suggested that adaptation level
     theory and the theory of signal detection may be satis-
     factory alternatives to the concept of threshold as
     approaches to a complete psychophysics.

300. Cory, Daniel, "The Kinds of Perception and Knowledge,"
     JP 32 (1935), 309-22.

301. _____, "The Private Field of Immediate Experience,"
     JP 36 (1939), 421-27.

302. _____, "Are Sense-Data 'in' the Brain?" JP 45
     (1948), 533-49.

303. Cotten, Jean-Pierre, "Les Lectures de Merleau-Ponty: A
     Propos de la 'Phenomenologie de la Perception',"
     Rev Metaphys et Morale 77 (1972), 307-28.

304. Cousin, D. R., "Naive Realism," PAS 55 (1955), 179-200.
     Naive realism is construed as a proposal about the
     philosophical uses of ordinary perceptual verbs.

305. _____, "Perceptual Assurance," M 49 (1940), 19-41,
     and 150-69.
     Part One is a discussion of how perception may provide us
     with reasonable assurance concerning the existence and
     nature of a material thing. Part Two concerns the jus-
     tification of such assurance.

306. _____, "Kant's Concept of Appearance, I and II,"
     P 16 (1941), 169-84 and 272-84.

307. _____, "On the Onwership of Images," A 30 (1970),
     206-08.
     Offers causal criterion for ownership of images.

308. Coval, Sam C. and Todd, D. D., "Adjusters and Sense-Data,"
     APQ 9 (1972), 107-112.
     An attempt to further support Grice's contention [#540]
     that 'looks'-statements can be logically detached from
     expression of doubt or denial. The dependency of 'seems'-
     statements on 'is'-statements reflects our need to fix a
     standard case to serve the needs of communication.

309. Cox, J. W. Roxbee, "Are Perceptible Qualities 'In' Things?"
     A 23 (1962), 97-103.
     The controversy between the "Objectivist" view ·(that
     qualities we ordinarily attribute to objects are really
     "in" those objects) and its scientific critics has been
     misconstrued. The scientific argument should be construed

more broadly than as a mere attack on objectivism.

310. _____, "Distinguishing the Senses," <u>M 79</u>
       (1970), 530-50.
       After rejecting the "sense organ" and "characteristic
       experience" accounts of the distinction between senses,
       author proposes a modified version of the "characteristic
       properties" view, according to which different qualities
       are sensed by sight, by touch, etc.

311. _____, "An Analysis of Perceiving in Terms of
       the Causation of Beliefs," in F. N. Sibley [#1218].
       Defends a causal analysis of perceiving according to which
       the primary notion is perceiving-that. Distinguishes
       between direct and indirect perception in terms of the
       causal account. Argues that what is caused in perception
       are beliefs--hence the account is more akin to Armstrong's
       than to Grice's.

312. Craig, E. G., "Berkeley's Attack on Abstract Ideas," <u>PR 77</u>
       (1968), 425-37.

313. Craig, F. I. M. and Lockhart, R. S., "Levels of Processing:
       A Framework for Memory Research," <u>J of Verbal Learning
       and Verbal Behavior 11</u> (1972), 671-84.

314. Crawford, Dan, "Bergmann on Perceiving, Sensing and
       Appearing," <u>APQ 11</u> (1974), 103-12.
       An attempt to make Gustav Bergmann's later theory of
       perception accessible. Constructs Bergmann's theories of
       veridical perception, the objects of perceptual acts,
       perceptual error, appearing and sensations.

315. _____, "Propositional and Nonpropositional Per-
       ceiving," <u>PPR 35</u> (1974), 201-10.
       A discussion of Chisholm's distinction between proposi-
       tional and non-propositional senses of 'perceive'. The
       two senses of 'perceive' are very similar--the only
       difference being that in the propositional sense the
       belief involved is both true and justifiably accepted.

316. Crites, S. D., "Vision," <u>Encyclopedia of Philosophy</u>, Vol.
       8, p. 252.

317. Culbertson, James T., "A Physical Theory of Sensation,"
       <u>PS 9</u> (1942), 197-26.
       Proposes a theory according to which the qualitative
       characteristics of sensations can be derived from postu-
       lated non-sensory physical entities.

318. Cummins, Philip, "Perceptual Relativity and Ideas in the
       Mind," <u>PPR 24</u> (1963), 202-14.
       Examines Berkeley's use of the argument from perceptual
       relativity and traces the origins of this argument in the

18th century sceptical literature.

319. Daniels, Charles B., "Colors and Sensations: Or How to
     Define a Pain Ostensively," APQ 4 (1967), 231-37.
     Argues that sensations can be shared, they are located
     in space, they are ontologically dependent on their
     owner(s) and that this dependence constitutes the rela-
     tion "being felt."

320. _____, "Seeing Through a Time-Gap," AJP 48
     (1970), 354-59.
     Reply to Carrier [#242]. When we "see" an object that
     has ceased to exist we actually see that object.

321. Danto, Arthur C., "Concerning Mental Pictures," JP 55
     (1958), 12-20.
     To deny that there are mental pictures is a factual claim
     and not, as Ryle holds, a logical or linguistic one.

322. David, G. E., "Common Sense and Sense-Data," PQ 4 (1954),
     229-46.
     Recent attacks on the sense-datum theory fail to take
     account of the interdependence of visual experience and
     tactile experience. Insofar as visual sense-data are said
     to vary with the position of the eye the sense-datum
     theory will have a toehold.

323. Davidson, Donald, "Mental Events," in L. L. Foster and
     J. W. Swanson, eds., Experience and Theory, (Amherst:
     University of Massachusetts Press, 1970), 79-101.
     Primarily devoted to reconciling the anomaly of mental
     events with the determination of physical events. Per-
     ception is a recurrent example of the apparent conflict
     generated by this attempt.

324. Day, J. P., "Unconscious Perception," ASSP 34 (1960), 47-
     66. Symposium with G. N. A. Vesey.

325. Day, R. N., Human Perception, (New York: Wiley, 1969).
     An introductory text.

326. Deikman, Arthur J., "Deautomatization and the Mystic
     Experience," P 29 (1966), 324-38.
     Discussion of the alteration of perception brought about
     by certain techniques of meditation, attention to sensory
     stimuli and shift in psychological attitude from defen-
     sive to receptive. Suggests that mystical experiences
     are results of an operation of new perceptual capacities
     that are responsive to dimensions of stimulus array
     previously ignored or blocked from consciousness.

327. Deitsch, Martin, "Seeing and Picturing," JP 68 (1971),
     338.
     Criticism of M. Perkins [#1028].

38

328. _____, "Visualizing," M 81 (1972), 113-15.
      There is a sense in which we can visualize something while
      seeing it at the same time.

329. Delaney, C. F., "Sellars and the Contemporary Mind-Body
           Problem," The New Scholasticism 14 (1971), 245-68.

330. Dember, William, Psychology of Perception, (New York:
           Holt, Rinehart and Winston, 1960).
      A widely used psychological textbook.

331. _____, Visual Perception: The Nineteenth Cen-
           tury, (New York: Wiley, 1964).
      Anthology, works by: Thomas Young, Charles Bell,
      Johannes Müller, Hermann Ludwig von Helmholtz, Louis
      Albert Necker, R. Adams, Silvanus Phillips Thompson, Ernst
      Mach, Thomas Brown, Charles Wheatstone, Hermann Lotze,
      George Malcolm Stratton, John Stuart Mill, Wilhelm Max
      Wundt, Alfred Binet, Herbert Spencer, John Dewey, Burtis
      Burr Reese.

332. Dennett, D. C., Content and Consciousness, (London:
           Routledge and Kegan Paul, 1969).
      An influential functionalist account of the nature of
      mind. In the second part questions directly related to
      perception are touched upon, e.g., colors and a perceiving
      machine.

333. Deutsch, J. A. and Deutsch, D., "Attention: Some Theor-
           etical Considerations," PR 70 (1963), 80-90.
      A study of the mechanisms involved in selecting wanted
      from unwanted messages. These are so complex as to raise
      problems for the filter theory. Authors propose an alter-
      native account of the mechanisms involved according to
      which there is a shifting reference standard which sorts
      for the most important stimulus.

334. Deutscher, Max, "David Armstrong and Perception," AJP 41
           (1963), 81-88. (Reply by Armstrong, p. 246).

335. DeValois, R. L. and Abramov, I., "Color Vision," ARP 17
           (1966), 337-362.
      A bibliography and discussion of current work in the topic
      of color vision, together with works in the topic of human
      vision.

336. Dicker, Georges, "Phenomenalism and the Causal Theory of
           Perception," (abstract) JP 70 (1973), 657.

337. _____, "Seeing Bodies Move," P 54 (1973), 111-
           112.
      Proposes an analysis of seeing a body move.

338. Dilman, Ilham, "Imagination," ASSP 41 (1967), 19-36.

39

Symposium with H. Ishiguro. Detailed discussion of the relationship between imagining and perceiving and between seeing a picture and having a mental image.

339.   _____, "Imagination," A 28 (1968), 90-97.
There is a different sense of 'see' involved in seeing a picture and seeing something in my mind's eye. "Seeing" a mental image is not seeing.

340.   _____, and Phillips, D. Z., Sense and Delusion, (London: Routledge and Kegan Paul, 1971).

341. Ditchburn, R. W. and Ginsborg, B., "Vision with a Stabilized Retinal Image," N 170 (1952), 36-37.
The contrast threshold for the stabilized image is very much higher than the normal threshold for the same brightness. Stabilization causes the image to disappear.

342.   _____, "Eye-movements in Relation to Retinal Action," Opt Acta 1 (1955), 171-76.
Argues that scanning by normal involuntary eye-movements is necessary for pattern perception.

343.   _____, and Fender, D. H., "The Stabilized Retinal Image," Opt Acta 2 (1955), 128-33.
Discusses techniques for retinal image stabilization, and shows how with a stabilized image normal vision is obtained by interrupting light near the flicker fusion frequency.

344. Dixon, N. F., Subliminal Perception: The Nature of the Controversy, (London: McGraw Hill, 1971).
This book reviews the data concerning subliminal perception and concludes there is information obtained by organisms when consciousness is not present.

345. Dobbs, H. A. C., "The Dimensions of the Sensible Present," Studium Generale 24 (1971), 108-26.

346. Dodwell, P. C., Visual Pattern Recognition, (New York: Holt, Rinehart and Winston, 1970).
Starts by reviewing various models of pattern recognition. A survey of the literature on contour coding. The argument is that perception must be studied as a series of fairly distinct stages; yet this accords with Gibson's theory of perception.

347.   _____, "On Perceptual Clarity," PR 78 (1972), 275-89.
An attempt to account for perceptual clarity by means of a model that specifies a form of correlation between consecutive time samples. The model is defended by appeal to the repetition clarity effect, fading and regeneration of stabilized images, visual acuity and short-term visual

storage and masking.

348.   Dolby, R. G. A., "Philosophy and the Incompatibility of
        Colours," A 34 (1973), 8-16.
        The statement "Nothing can be red and green all over" is
        contingent, and if read as "Nothing can appear red and
        green all over," is false.

349.   Donderi, D. and Zelnicker D., "Parallel Processing in
        Visual Same-Different Decisions," Perception and
        Psychophysics 5 (1969), 197-200.

350.   _____, and Case, B., "Parallel Visual Processing:
        Constant Same-Different Latency With Two to Fourteen
        Shapes," Perception and Psychophysics 8 (1970), 373-
        75.
        Results of an experiment with 200-millisecond exposure to
        2 to 14 geometric shapes (which varied from one being
        different to there being 3 different shapes) show that
        decisions about whether the shapes were the same or
        different are made with information processed in parallel
        from many stimuli.

351.   Doppelt, Gerald, "Dretske's Conception of Perception and
        Knowledge," PS 40 (1973), 433-46.
        A discussion and criticism of Dretske's analysis of 'S
        sees that b is P'; Dretske has failed to provide an
        adequate account of the role of "proto-knowledge" (ante-
        cedent knowledge concerning b which S brings to the per-
        ceptual situation) in generating perceptual knowledge.
        Doppelt proposes an alternative analysis according to
        which S's proto-beliefs about b conjoined with the fact
        that b looks a certain way to S, justifies (serves as
        evidence for) S's taking b to be P.

352.   Dore, Clement, "Ayer on the Causal Theory of Perception,"
        M 73 (1964), 287-90.
        Discussion of Ayer's rejection of the causal theory as an
        adequate theory of perception [#81]. Argues that accep-
        tance of the causal theory does seem to commit one to a
        certain analysis of the meaning of perceptual judgments.

353.   _____, "Seeming to See," APQ 2 (1965), 312.

354.   Dowling, Eric, "Intentional Objects, Old and New," R 12
        (1970), 95-107.
        Discusses relationships between Anscombe's treatment of
        intentional objects and that of Aquinas.

355.   Dretske, Fred, "Observational Terms," PR 73 (1964), 25-42.
        Discussion of the distinction between observational and
        theoretical terms. Introduces a success-verb sense of
        'see' and argues that what one sees in this sense is
        relative to a background of scientific information against

41

which there are defining conditions for detecting certain
things simply by looking.

356. _____, "Ziring Ziderata," M 75 (1966), 211-23.
Analysis of 'S desires x' (desire = "zire"; x = "ziderat-
tum") so that the zideratum can be made real in the context of a sense-datum theory of desired objects.

357. _____, Seeing and Knowing, (Chicago: University
of Chicago Press, 1969).
Controversial and influential attempt to defend the claim
that non-epistemic seeing--i.e., seeing that does not
involve beliefs or dispositions to believe--is basic and
is involved in various types of epistemic seeing.

358. _____, "Seeing and Justification," in N. S. Care
and R. H. Grimm, eds., Perception and Personal Identity, (Cleveland: Case Western Reserve University
Press, 1969), 42-81. Comments by Philip Hugly.
Analysis of the informational content of a statement of the
form 'S sees that b is P.'

359. _____, "Perception From an Epistemological Point
of View," JP 68 (1971), 584-91.
Reply to A. Shimony [#1209]. Even if we accept the causal
theory, the question of how knowledge can be acquired in
perceptual situations is unanswered.

360. _____, "Epistemic Operators," JP 67 (1970), 1007-
23.
Argues that epistemic operators ('knows that,' 'has a
reason to believe that') are "semi-penetrating"--i.e.,
that if P entails Q, it is not always the case that 'S
knows that P' entails 'S knows that Q'. The argument is
extended to cover the operators 'looks so-and-so to S'.
and 'is so-and-so'.

361. _____, "Perception and Other Minds," N 7 (1973),
34-44.
The problem of other minds is essentially a version of the
same epistemic difficulties raised by our perceptual knowledge of physical objects and of the past and the future;
viz., how mediate or indirect knowledge is possible.

362. Dreyfus, H. L., and S. J. Todes, "The Three Worlds of
Merleau-Ponty," PPR 22 (1961), 559-65.

363. Ducasse, Curt J., "Introspection, Mental Acts and Sense,"
M 45 (1936), 181-92.

364. _____, "Objectivity, Objective Reference and
Perception," PPR 2 (1941), 43-78.
Discusses how thoughts and sensations objectively refer to
objects.

42

365. _____, "Minds, Matter and Bodies," in J. R.
           Symthies, ed., Brain and Mind, (London: Routledge and
           Kegan Paul, 1965), 81-96. Comments by Brain, Flew,
           Price, and Snythies.
       Minds and bodies are substances whose natures consist of
       integrated sets of capacities.

366. _____, "Causation: Perceivable? Or Only
           Inferred?" PPR 26 (1965), 173-79.
       He answers it is directly perceivable.

367. _____, "How Literally Causation is Perceivable,"
           PPR 28 (1967), 271-73.

368. Dufrenne, Mikel, Phenomenologie de l'Experience Esthet-
           ique, (Paris: Presses Universitaires de France,
           1953).
       A French phenomenologist's treatment of aesthetics,
       especially Volume II, La Perception Esthetique.

369. Duggan, Timohy and Taylor, Richard, "On Seeing Double,"
           PQ 8 (1958), 71-74.
       Discussion of Thomas Reid's claim that most of the things
       visible to us in normal circumstances actually appear
       double, though we do not notice it. Authors present
       implications and a defense of this claim.

370. _____, "Thomas Reid's Theory of Sensation," PR
           69 (1960), 90-100.

371. Duncan, H. F., Goutlay, N., and Hudson, W., A Study of
           Pictorial Perception among Bantu and White Primary
           School Children in South Africa, (Johannesburg:
           Witwatersrand University Press, 1973).
       There were differences, especially with rural Bantu
       children.

372. Duncker Karl, "Phenomenology and Epistemology of Con-
           sciousness of Objects," PPR 7 (1946), 505-41.
           Translated by Loise Haessler.

373. Eames, Elizabeth R., "Is There a Philosophical Problem of
           Perception?" MS 48 (1970), 53-58.
       Discussion of Austin's criticisms of sense-datum theories.
       Author contrasts Austin's attack on such theories with
       Dewey's and argues that Dewey's approach is philosophi-
       cally sounder.

374. Ebersole, Frank B., "On Seeing Things," PQ 11 (1961), 289-
           300.
       Argues that there are no such things as statements which
       are descriptions of immediate visual experience.

375. _____, "How Philosophers See Stars," M 74
     (1965), 509-19.
     Attack on sense-datum theories and the phenomenalist
     reconstruction of physical objects out of sense-data.
     Hallucinations are analyzed as reports of experiences
     rather than as perceptions.

376. Eccles, Sir John, The Brain and the Unity of Conscious
     Experience, (Cambridge: Cambridge University Press,
     1965).
     In this lecture a neurologist develops a Kantian type
     theory.

377. _____, Facing Reality: Philosophical Adventures
     by a Brain Scientist, (New York, Heidelberg and Ber-
     lin: Springer-Verlag, 1970).
     Tries to integrate scientific work on the brain with
     reflections on the nature of self, the unity of conscious
     experience, evolution, freedom, creativity, the soul and
     the nature of scientific explanation.

378. _____, The Inhibiting Pathways of the Central
     Nervous System,(Liverpool: Liverpool University
     Press, 1969).

379. Edie, James M., "William James and Phenomenology," RM 23
     (1970), 481-526.

380. Edmonds, E. M., Evans, S. H., and Mueller, M. P. "Learning
     How to Learn Schema," Psychonomic Sciences 6 (1966),
     377-78.

381. _____, "Effects
     of Knowledge of Results on Mixed Schema Learning,"
     Psychonomic Science 10 (1968), 75-76.

382. Edwards, Paul, Encyclopedia of Philosophy, (editor-in-
     chief), (New York: Macmillan Company and The Free
     Press, 1967). Volumes 1-8.
     Includes articles concerning perception by: Beardsley,
     M. C., Sprague, E., Wolf, E., Grant, E. M., Cahn, S. M.,
     Hamlyn, D. W., Kenny, A., Harrison, J., Hick, J., Blau,
     J. L., Markus, R. A., Hirst, R. J., Furley, D. J., Austeda,
     F., Reale, M., Wright, J. R. G., Lloyd, A. C., Smart, J.
     J. C., Crites, S. D.

383. Egeth, H., and Smith E. E., "Perceptual Selectivity in a
     Visual Recognition Task," J. Exp. Psych. 74 (1967),
     543-49.
     Replicates Lawrence and Coles' (1954) experiment but uses
     pictorial alternatives; found superior performance for
     before and after condition and that magnitude of advantage
     was greatest for similar alternatives as Lawrence and
     Coles had predicted.

384. Egeth, Howard, "Selective Attention," <u>Psych Bull 67</u> (1967), 41-57.

385. Einstein, Albert, "Remarks on Bertrand Russell's Theory of Knowledge," in P. Schilpp, <u>The Philosophy of Bertrand Russell</u>, (Evanston, Illinois: Northwestern University Press, 1944).

386. _____, "Reply to Critics," in P. Schilpp, <u>Albert Einstein</u>, (Evanston, Illinois: Northwestern University Press, 1949).
See especially his reply to Bohr on questions of observation and the quantum theory.

387. Eisner, W., <u>Educating Artistic Vision</u>, (London: Collier-Macmillan, 1972).

388. Ellis, Brian, "Physical Monism," <u>S 17</u> (1967), 141-61.
Argues for a realistic theory of perception and a physicalistic theory of mind. What is immediately perceivable is dependent upon the immediate neural responses we have acquired the capacity to make.

389. Ellis, Willis D., ed., <u>A Source Book of Gestalt Theory</u>, (London: Routledge and Kegan Paul, 1950 and 1955).
Anthology, works by: Wertheimer, Köhler, Fuchs, Benary, Gottschaldt, Wulf, Ternus, Duncker, Lindemann, Hartmann, Frey, Gelb, Hornbostel, Hertz, Lewin, Zeigarnik, Goldstein, Schulte, Koffka.

390. Ellison, D. G., "The Scientists' Criterion of True Observation," <u>PS 30</u> (1963), 41-52.
True observation defined in terms of inter-observer agreement. Rejects a correspondence theory of truth.

391. Emmett, E. R., "The Philosophy of Resemblance," <u>P 29</u> (1954), 145-51.
Discussion and criticism of the account of resemblance given by H. H. Price [#1092].

392. Epstein, Joseph, "Professor Ayer on Sense-Data," <u>JP 53</u> (1956), 401-15.

393. Epstein, W. and Park, J., "Examination of Gibson's Psychophysical Hypothesis," <u>Psych Bull 62</u> (1964), 180-96.

394. Epstein, William, <u>Varieties of Perceptual Learning</u>, (New York: McGraw Hill, 1967).
Attempts to present descriptive generalizations based upon empirical data. Classifies five different kinds of perceptual training and reviews the literature of perceptual learning.

395. Evans, C. R., "Some Studies of Pattern Perception Using a Stabilized Retinal Image," <u>British Jour of Psych 56</u>

(1965), 121-33.

396. _____, The Subject of Consciousness, (London: Allen and Unwin, 1970).

397. Evans, R., An Introduction to Color, (New York: Wiley, 1948).

398. Evans, S. H., "A Brief Statement of Schema Theory," Psychonomic Science 8 (1967), 87-88.
A schema is a characteristic of some population of objects, or a set of rules for producing a population prototype. Humans abstract schema from the environment. The notion of a schema family is needed to adequately account for ordinary human perception.

399. _____, "Redundancy as a Variable in Pattern Perception," Psych Bull 67 (1967), 104-13.
A modified schema theory and the research relevant to it.

400. Ewing, A. C., "Knowledge of Physical Objects," M 52 (1943), 97-121.
Argues that any general doubts about the existence of physical objects may be meaningless and attempts to provide grounds for thinking so that do not presuppose the truth of the verification principle.

401. _____, "The Causal Argument for Physical Objects," ASSP 19 (1945), 32-56. Symposium with Aaron and McNabb.
Defends phenomenalism. Argues that the most reasonable conclusion to draw from the causal argument is that the external causes of our perceptions are groups of unsensed sensibilia. Realist's belief in physical objects is justified if taken as a probable hypothesis that is confirmed by the success of predictions based upon it.

402. Fann, K. T., ed., Symposium on J. L. Austin, (New York: Humanities Press, 1969).
Collection of critical essays on the work of J. L. Austin. The following are specifically concerned with Austin's Sense and Sensibilia:
Hirst, R. J., "A Critical Study of Sense and Sensibilia," 243-253. Firth, Roderick, "Austin's Argument From Illusion," 254-266. Bennett, Jonathan, "'Real'," 267-283. Ayer, A. J., "Has Austin Refuted Sense-Data?" 284-308. Forguson, L. W., "Has Ayer Vindicated the Sense-Datum Theory?" 309-341. Ayer, A. J., "Rejoinder to Professor Forguson," 342-348.

403. Fantz, Robert L., "The Origin of Form Perception," Sci. Amer. (May, 1961), 66-72.
Infants were tested for ability to perceive shape,

46

pattern, size and solidity. It was found that the
ability to perceive form as so measured may be innate.

404. Farberg, M. and T. Nordenstam, "If I Carefully Examine a
Visual After-Image, What am I Looking At, and Where
Is It?" A 19 (1958), 99-100.

405. Farrell, B. A., "Experience," M 59 (1950), 170-98.
A discussion of the awkwardness of sensations of experiences incurrent psychology. Argues that experiences
are not peculiar "sorts of things," that need to be
accounted for or rejected. Hence materialism need not be
reductive.

406. _____, "A Psychological Look at Some Problems of
Perception," in Knowledge and Necessity, Royal Institute of Philosophy Lectures, Vol. 3, (London: Macmillan, 1970), 51-72.
Sketches some recent psychological and physiological work,
e.g., Hubel and Weisel, and argues that works by Quinton
and Don Locke can be seen to be fallacious on that basis.

407. Feigl, Herbert, "Correspondence with Aldrich," PS 2
(1935), 256-61.

408. Feldman, Fred and Heidelberger, Herbert, "Tormey on
Access and Incorrigibility," JP 70 (1973), 297-98.
The conclusion that another can have incorrigible knowledge of my being in pain does not follow from the pre-
misses Tormey uses [#1324].

409. Fellows, Brian J., The Discrimination Process and Development, (Oxford: Pergamon Press, 1968).
Discrimination is the process by means of which an organism
responds to differences between stimuli. Perception is
the process by means of which an organism receives and
analyzes sensory information. Using these concepts the
author reviews much of the literature on children's perception.

410. Festinger, L., Ono, H., Brunham, C., and Bamber, B.,
"Efference and the 'Conscious' Experience of Perception," J. Exp. Psychol. Monograph 74 (1967), 1-36.

411. Feyerabend, P. K., "An Attempt at a Realistic Interpretation of Experience," PAS 58 (1958), 143-70.
Argues that even color words change their meaning when
related theories change; this is argued persuasively by
examining the Doppler effect on light.

412. _____, "Patterns of Discovery," PR 69 (1960),
247-52.
Review of Hanson's book by the same title.

413.   _____, "Knowledge Without Foundations,"
       (Oberlin, Ohio: Oberlin College, 1961).
       An attack on foundationalist theories of knowledge and the
       idea of perceptual givenness.

414.   Fieandt, K. von, and Gibson, J. J., "The Sensitivity of
       the Eye to Two Kinds of Continuous Transformations of
       a Shadow-Pattern," Jour. of Exp. Psych 57 (1959),
       344-47.

415.   Findlay, J. N., "On Having in Mind," P 28 (1953), 291-310.
       Discussion of the problems of intentionality--investigates
       what it is to "have something in mind."

416.   Fingarette, Herbert, Self-Deception, (London: Routledge
       and Kegan Paul, 1969).
       Explains the paradoxical phenomenon of self-deception in
       terms of what it is to become explicitly conscious of
       something. Shift from visual-language metaphor to action
       and volition-language metaphor suggestion in explaining
       consciousness of. To be conscious of something is the
       exercise of a skill called "spelling out" some feature of
       the world. Link to neurophysiological discoveries offered
       in support of philosophical analysis.

417.   Firth, Roderick, "Sense-Data and the Percept Theory," M 58
       and 59 (1959 and 1950), 434-65 and 35-56. Reprinted
       in Swartz [#1292].
       A discussion of the reasons underlying a rejection of a
       sense-datum theory in favor of what Firth terms the per-
       cept theory. The percept theory is based on a rejection
       of a sense-datum or a sensation which is the content of a
       perception. Distinguishes two versions of the sense-datum
       theory and how the percept theory provides for a rejec-
       tion of each.

418.   _____, "Radical Empiricism and Perceptual Rela-
       tivity," PR 59 (1950), 164-83 and 319-31.
       Formulation and discussion of the argument from perceptual
       relativity. Criticism of C. I. Lewis' attempt to refute
       the argument. Firth proposes alternative answer which, he
       claims, does succeed in refuting it.

419.   _____, "Ultimate Evidence," JP 53 (1956), 732-
       39. Comment on Chisholm [#263]. (Reprinted in Swartz
       [#1292].)
       Argues against Chisholm that sense experience, rather than
       perceptual takings are essential to an adequate justifica-
       tion of perceptual statements.

420.   _____, "Phenomenalism," in Science Learning and
       Human Rights, (Philadelphia: University of Pennsyl-
       vania Press, 1952). Symposium with M. Black.

421. _____, "Chisholm and the Ethics of Belief," PR
       68 (1959), 493-506.
       Discussion of the ethical interpretation of epistemologi-
       cal terms.

422. _____, "Austin and the Argument from Illusion,"
       PR 73 (1964), 372-82.
       Critical discussion of Austin's attack on the Cartesian
       distinction between sensory and judgmental content of
       sense-experience in Sense and Sensibilia. Austin succeeds
       in showing that the argument from illusion, on which this
       distinction is based, embodies serious conceptual con-
       fusions. He failed to prove that perceptual experience
       lacks a sensory component; this failure is attributed to
       Austin's acceptance of the basic terms in which the argu-
       ment from illusion is stated.

423. _____, "Coherence, Certainty, and Epistemic
       Priority," JP 61 (1964), 545-57. Comments by Richard
       B. Brandt.
       Characterizes several types of coherence theory. Argues
       that C. I. Lewis was primarily concerned to attack a
       coherence theory of justification, and attempts to char-
       acterize the nature of the dispute between this and Lewis'
       views.

424. _____, "The Anatomy of Certainty," PR 76 (1967),
       3-27.
       Analysis of kinds of certainty of the sort expressed in an
       assertion of the form "Statement S (an empirical claim),
       made by A at t, is certain for A at t.' He distinguishes
       three epistemological uses of 'certain' in such assertions:
       (1) truth-evaluating uses; (2) warrant-evaluating uses; and
       (3) testability-evaluating uses. After discussing rela-
       tionships between these three uses Firth turns to a criti-
       cal discussion of Malcolm's arguments to show that a claim
       like 'This is an inkbottle' is certain, regardless of pos-
       sible outrageous behavior on the part of that object.

425. _____, "The Men Themselves: or the Role of
       Causation in Our Concept of Seeing," in H-N.
       Casteneda (ed.), Intentionality, Minds and Percep-
       tion, (Detroit: Wayne State University Press, 1967).
       Comments by Charles Caton.
       Discusses the necessary and sufficient conditions for
       seeing something itself and just seeing a part of it or a
       surface or covering.

426. Flay, Joseph C., "Hegel's "Inverted World"," RM 23 (1970),
       662-78.

427. Fleming, B. Noel, "Recognizing and Seeing As," PR 66
       (1957), 161-79.

A necessary but not a sufficient condition of recognizing x as y by sight is seeing x as y. Attempts to account for the difference between recognizing x as y and knowing x to be y at the same time.

428. _____, "The Nature of Perception," RM 16 (1962), 259-95.
Critical study of D. M. Armstrong [#41] and D. W. Hamlyn [#574].

429. _____, "The Idea of a Solid," AJP 43 (1965), 131-43.
Defends Lockean claim that it is logically possible for a physical object to possess only primary qualities, (including solidity) and presents a criticism of Hume's argument against Locke.

430. _____, "Price on Infallibility," M 75 (1966), 193-219.

431. _____, "Mind as the Cause of Motion," AJP 47 (1969), 220-42.
Discussion and review of D. M. Armstrong [#46].

432. Flew, Annis, "Images, Supposing and Imagining," P 28 (1953), 246-54.
Distinguishes three senses of 'imagine,' offers an analysis of Hume's views on the imagination and suggests that these are linguistic rather than psychological insights. Comments on Ryle's discussion of imagination in The Concept of Mind.

433. Flew, Antony G. N., "Unaesthetized Materialism: Completing Don Locke's Defence," PQ 22 (1972), 53-54.
A discussion of the distinction between seeing and "seeing." "Seeing" a pink rat does not, though seeing a pink a rat does, entail that there is a (publicly observable) pink rat to be seen.

434. Flock, H. R. and Moscatelli, A., "Variables of Surface Texture and Accuracy of Space Perceptions," Perceptual and Motor Skills 19 (1964), 327-34.

435. _____, "A Possible Optic Basis for Monocular Slant Perception," Psych.Rev. 71 (1964), 380-91.

436. _____, "Optical Texture and Linear Perspective as Stimuli for Slant Perception," Psych Rev 72 (1965), 505-14.

437. Fodor, J. A., "Could There Be a Theory of Perception?" JP 63 (1966), 369-80.
Argues that psychological data and theorizings are relevant to philosophical theories of perception.

438. _____, "The Appeal to Tacit Knowledge in Psychological Explanation," JP 65 (1968), 627-40.

439. Ford, Lewis, "On Some Difficulties with Whitehead's Definition of Abstract Hierarchies," PPR 30 (1969), 453-
55.

440. Forgus, Ronald H., Perception: The Basic Process in Cognitive Development, (New York: McGraw Hill, 1966).
An undergraduate text. Perception is information extraction. Has sections on psychophysics and methodology.

441. Forguson, Lynn W., "Has Ayer Vindicated the Sense-Datum
Theory?" in K. T. Fann, Symposium on J. L. Austin,
(New York: Humanities Press, 1969), 309-41.
An Austinian reply to Ayer [#83].

442. Foss, Brian M., ed., New Horizons in Psychology, (Bungay,
Suffolk England: The Chaucer Press Ltd., 1967).
Anthology, works by: P. C. Dodwell, N. F. Dixon, R. L.
Gregory, Anne Treisman, John Brown, P. C. Wason, E.
Dalrymple-Alford, Moya Tyson, Kevin Connolly, J. D.
Carthy, W. Sluckin, P. M. Milner, Robert Wilkinson, C. R.
B. Joyce, Roger Strech, John Annett, N. O'Connor, H. R.
Beech, D. Bannister, M. L. J. Abercrombie, D. Price-
Williams.

443. Foss, Laurence, "Language, Perception and Fact," IPQ 8
(1968), 513-46.
Proposes a way of distinguishing description and explanation and explains the former in terms of scientific expec-
tation-producing paradigms. Observation (description)
held to be a function of shifting explanatory paradigms--
hence meaning of descriptive terms is held to shift as do
the paradigms. Proposes a three-part criterion for 'being
facutally the case'.

444. _____, "The Myth of the Given," RM 22 (1968), 36-
57.
Discusses relationship between ordinary language, scientific theory and observation (emphasis on former).

445. Franks, J. J. and Bransford, J. D., "Abstraction of Visual
Patterns," J. Exp. Psychol. 90 (1971), 65-74.

446. Frantz, John J., "Merleau-Ponty's Notion of "Flesh": A
Look at the Development of a New Philosophical
Insight," Dialogue (Phi Sigma Tau) 14 (1972), 46-51.
Argues Merleau-Ponty's philosophy progressed from a position holding perception is primary, through stages of his
philosophy of vision, culminating in his final notion of
flesh.

447. Freed, Bruce, "Beliefs About Objects," Phil. Studies 21

(1970), 41-47.
Gives an analysis of belief sentences so that such sentences can be construed as implying that 'believes x' is a one-place predicate while also implying that some of our beliefs are about objects.

448.   Freeman, R. B., Jr., "Ecological Optics and Visual Slant," Psych Rev 72 (1965), 501-04.

449.   _____, "Optical Texture Versus Retinal Perspective: A Reply to Flock," Psych Rev 73 (1966), 365-71.
        Reply to Flock [#435].

450.   _____, "Function of Cues in the Perceptual Learning of Visual Slant: An Experimental and Theoretical Analysis," Psychological Monographs 80 (Z, Whole No. 610) (1966).

451.   Fried, Peter A., ed., Readings in Perception: Principle and Practice, (Lexington, Massachusetts: D. C. Heath, 1974).
        A good book of readings includes articles by Gibson, Garner, Hake and Eriksen, Hekts, Kohler, Helson, Attneave, Elkind, Postman, Hubel and Wiesel and many others.

452.   Fries, Horace, "The Spatial Location of Sensa," PR 44 (1935), 345-53.
        Sensa are located physically within the body of the percipient.

453.   Fritz, Charles A., "Sense Perception and Material Objects," PPR 16 (1955), 303-16.
        Statements about sense-data are indispensible in an adequate theory of knowledge; statements about material things are also essential and cannot be reduced to sense-datum statements.

454.   _____, "Contextual Properties and Perception," PPR 20 (1959), 338-51.
        The argument from illusion presupposes a metaphysical claim about the status of properties of material things. Examining the notion of a property provides a useful starting-point for theories of perception.

455.   Frohlich, Fanchon, "Primary Qualities in Physical Explanation," M 68 (1959), 209-17.
        Proposes explanation for the fact that primary qualities are implicitly selected to be those in terms of which we understand and evaluate explanations of physical phenomena.

456.   Furley, D. J., "Memory," Encyclopedia of Philosophy, Vol. 5, p. 267.

457. Furlong, E. J., "Memory and the Argument from Illusion,"
      PAS 54 (1954), 131-44.

458. _____, "Berkeley and the 'Knot About Inverted
      Images," _AJP 41_ (1963), 306-16.
      Discusses Berkeley's solution to the problem of inverted
      retinal images between _The Essay Towards a New Theory of
      Vision_ and _The New Theory of Vision Vindiated and
      Explained_. Criticizes D. M. Armstrong's account of
      Berkeley's solution [#40].

459. _____, "Berkeley and the Tree in the Quad," _P 41_
      (1966), 169-73.
      As against a claim made by J. Bennett [#117], Furlong
      argues that Berkeley had resolved the issue regarding
      intermittancy of external objects in the _Principles_.

460. _____, "Mental Images and Mr. O. Hanfling," _A 30_
      (1969), 62-64.
      Criticism of [#583].

461. Gale, Richard M., "Has the Present Any Duration?" _N 5_
      (1971), 39-47.
      Symposium with Laird Addis and Jay Rosenberg.

462. Gallois, Andre, "Berkeley's Master Argument," _PR 83_ (1974),
      55-69.
      Defense of Berkeley's argument that a possible object of
      perception may exist unperceived.

463. Gardner, Howard, "On Figure and Texture in Aesthetic
      Perception," _British J. Aes. 12_ (1972), 49-59.
      Texture is a microstructural regularity exhibited by both
      figure and ground. As aesthetic perception matures it is
      characterized by increasing attention to textural rather
      than figural aspects of the work.

464. Garner, Wendell R., H. W. Hake, and C. W. Eriksen,
      "Operationalism and the Concepts of Perception,"
      Psych Rev 63 (1956), 149-59.
      Operationists have accepted a narrow concept of perception
      such that perception is defined in terms of perceptual
      responses. They argue that introspection can also provide
      necessary data in investigating perception, and they con-
      strue introspection as grounded in operational terms.

465. _____, _Uncertainty and Structure as Psycho-
      logical Concepts_, (New York: Wiley, 1962).
      Uses the concept of information to develop a programmatic
      theory of psychological inquiry. Uncertainty is
      associated with any particular outcome of an event. These
      concepts are used to define various perceptual and linguis-
      tic characteristics, e.g., contingent uncertainty is used

as a measure of perceptual discrimination.

466. _____, and Morton, J., "Perceptual Independence: Definitions, Models and Experimental Paradigms," Psych Bull 72 (1969), 233-59.
The concept of perceptual independence is clarified.
Implications of the analysis offered are that perceptual
independence is not a single concept, but can be studied
most effectively by the use of experiments using ortho-
gonal inputs. Instead of trying to discover whether such
independence exists we should instead try to find the
locus of interaction.

467. _____, and Felfoldy, Gary L., "Integrality of
Stimulus Dimensions in Various Types of Information
Processing," Cognitive Psychol 1 (1970), 225-41.
Discusses differences in processing correalted with
dimensions of stimuli.

468. _____, The Processing of Information and Structure, (New York: Wiley, 1974).
The concepts of stimulus information and stimulus structure
are primary in perception. There are different kinds of
structure and all are properties of the stimuli. These
structures are processed. Includes a defense of a version
of critical realism.

469. Garnett, A. Campbell, "Mind as Minding," M 61 (1952), 349-
58.
Criticism of Ryle's notion of observation.

470. _____, The Perceptual Process, (London:
Allen and Unwin, 1965).
A critique of mid-century literature; argues that perception is a process and, thus, sense-data and other state
theories are wrong.

471. Garnett, Maxwell, "Gestalt Psychology," P 18 (1943), 37-49.
Psychology is concerned with formulating and testing "laws
of thought." Criticizes Koffka for details of the program
presented in Principles of Gestalt Psychology [#772].

472. Gauld, Alan, "Could a Machine Perceive?" BJPS 17 (1966),
44-58.
Raises doubts concerning the possibility of constructing a
machine that would be able to perceive an object as an
object.

473. Geach, Peter, Mental Acts, (London: Routledge and Kegan
Paul, 1957).
Argues against abstractionism as a theory of concept for-
mation.

474. Gentry, George, "Broad's Sensum Theory and The Problem of the Sensible Substratum," <u>Monist 45</u> (1935), 131-49.

475. _____, "The Logic of the Sensum Theory," <u>PS 10</u> (1943), 81-89.
The objective constituent of a perceptual experience is a sense field with a certain outstanding sensa rather than a physical object. Criticizes C. D. Broad's views concerning the probabilistic nature of evidence.

476. George, F. H., <u>Cognition</u>, (London: Methuen, 1952).
Examination of traditional psychological theories of cognition; author defends a cybernetic approach.

477. _____, "Epistemology and the Problem of Perception," <u>M 66</u> (1967), 491-506.
Discusses the distinction between an empirical theory of perception and a logical theory of perception. Philosophers who are concerned with the latter are interested in perception in a different way than are psychologists.

478. Gesell, Arnold, "Infant Vision," <u>Sci. Amer. 182</u> (1950), 20-22.
The development of an infant's visual system is closely connected with evolutionary development of the eye, and with increasing neuro-muscular control.

479. Gex, Maurice, "Philosophies, de L'experience," <u>RIP 24</u> (1970), fasc 3, 4).

480. Gibs, Benjamin, "Putnam on Brains and Behavior," <u>A 30</u> (1969), 53-55.

481. Gibson, E. Gibson, J. J., Smith, O. W., and Block, H., "Motion Parallax as a Determinant of Perceived Depth," <u>Jour. of Exp. Psych. 58</u> (1959), 40-51.
A study of what kinds of motion in the light entering an eye arouse judgments of depth and what kinds do not.

482. Gibson, Eleanor, J., and Walk, Richard D., "The 'Visual Cliff'," <u>Sci. Amer. 202</u> (1960), 64-71.
Experiments with this device indicate that a seeing animal can perceive depth when it has acquired locomotion, even when locomotion begins at birth. Some report of findings concerning the types of visual clues used in perceiving depth.

483. _____, "Learning to Read," <u>Science 148</u> (1965), 1066-72.

484. _____, <u>Principles of Perceptual Learning and Development</u>, (New York: Appleton-Century-Crofts, (1969).

Perception is the process of attaining information about the world. Perception is selective. The text reviews an attempt to adjudicate between various theories of perceptual learning, analyze various experimental paradigms and to discuss the literature of infant and child perception. An important book.

485. Gibson, James J., _The Perception of the Physical World_, (Boston: Houghton Mifflin, 1959).
Perception is of the visual world and not of the visual field. Observers are active. This is an early version of the theory elaborated in Gibson's influential and important later works.

486. _____, "The Perception of Visual Surfaces," _American Journal of Psychology_ 63 (1950), 367-84.
Further evidence in support of the author's view that visual space-perception is reducible to the perception of visual surfaces. Here he attempts to give the essential properties of a surface that serve as effective stimuli for space perception.

487. _____, "What is a Form?" _Psych Rev_ 58 (1951), 403-12.
Perception is of the forms in the world.

488. _____, "Optical Motions and Transformations as Stimuli for Visual Perception," _Psych Rev_ 64 (1957), 288-95.
Perception can be of motions and optical transformations.

489. _____, and Gibson, E., "Continuous Perspective Transformations and the Perception of Rigid Motion," _Jour. of Exp. Psych._ 54 (1957), 129-38.
Describes an experiment which seeks to determine what sorts of optical arrays yield perception of motion of a rigid surface. Conclusions show that the changing form of a stimulus object is sometimes perceived as a constant form with changing slant. It is suggested that such findings are relevant for discussions of shape perception, and of identifying objects by their shapes.

490. _____, "Perception as a Function of Stimulation," in S. Koch, ed., _Psychology: A Study of Science_, Vol. 1 (New York: McGraw Hill, 1959), 456-501.
Perception is directly of the world; a direct response to stimulation.

491. _____, "The Useful Dimension of Sensitivity," _Amer. Psychol._ 18 (1963), 1-15.
Constancy of phenomenal objects are often enhanced by variations of momentary sensations.

492.   _____, The Senses Considered as Perceptual
          Systems, (Boston: Houghton Mifflin, 1966).
          Perception is the direct pickup of information from the
          environment. Thus, perception is of the world and
          sensations and constructive processes need not be included
          in a theory of perception. Gibson's theory spells out a
          theory of ecological optics in which there is a direct
          psychophysical link between information present in the
          environment and that picked up by a perceiver.

493.   _____, "The Problem of Temporal Order in
          Stimulation and Perception," J. Psychol. 62 (1966),
          141-49.
          Argues that the traditional distinction between percep-
          tion and memory is mistaken. Perception is not just of the
          present. Offers a set of five new theorems for perception
          all designed to include a temporal variable for a percep-
          tual stimulus.

494.   _____, "New Reasons for Realism," S 17 (1967),
          162-72.
          Argues against the view that sensations are needed as
          mediators in perception.

495.   _____, "On the Relation Between Hallucination
          and Perception," Leonardo 3 (1970), 425-27.
          Hallucinations can be distinguished from percepts when
          perception takes place over a period of time.

496.   _____, The Information Available in Pictures,"
          Leonardo 4 (1971), 27-35.
          Argues against current theories of pictorial perception in
          favor of a theory that light conveys information about
          the world. Perception of pictures is called mediate per-
          ception, as contrasted with direct perception of the
          environment.

497.   _____, "The Legacies of Koffka's Principles,"
          in J. of Hist. of the Behavioral Sciences 7 (1971),
          3-9.
          Analysis of Koffka's contribution to the theory of percep-
          tion.

498.   _____, "A Theory of Direct Visual Perception,"
          in Joseph R. Royce and William W. Rozeboom, eds.,
          The Psychology of Knowing, (New York: Gordon and
          Breach, 1972), 215-27.
          The visual system explores and detects information present
          in the stable, unbounded and permanent stimulus-information
          in the ambient optic array. Comments follows pps. 228-40.

499.   Gibson, Quentin, "Is There a Problem About Appearance?"
          PQ 16 (1966), 319-28.

57

Answers there is.

500. Ginet, Carl, "How Words Mean Kinds of Sensations," PR 77
      (1968), 3-24.
      Discussion of how words mean sensations in order to resolve
      the problem of how I can mean the same thing by my use of
      a sensation-word as someone else does.

501. Givner, David A., "Berkeley's Ambiguity," Dialogue 8
          (1970), 646-62.
      Berkeley's arguments against matter rest on an ambiguity
      in the term 'perceivable' or 'sensible'.

502. _____, "To Be is to Be Distinguished," Idealis-
          tic Studies 4 (1974), 131-44.
      Uses J. J. Gibson's theory as a basis to defend the claim
      that differentiation is essential to perception, and that
      this ability is a sensible property of a perceiving state.

503. Glasgow, W. D., and Pilkington, G. W., "Other Minds on
          Evidential Necessity," M 79 (1970), 431-35.

504. Gogel, W. C., "Perception of the Relative Distance Posi-
          tion of Objects as a Function of Other Objects in
          the Field," Jour. of Exp. Psych 47 (1954), 335-42.
      Reports of depth illusions similar to the "moon illusion."

505. Goldberg, Bruce, "The Linguistic Expression of a Feeling,"
          APQ 8 (1971), 87-92.

506. Goldman, Alan H., "Criteriological Arguments in Percep-
          tion," M 84 (1975), 102-05.
      Questions the claim that there is a necessity connection
      between the secondary qualities of physical objects and
      the ways they appear to perceivers in normal conditions.
      One may intelligibly ask whether objects really have the
      colors they appear to have in normal conditions.

507. Goldmeier, Erich, "Similarity in Visually Perceived Forms,"
          Psychological Issues Vol. 28, Number 1, Monograph 29
          (1972).
      An experimental investigation of the perceived similarity
      between objects.

508. Gombrich, E. H., Hochberg, Julian and Black, Max, Art,
          Perception and Reality, (Baltimore: Johns Hopkins
          Univeristy Press, 1972).
      Preface by Maurice Mandelbaum. Contents: E. H. Gombrich,
      "The Mask and the Face: The Perception of Physiognomic
      Likeness in Life and Art," Julian Hochberg, "The Represen-
      tation of Things and People," Max Black, "How Do Pictures
      Represent?"

509.   _____, Art and Illusion, (London: Phaidon: 2nd
            edition, 1962).
        Artists must learn representative techniques in order to
        provide illusions of reality. These techniques change over
        time. Perceivers, too, must acquire schema for perceiving
        two-dimensional objects as three-dimensional represen-
        tations of reality.

510.   Goodman, Nelson, The Structure of Appearance, (Indianapo-
            lis: Bobbs-Merrill Company, 1951; 2nd edition,
            Bobbs-Merrill, 1966).
        Construction of a formal system in which the primitives
        are qualities--construed as individuals. The methodologi-
        cal advantages of this procedure are discussed in detail
        and author compares results of his choice of primitives
        with alternatives. Although the system is phenomenological
        and nominalistic the system is neutral as between nominalism
        and realism.

511.   _____, "Sense and Certainty," PR 61 (1952), 160-
            67.
        APA Symposium with Reichenbach and C. I. Lewis.

512.   _____, "Letter," M 66 (1957), 78.
        Reply to Clement [#279].

513.   _____, "Review of Gombrich's Art and Illusion,"
            JP 57 (1960), 595-99.

514.   _____, "The Way the World Is," RM 14 (1960), 48-
            56.
        There is no one true description or picture or linguistic
        representation of the world because there are many.
        Rejects the picture (structural isomorphism) theory of
        language in favor of "a language theory of pictures."

515.   _____, Languages of Art, (Indianapolis: Bobbs-
            Merrill, 1968).
        Concerned with problems of pictoral perception and
        expression in art. Pp. 10-19 contain an explanation of
        seeing in perspective that does not involve sense-data.

516.   Götlund, Erik, "Some Comments on Mistakes in Statements
            Concerning Sense-Data," M 61 (1952), 297-306.
        Argues that statements about sense-data can involve
        mistakes in the use of descriptive terms.

517.   Gotshalk, D. W., The Structure of Awareness,(Urbana,
            Illinois: University of Illinois Press, 1969).
        Observation in sense-monitored cognition, such as,
        knowing and symbolizing. Criticizes empiricist theories.

518.   Goudge, Thomas A., "The Views of Charles Peirce on the

Given in Experience," <u>JP 32</u> (1935), 533-44.

519. Graham, Clarence H., "Behavior, Perception and the Psychophysical Methods," <u>Psych Rev 57</u> (1950), 108-20.
Consideration of stimulus operations and responses
encountered in psychophysical experiments with special
attention to theoretical aspects of psychophysical
research in visual perception. Includes bibliography.

520. _____, "Sensation and Perception in an
Objective Psychology," <u>Psych Rev 65</u> (1958), 65-76.
Discussion of the role of sensation and perception in the
structure of a behavioristic psychology. Author argues
that the terms 'sensation' and 'perception' do not refer
to two distinct operationally specifiable concepts.

521. _____, and Ratoosh, Philburn, "Notes on
Some Interrelations of Sensory Psychology, Perception, and Behavior," in S. Koch, ed., <u>Psychology:
A Study of a Science</u>, (New York: McGraw Hill,
1962), vol. 4, 483-514.
A specification of the kinds of stimulus-response functions characterizing experiments in the areas of sensation and perception motivated by desire for consistent
behavioral approach to these areas. Discussion of problems in translating phenomenological claims into
behavioristic claims, especially in describing color
vision. Argues that sensation and perception constitute a single area of investigation. Value of
establishing psychophysical scales questioned. Argues
that no measurement is fundamental to psychology.
Includes bibliography.

522. _____, ed., <u>Vision and Visual Perception</u>,
(New York: Wiley, 1965).
Chapters by Neil Bartlett, John Lott Brown, Yun Hsia,
Conrad G. Myeller and Lorrin A. Riggs.

523. Gram, Moltke S., "Transcendental Arguments," <u>N 5</u> (1971),
15-26.
APA Symposium with Roger C. Buck and Arthur C. Danto.

524. _____, "Causation and Direct Realism," <u>PS 39</u>
(1972), 388-96.
Argues that Pitcher's epistemological version of direct
realism founders on the phenomenon of hallucination
because false perceptual beliefs cannot be accounted for
in such a way that they meet the criterion of no intrinsic difference between a veridical and hallucinatory
experience. The failure of Pitcher's theory is a result
of confusing epistemological with psychophysical dualism.

525. Granit, Ragnar, <u>Receptors and Sensory Perception</u>: A
Discussion of Aims, Means, and Results of

Electrophysiological Research into the Processes of
Reception, (New Haven: Yale University Press, 1955).
A very sophisticated review of the state of electrical
studies in the physiology of perceptual receptors.

526. Grant, L. B., "Review of D. M. Armstrong's Perception and
the Physical World," AJP 40 (1962), 220-29.

527. Grant, R. M., "Appearance and Reality," Encyclopedia of
Philosophy, Vol. 1, p. 135.

528. Greenway, A. P., "Psychological Findings and Sensory
Experience," IPQ 13 (1973), 99-110.
An adequate description of sensing must account for both
the reality and concreteness of sensory appearances (how
they embody direct contact with objects) as well as their
cognitive, experiential aspects.

529. Gregory, Joshua C., "The Concept of Mind and the Unconscious," BJPS 2 (1951), 52-57.
Ryle's arguments in The Concept of Mind virtually ignore
the operations of the unconscious, to the detriment of
the explanatory power of Ryle's views.

530. Gregory, Richard L., Eye and Brain, (New York: McGraw-
Hill, 1966).
A very readable work presenting in summary theories of
vision from Descartes, Berkeley and Helmholtz to those of
modern psychologists and physiologists. Argues that the
senses do not give us a picture of the world--rather they
provide clues which we use as evidence in checking hypotheses. Includes chapters on light, the eye, the brain,
seeing brightness, movement and color, illusions, vision
and art, whether seeing is a learned ability, the relation between vision and beliefs and the particular problems posed by space travel. Many diagrams and illustrations.

531. _____, "Visual Illusions," Sci Amer 219
(1968), 66-76.
The relatively widespread occurrence of visual illusions
of perspective suggests that they result from the attempts
of a data-handling system faced with ambiguous images to
establish a consistent interpretation of external reality.
If so, similar illusions should also occur in suitably-
constructed robots.

532. _____, The Intelligent Eye,(New York: Mc-
Graw-Hill, 1970).
Perception held to be a kind of thinking--in particular a
kind of problem-solving--whereby one infers the nature
and existence of objects from sensed visual patterns.
Perception of pictures regarded as a special case of
object perception. The skills involved in perception of

pictures is directly related to the development of abstract thinking. Includes many illustrations and stereoscopic glasses which enable viewer to perceive three-dimensional effects from two-dimensional drawings.

533. _____, "Perception as Pickup of Information," Contemporary Psychology 16 (1971), 555-56.
Review of Eleanor J. Gibson's Principles of Perceptual Learning and Development.

534. _____, and Gombrich, E. H., eds., Illusion in Nature and Art, (New York: Charles Scribner's Sons, 1973).
Articles on illusion by Blakemore, Gregory, Hinton, Deregowski, Gombrich, and Penrose.

535. _____, "Perceptions as Hypotheses," in S. C. Brown, ed., Philosophy of Psychology, (New York: Barnes and Noble, 1974), 195-210. Comments, same volume, by G. E. M. Anscombe and G. N. A. Vesey.
Argues that perceptions share many characteristics of hypotheses in science by leading beyond available sensory information. Certain assumptions are made by perceivers in order to account for sensory information; these assumptions may differ from and even conflict with those we would accept intellectually. This accounts for perception of apparently impossible figures.

536. Green, R. T., and Courtis, M. C., "Information Theory and Figure Perception: The Metaphor That Failed," Acta Psychologica 25 (1966), 12-36.
Attack on Attneave's information theory of perception. Argues the concept of information in psychology is not that used in mathematical information theory, so parallels are misleading.

537. Grene, Marjorie, The Knower and the Known, (London: Faber and Faber, 1966).
Argues against a "Cartesian-Newtonian" view of the world in favor of a thesis that knowledge is active conjecture; a Polanyi-style approach.

538. _____, "The Aesthetic Dialogue of Sartre and Merleau-Ponty," The Journ of the Brit Soc for Phenom 1 (1970), 59-72.
An unusually readable essay including long discussion of Merleau-Ponty's "The Eye and the Mind." Author contrasts Sartre and Merleau-Ponty and relates their differences in perceptual orientation to political and other philosophical differences.

539. Grice, H. P., "Some Remarks About the Senses," in R. J. Butler, ed., Analytical Philosophy, 2nd series (New York: Barnes and Noble, Inc., 1962), 133-53.

Under what conditions would we say that a Martian possesses a sense that we do not, rather than that it exercises a faculty of, e.g., seeing through some non-optical means? By way of this question Grice distinguishes several possible meansof distinguishing our senses from one another. The origin of a number of controversial issues.

540.   _____, "The Causal Theory of Perception," ASSP 35
           (1961), 121-52.
Sense-datum statements are a class of statements of the form "x looks (feels, etc.) Ø to A." These are to be analyzed in causal terms.

541. Griffiths, A. Phillips, "Ayer on Perception," M 59 (1960), 486-98.

542. Grossman, Neal, "Empiricism and the Possibility of Encountering Intelligent Beings with Different Sense-Structures," JP 61 (1974), 815-21.

543. Grossman, Reinhardt, "Sensory Intuition and the Dogma of Localization," I 5 (1962), 238-51.
Argues against the thesis that all objects of sensory intuition are localized in space and time. This thesis held to be the epistemological foundation for conceptualism and certain forms of nominalism.

544.   _____, The Structure of Mind, (Madison: University of Wisconsin Press, 1965).
Proposes a defense of realism based on an analysis of intentionality. Suggests that there is a relation between mental acts and their contents that avoids the problems inherent in a representative theory.

545.   _____, "Non-Existent Objects: Recent work on Brentano and Meinong," APQ 6 (1969), 17-32.

546. Gurwitsch, Aron, The Field of Consciousness, (Pittsburgh: Duquesne University Press, 1964).
A phenomenological study of consciousness.

547.   _____, "Contribution to the Phenomenological Theory of Perception," in his Studies in Phenomenology and Psychology, (Evanston, Illinois: Northwestern University Press, 1966).

548.   _____, "On A Perceptual Root of Abstraction," in his Studies in Phenomenology and Psychology, (Evanston, Illinois: Northwestern University Press, 1966).

549.   _____, "Toward A Theory of Intentionality," PPR 30 (1969-1970), 354-67.

550. _____, "Substantiality and Perceptual Coherence,"
      Res Phenomenol 2 (1972), 29-46.

551. Gustafson, Donald, "A Note on a Misreading of Wittgen-
      stein," A 28 (1968), 143-44.

552. Gyr, John W., Brown, John S., Willey, Richmond, and
      Zivian, Arthur, "Computer Simulation and Psychologi-
      cal Theories of Perception," Psych Bull 65 (1966),
      174-92.

553. _____, "Is a Theory of Direct Visual Perception
      Adeqaute?" Psych Bull 77 (1972), 246-61.
      Reply by Gibson, same journal, 79 (1973), 396-7.
      Gibson's theory does not take account of neuropsychologi-
      cal and experimental evidence that suggests perception
      also involves the activity of the perceiver.

554. _____, "Perception as Reafference and Realted
      Issues in Cognition and Epistemology," in Joseph R.
      Royce and William W. Rozeboom, eds., The Psychology
      of Knowing, (New York: Gordon and Breach, 1972).
      Argues that Gibson leaves out of his theory the
      activity of the organism and reafference.

555. Haber, Ralph Norman, "Nature of the Effect of Set on
      Perception," Psych Rev 73 (1966), 335-51.
      Reviews findings concerning alternative hypotheses con-
      cerning the effects of set on reports of perceptual
      experience: 1) attending to a particular attribute of a
      stimulus results in more vivid perception of that attri-
      bute; and 2) set affects memory organization, so that what
      is attended to tends to be reported more accurately. This
      issue bears on the distinction between perceptual and
      mnemonic tasks.

556. _____, "Perception and Thought: An Infor-
      mation-Processing Analysis," in James F. Voss, ed.,
      Approaches to Thought, (Columbus, Ohio: Charles E.
      Merrill, 1969), 1-26. (Discussion of Haber by
      Michael I. Posner, same volume, 27-37.) (General
      discussion of Haber and Posner, same volume, 38-39.)
      Assumptions of an information-processing analysis of
      visual perceptions set out and defended. Visual exper-
      ience is not immediate, but is composed of numerous dis-
      tinct successive operations, limited by capacities of the
      nervous system for channeling and storing information.
      Memory is also subjected to processing analysis. Tech-
      niques of research design discussed, including backward
      masking and post-stimulus sampling. Concepts of short-
      term visual storage and interference processes discussed
      in terms of recent experiments. Includes bibliography.

557. _____, ed., Contemporary Theory and Research

in _Visual Perception_, (New York: Holt, Rinehart and
Winston, 1968).
An excellent anthology with articles by Boynton,
Natsoulas, Broadbent, Corso, Spigel, Kolers, Matin and
MacKinnon, McFarland, Barlow and Hill, Hubel and Wiesel,
Miller, Averbach and Sperling, Neisser, Sternberg,
Hochberg, Melas, Gregory, Ganz, Mackworth, Epstein,
Julesz, Kohler, von Holst, Rock, Wapner, Bower, Held,
Bruner, Gibson, Pick, Swets, Haber and many others.

558. _____, ed., _Information-Processing
Approaches to Visual Perception_, (New York: Holt,
Rinehart and Winston, 1969).
An athology including sections on short-term visual
storage models, visual maskings, simultaneity, reaction
time, visual scanning and searching, sequential and
repetition processes, microgenetic and ontogenetic
processes, encoding, rehearsal, storage and retrieval,
and attention. Authors include: Sperling, Mackworth,
Posner, Keele and Chase, Posner and Keele, Eriksen and
Collins, Hubert, Kahneman, Schiller and Chorover, Fehrer
and Raab, Eriksen, Weisstein, Harter, Rutschmann,
Kristofferson, Bartlett, Hatter, White, Fraisse, Smith,
Kaswan and Young, Sekuler, Raab, Fehrer, Hershenson,
Williams, Sternberg, Egeth, Corvitz and Davies, Hyman
and Kaufman, Nickerson, Mayzner, Tresselt and Helfer,
Haber, Heckenmueller, Armington, Gardner and Schick,
Broadbent, Mewhort, Corballis, Tresman and Geffen,
Deutsch and Deutsch, Spong, Haider and Lindsley, and
others.

559. _____, and Hershenson, M., _The Psychology
of Visual Perception_, (New York: Holt, Rinehart
and Winston, 1973).
A useful undergraduate text that reviews the various
psychological theories of perception, but essentially is
a processing approach. It is suggested that the visual
system integrates information or constructs percepts.

560. _____, "How We Remember What We See," _Sci
Amer 222_ (1970), 104-112.
On recognition processes in perception; a description
of the memory systems involved therein.

561. Hacker, P. M. S., _Insight and Illusion_, (Oxford:
Clarendon Press, 1972).
A study of Wittgensteinian themes.

562. Hahn, Lewis E., "Neutral, Indubitable Sense-Data as the
Starting Piont for Theories of Perception," _JP 36_
(1939), 589-600.

65

Argues that sense-data as conceived by H. H. Price are neither theory-neutral nor is their existence indubitable.

563. _____, "Psychological Data and Philosophical
Theories of Perception," JP 39 (1942), 296-301.
Contends that the choice of what psychological data is to
be accounted for in a philosophical theory of perception
represents and reflects a certain metaphysical bias.

564. _____, A Contextualistic Theory of Perception,
Published in Philosophy, Vol. 22, (Berkeley and Los
Angeles: University of California Press, 1942).

565. Hall, Everett W., "Perception as Fact and as Knowledge,"
PR 52 (1943), 468-89.
Distinguishes the psychology of perception from the
philosophy (epistemology) of perception and suggests
these have been in danger of being collapsed. Outlines a
philosophical theory of perception.

566. _____, "The Adequacy of a Neurological Theory
of Perception," PPR 20 (1959), 75-84.
Neurophysiology and philosophers have distinct interests
in perception--author argues for a clear division of
labor.

567. Hall, R., "The term 'sense-datum'," M 73 (1964), 130.

568. Hallett, H. F., "The Essential Nature of Knowledge," P 20
(1945), 227-43.
Argues that visual perception is a kind of prima facie
knowledge.

569. Halsbury, Earl of, "Epistemology and Communication Theory,"
P 34 (1959), 289-307.
Proposes coding-decoding model to explain functioning of
nervous system in learning. Scientific and common sense
knowledge exhibit the same structure. Discusses the
difference between human nervous systems and computers.

570. Hamlyn, D. W., "Psychological Explanation and the Gestalt
Hypothesis," M 60 (1951), 506-20.
Argues that Gestaltists have asked the wrong sorts of
questions, particularly in studying perception.

571. _____, "A Note on Experience," A 14 (1953), 90-94.
A reply to Hartnack [#612]. There is a sense in which
experiences are private.

572. _____, The Psychology of Perception, (London:
Routledge and Kegan Paul, 1957).
An attack on the conceptual claims found in the Gestalt
theories of perception.

573.　＿＿＿＿＿＿, "The Visual Field and Perception," <u>ASSP 31</u>
　　　　(1957), 107-24. Symposium with A. C. Lloyd.
　　　Discussion of J. J. Gibson's distinction between a visual
　　　field and a visual world.

574.　＿＿＿＿＿＿, <u>Sensation and Perception</u>, (London:　Rout-
　　　　ledge and Kegan Paul, 1961).
　　　Historical survey of theories of perception and sensation
　　　from classical Greek times through the early part of the
　　　twentieth century. Attempts to adjudicate between various
　　　claims that sensations are involved in perceptions and how.

575.　＿＿＿＿＿＿, "Seeing Things as They Are," Inaugural
　　　　Lecture, Birkbeck College (London; 1965).

576.　＿＿＿＿＿＿, <u>Aristotle's De Anima, Books II and III</u>,
　　　　(Oxford: 1968).

577.　＿＿＿＿＿＿, "Koine Aisthesis," <u>Monist 52</u> (1968), 195-
　　　　209.
　　　Discussion of the role of common sense, or the sense by
　　　means of which the common sensibles are apprehended, in
　　　Aristotle.

578.　＿＿＿＿＿＿, "Continuity," <u>Encyclopedia of Philosophy</u>,
　　　　Vol. 2, 205.

579.　＿＿＿＿＿＿, <u>The Theory of Knowledge</u>, (Garden City:
　　　　Doubleday, 1970).
　　　An introductory book on epistemology that reviews and
　　　rehearses the traditional pro and con arguments for
　　　sense-data.

580. Hammond, Albert L., "On 'Sensation'," <u>PR 53</u> (1955), 260-
　　　　85.
　　　Perceived colors should not be treated on a par with
　　　bodily sensations. Proposes explanation of why philoso-
　　　phers are tempted to do so.

581. Hampshire, Stuart, "Identification and Existence," in
　　　　H. D. Lewis, ed., <u>Contemporary British Philosophy
　　　　III</u>, (London: Allen and Unwin, 1956).

582.　＿＿＿＿＿＿, "Perception and Identification,"
　　　　<u>ASSP 35</u> (1961), 81-96. Symposium with P. F. Strawson.
　　　Claims there are pure noncommital descriptions of objects
　　　possible, and that these descriptions will qualify as a
　　　harmless variety of sense-data.

583. Hanfling, O., "Mental Images," <u>A 29</u> (1969), 166-73.
　　　Discussion of claim that the identity of mental images is
　　　logically dependent on their owner's identification of
　　　them.

584. Hannay, Alastair, "Wollheim and Seeing Black on White As A Picture," Brit J Aes 10 (1970), 107-18.
The distinction between two ways of seeing black paint on a white surface is not absolute. They are (1) seeing the black as concealing part of a white surface and (2) seeing black and white "pictorially" or "phenomenologically." Critical of Wollheim [#1450].

585. _____, Mental Images: A Defence. (London: Allen and Unwin, 1971).

586. _____, "To See a Mental Image," M 82 (1973), 161-82.
We see two things when our eyes are shut: what we imagine and the image by which we imagine it. It is "proper" to describe visual imagining as seeing things in their per- ceptual absence, and to say that in visual imagining we can and do see a mental image.

587. Hansen, Robert, "This Curving World: Hyperbolic Linear Perspective," J Aes Art Crit 32 (1973), 147-61.
Challenges the traditional assumption that classical linear perspective actually represents the way the world appears. Gombrich and others have not paid sufficiently close attention to their fields of vision. Suggests a "law" of linear perspective whch, if followed by visual artists, would make their linear representations more faithful to actual perceptual experience.

588. Hanson, Norwood Russell, Patterns of Discovery, (Cambridge: Cambridge University Press, 1958).
Argues that observations are laden with theories and that interpretation is not involved in seeing in all cases. A Wittgensteinian treatment of topics in the philosophy of science.

589. _____, "On Having the Same Visual Experience," M 69 (1960), 340-50.
Argues against those who hold a privacy of sensation view, that one person can be said to have the same visual experiences as another.

590. _____, "Observation and Interpretation," in Voice of America, Forum Lectures, Philosophy of Science Series, No. 9, 1964. (Reprinted in S. Morgenbesser, ed., Philosophy of Science Today, New York: Basic Books, 1967.)
Argues the point made in his Patterns of Discovery that all perceptions and observations are theory-laden; interpre- tation is held not to be an essential aspect of percep- tion.

591. _____, Perception and Discovery, (San

Francisco, Freeman Cooper, 1970).
A neo-Wittgensteinian look at the concept of observation
and a Peircean abductive account of discovery in science.

592. Hardie, W. F. R., "Ordinary Language and Perception,"
PQ 5 (1955), 97-108.
Examines arguments based on facts about ordinary language
that purport to solve or dissolve traditional problems
in perception and finds them unsuccessful. Considers
arguments advanced by Stebbing, Warnock and Ryle.

593. _____, "The Paradox of Phenomenalism," PAS 46
(1946), 127-54.
An attack on the phenomenalist contention that the statement that a material object exists is to be understood as
equivalent to a certain hypothetical claim about possible
sense-experiences.

594. _____, "Austin on Perception," P 38 (1963),
253-63.
A sympathetic discussion of Austin [#72].

595. Hare, P. and Koehl, Richard, "Moore and Ducasse on the
Sense Data Issue," PPR 28 (1968), 313-31.

596. Harman, Gilbert, Thought, (Princeton, New Jersey: Princeton University Press, 1973).
Discusses the relation between seeing and knowing (in
chapter 10) and argues that for a perceptual belief to
be reasonable an inference must be involved, based upon
one's background beliefs. Perceptions provide the data
for perceptual knowledge.

597. Harris, C. S., "Perceptual Adaptation to Inverted,
Reversed, and Displaced Vision," Psych Rev 72 (1965),
419-44.
Adaptation to prism-produced displacement of the visual
field has been shown to be primarily proprioceptive (a
change in the felt position of a limb as seen through the
prism) rather than a visual change. This shows that,
contrary to an empiricist assumption, vision is stable
while the sense of position is flexible.

598. _____, and Gibson, A. R., "Is Orientation-specific
Colour Adaptation in Human Vision Due to Edge
Detectors, Afterimages, or Dipoles?" Science 162
(1968), 1506-07.

599. Harris, Errol E., Nature, Mind and Modern Science, (New
York: MacMillan, 1954).
An historical survey of theories of the nature of mind and
knowledge. Critique of the empiricist's program.

600. _____, "The Mind-Dependence of Objects," PQ 6

69

(1956), 223-35.
An attempt to answer questions raised by Brand Blanshard
in his review of Nature, Mind and Modern Science [#150]
concerning the relationship between qualities of things
and the mind.

601.   _____, Hypothesis and Perception, (New York:
        Humanities, 1970).

602. Harris, N. G. E., "On Seeing Everything Upside Down,"
        A 33 (1972), 28-31.
        The inverted spectrum case is inscrutable whereas two
        persons seeing everything upside down relative to each
        other would not be. Author suggests several ways in which
        this inversion might be discovered.

603. Harrison, Bernard, "On Describing Colours," I 10 (1967),
        38-52.
        Argues that one who experienced systematic transpositions
        of colours is not unlike one who is colour-blind. The
        sceptic can be answered by showing that colour-vocabulary
        will be affected in both cases.

604. Harrison, J., "Ethical Objectivism," Encyclopedia of
        Philosophy, Vol. 3, 73.

605. Harrison, Ross, "Strawson on Outer Objects," PQ 20 (1970),
        213-21.

606. Harrod, Sir Roy, "Sense and Sensibilia," P 38 (1963), 227-
        42.

607. Hartland-Swann, John, "On Describing the World," AJP 34
        (1956), 106-17.
        Discussion of the question whether anything exists
        independently of perception and if so how it is to be
        described without counterfactuals.

608.   _____, "'Being Aware of' and 'Knowing',"
        APQ 7 (1957), 216-35.
        Discussion of 'awareness' as it is used in theories that
        rely on the notion of "direct awareness."

609. Hartline, H. K., and Ratliff, F., "Inhibitory Interaction
        of Receptor Units in the Eye of Limulus," J Gen
        Physiol 40 (1957), 357-76.

610.   _____, "Visual Receptors and Retinal Inter-
        action," Science 164 (1969), 270-78.

611. Hartnack, Justus, Analysis of the Problems of Perception
        in British Empiricism, (Copenhagen: Munksgaard,
        1950).

612.   _____, "Remarks About Experience," A 13 (1952),
        117-20.
        To describe what we see is to say what we have found out
        by using our eyes. Experiences are not entities. This
        claim can be used as reason for preferring language of
        appearing to talk of sense-data.

613.   _____, "The Alleged Privacy of Experience," JP
        49 (1952), 405-11.
        The claim that one's experiences are private violates the
        logical grammar of our language.

614.   _____, "Remarks on the Concept of Sensation,"
        JP 56 (1959), 111-17.
        Sensations are not non-physiological occurrences that are
        caused by physiological processes.

615.   Hartshorne, Charles, The Philosophy and Psychology of Sen-
        sation, (Chicago: University of Chicago Press, 1934).
        Presents an "affective continuum" theory of sensory
        qualities. Good reviews of the philosophical and
        psychological literature then current.

616.   _____, "Professor Hall on Perception,"
        PPR 21 (1960), 563-71.
        Reply to E. Hall [#566].

617.   Hausman, Alan, "Solipsism and Berkeley's Alleged Realism,"
        RIP 22, No. 85-86, Fasc. 3-4, (1968), 403-12.
        Berkeley cannot escape solipsism by embracing realism
        with respect to the ideas (qualities), the collections of
        which constitute material objects.

618.   Hawley, Gessner G., Seeing the Invisible, (New York: Knopf,
        1945).
        A popular account of the workings of the electron micro-
        scope.

619.   Hay, John C., "Optical Motions and Space Perception: An
        Extension of Gibson's Analysis," Psych Rev 73 (1966),
        550-65.

620.   Hayek, Friederich A., The Sensory Order: An Inquiry into
        the Foundations of Theoretical Psychology, (Chicago:
        University of Chicago, 1952).
        The nervous system classifies sensory impulses and higher
        order data; these are then related to hierarchical
        patterns of motor responses or behaviors. An early
        "evolutionary" theory of perception. This model shows
        the relation between the two different orders, sensory
        and physical, better than alternative theories, e.g.,
        behaviorism.

71

621. Haymond, William S., "The Argument from Illusion," MS 46 (1969), 109-35.
The basis for the continuing influence of the argument from illusion is located in the Cartesian tendency to equate epistemic certainty with logical necessity.

622. Heaton, J. M., The Eye: Phenomenology and Physiology of Function and Disorder, (London: Tavistock, 1968).

623. _____, "The Phenomenology of Eyestrain," Human Context 5 (1973), 345-56.
In eyestrain one experiences an unusual sense of relationship between mind and body. The eyes are felt as "external"--something to be controlled by will "from the mind inside" as it were.

624. Hebb, D. O., The Organization of Behavior, (New York: Wiley, 1949).
The human capacity for recognizing patterns is the result of an intensive visual training that goes on from the moment of birth. Schema are established and reconstructed by further experiences.

625. _____, "A Neurophysiological Theory," in S. Koch, ed., Psychology: A Study of a Science, (New York: McGraw-Hill, 1963), Volume 1, 622-43.
Author discusses the development, assumptions and results of his work in [#624].

626. _____, A Textbook of Psychology, 2nd edition, (Philadelphia: Saunders, 1966).

627. _____, "Concerning Imagery," Psych Rev 75 (1968), 466-77.
A physiological analysis of imagery. Eidetic imagery, hallucinations and hypnagogic imagery compared to memory images, and peculiar features of the memory image are discussed.

628. Heckenmueller, S. G., "Stabilization of the Retinal Image: A Review of Method, Effects and Theory," Pysch Bull 63 (1965), 157-69.
Three basic methods used in reducing involuntary eye movements in order to produce a stable retinal image are presented. Stabilizing the retinal image is found to produce some fading or actual disappearance of the object being viewed. Other effects on the disappearance are considered, and some explanations for this phenomenon are suggested.

629. Heidelberger, Herbert, "Chisholm's Epistemic Principles," N 3 (1969), 73-82.
A discussion of four of Chisholm's principles of evidence.

630. Heil, John, "Sensations, Experiences and Brain Processes,"
P 45 (1970), 221-26.
An attack on Armstrong's version of the identity theory
on the grounds that Armstrong cannot account for three
experimental test subjects being able to tell graphs of
their own neural activity from those of the others.

631. Heisenberg, Werner, The Physicist's Conception of Nature,
(London: Hutchinson, 1958). (originally 1955)

632. _____, Physics and Philosophy, (London:
Allen and Unwin, 1959). (originally 1958).
A physicist's look at philosophical problems with quantum
theory, especially those concerned with ordinary versus
scientific uses of language and in what sense they are
compatible.

633. Held, Richard, ed., Image, Object and Illusion, (San
Francisco: W. H. Freeman, 1974).
Readings obviously published in Scientific American
on the topics of the general processes of vision, color
and contrast, spatial perception and form analysis.

634. Helson H., "Adaptation Level Theory," in S. Koch, ed.,
Psychology: A Study of a Science, Vol. 1, (New York:
McGraw-Hill, 1963), 565-621.
Outline of adaptation level theory and applications to
some main areas of psychology, especially to non-deviant
sensory behavior.

635. _____, Adaptation-level Theory, (New York: Harper
and Row, 1964).
Attempts to use adaptation as the basic theoretical concept for studying behavior. It is extended from perceptual contexts to cover such areas as motivation, personality and interpersonal behavior.

636. Hempel, Carl G., "Reflections on Nelson Goodman's The
Structure of Appearance," PR 62 (1953), 108-26.

637. _____, "The Theoretician's Dilemma," in Feigl,
Scriven and Maxwell, eds., Minnesota Studies in
the Philosophy of Science II, (Minneapolis, Minnesota: University of Minnesota Press, 1958).

638. Henle, Paul, "On the Certainty of Empirical Statements,"
JP 44 (1947), 625-32.
Reply to Stace, [#1280].

639. Henson, R. G., "Ordinary Language, Common Sense, and the
Time-Lag Argyment," M 76 (1967), 21-33.
An attack on the time-lag argument by appealing to
ordinary language in philosophical discourse.

640. Henze, Donald F., "Berkeley on Sensations and Qualities,"
     _T 31_ (1965), 174-80.

641. Hershenson, Maurice, "Development of the Perception of
     Form," _Psych Bull 67_ (1967), 326-36.

642. Hesse, Mary, "Theories, Dictionaries and Observation,"
     BJPS 9 (1958), 12-28. Comments by Alexander.
     If observation statements are to serve as tests for the
     truth of a scientific theory the distinction between
     direct observation and theoretical inference cannot be
     maintained.

643. _____, _The Structure of Scientific Inference_,
     (Berkeley: University of California Press, 1974).
     Section 1 is on theory and observation; argues that the
     traditional theory/observation distinction is misguided
     but that its positive points can be captured by a network
     model of theories.

644. Hick, J., "Fallacies," _Encyclopedia of Philosophy_, Vol. 3,
     176.

645. Hickes, G. Dawes, _The Nature of Perception and its
     Objects_. Proceedings of the Seventh International
     Congress of Philosophy, Oxford, 1931.

646. _____, _Critical Realism: Studies in the
     Philosophy of Mind and Nature_, (London: Macmillan,
     1938).
     Contains an analysis of Broad's theory of sensa, and
     concludes by asking how one insight into the world arose
     since all we know (on Broad's view) are sensa.

647. Higginson, Glenn D., "Stimulus, Sensation and Meaning,"
     _JP 32_ (1935), 645-50.
     Argues against the sensation/perception distinction and
     makes a case for regarding perception as a functional
     state of an organism.

648. Hill, Thomas English, _Contemporary Theories of Knowledge_,
     (New York: Macmillan, 1961).
     A useful review of early to mid-twentieth century theories
     of knowledge: Idealist, Realistic, Mediating, Pragmatist,
     and Analytic theories.

649. Hinckfuss, I. C., "J. M. Hinton on Visual Experiences,"
     _M 79_ (1970), 278-80.
     Critical comment on Hinton [#656]. There are psi-events:
     events entailed by either of the claims 'I see a flash' or
     'I have a visual experience of a flash.'

650. Hinshaw, Virgil C., _An Inquiry into the Factual Basis of_

Human Knowledge, (Princeton University Library, 1945).

651. _____, "Basic Propositions in Lewis' Analysis
      of Knowledge," JP 46 (1949), 176-84.

652. _____, "The Given," PPR 18 (1957), 312-25.
      Distinguishes several senses of 'the given'.

653. Hintikka, Jaako, "On the Logic of Perception," (with
      comments by Romane Clark) in N. S. Care and R. H.
      Grimm, eds., Perception and Personal Identity,
      (Cleveland: Case Western Reserve University Press,
      1967), 140-96. Also in Models for Modalities, 151-
      83.
      Shows that perceptual terms can be treated as modal
      notions, on a par with verbs of propositional attitudes.
      The semantics for perceptual terms is laid out and used
      to clarify the argument from illusion, the status of
      sense-data and the nature of objects of immediate per-
      ception.

654. Hinton, J. M., "Seeming and Causes," P 41 (1966), 348-55.
      Critical discussion of F. G. Ebersole [#375].
      Seeing is something that happens--an event--and is
      something that light rays bring about.

655. _____, "On Not Having What You Are Given," I 10
      (1967), 313-16.
      Rejects current tendency to distinguish philosophers'
      theories of perception according to whether or not they
      accept a "given" element in perception.

656. _____, "Visual Experiences," M 76 (1967), 217-27.
      Argues against the idea that there is a visual experience,
      called psi-ing, that necessarily occurs either when one,
      e.g., sees a flash of light, has an experience which is
      like seeing a flash of light or seeming to see a flash of
      light. Suggests that introducing such events in non-
      veridical cases is as misguided as introducing sense-data
      as the objects of non-veridical experiences.

657. _____, "Perception and Identification," PR 76
      (1967), 421-35.
      Argues that remarks such as "The speck moving slowly
      over that radio mast is the plane we're waiting for" and
      "That speck...is identical with the plane" can be per-
      fectly in order and can, furthermore, sometimes be true.

658. _____, "Illusions and Identity," A 27 (1967), 65-
      76.
      Attempt to propose satisfactory criteria of identity for
      neurophysiological events and phosphenes (illusions of
      flashes of light resulting from electrical stimulation of

the brain.)

659. _____, "Experiences," PQ 17 (1967), 1-13.
Whether experience of seeing blue is a non-physical event
still in question if certain arguments for the identity-
thesis are false.

660. _____, "Visual Experiences: A Reply to I. C.
Hinckfuss," M 82 (1973), 278-79.
Is there an experience (of psi-ing) which is common to
both perceiving that p and having the illusion that you
do? Reply to Hinckfuss [#649].

661. Hirsch, Helmut V. B., and Spinelli, D. M., "Visual
Experience Modifies Distribution of Horizontally and
Vertically Oriented Receptive Fields in Cats,"
Science 168 (1970), 869-71.
Report of experiments done with cats raised from birth
with one eye viewing horizontal lines and one eye viewing
vertical lines. It was found that environments with
horizontal fields activated only the eye exposed to
horizontal lines and those with vertical fields activated
only the eye exposed to vertical lines.

662. Hirst, R. J., The Problems of Perception, (London: Allen
and Unwin, 1959).
A critical discussion of the traditional philosophical
positions in philosophy (sense-data, phenomenalist,
linguistic, representative theories). Relates these
philosophical problems to wider philosophical issues
(mind-body problem) and to psychological and physiological studies. An early version of his version of direct
realism.

663. _____, "Critical Study of Austin's Sense and
Sensibilia," PQ 13 (1963), 162-70.

664. _____, "Perception, Science and Common Sense," M 60
(1951), 481-505.
Criticizes the argument from illusion and argues that the
main problem of perception is that of giving adequate
accounts of physiological facts.

665. _____, "Form and Sensation," ASSP 39 (1965), 155-
72.
Symposium with C. J. F. Williams.

666. _____, ed., Perception and the External World,
(New York: Macmillan, 1965).
Anthology, mostly excerpts from classical and early to
mid-twentieth century sources. Sections are problems.
Sense-datum theory, types of Realism and Radical theories
(Idealism, permanent possibilities, phenomenalism).
Includes articles by Lovejoy, Brain, Helmoltz, Koffka,

Moore, Price, Russell, Ayer, Austin, Ryle, Price,
Locke, Montague, McGilvary, R. W. Sellars, Berkeley,
Hume, and Mill.

667. _____, "Images," Encyclopedia of Philosophy, Vol.
4, 133.

668. _____, "Sensa," The Encyclopedia of Philosophy,
Vol. 7, 407-15.
Distinguishes sensa (objects of immediate awareness) into
sensations and sensa-data. Reviews arguments historically
adduced for introducing latter and criticisms of the
sense-datum theory. Includes extensive bibliography on
the topic.

669. Hochberg, Herbert, "Ontology and Acquaintance," Phil
Studies 17 (1966), 49-55.

670. Hochberg, Julian, "Perception: Toward the Recovery of a
Definition," Psych Rev 63 (1956), 400-05.
Attempts to determine operations that will define "perception": psychophysical scaling in terms of immediacy
or perceptual quality of aroused experience and responses
that cannot be obtained in the absence of the stimulus.

671. _____, Perception, (Englewood Cliffs, New
Jersey: Prentice-Hall, 1964).
Introductory text for a course in psychology or perception.
Includes discussions of measurement of sensations by
methods of sensory psychophysics and analytic introspection, functioning of the visual system, structuralism,
the nature-nurture debate, gestaltist laws of organization, space-perception and social perception. Many
diagrams and illustrations.

672. _____, "In the Mind's Eye," in R. N. Haber,
ed., Contemporary Theory and Research in Visual
Perception, (New York: Holt, Rinehart and Winston,
1968), 309-31.
Attempt to analyze structure of visually perceived form
and to identify the elements of perceptual processing.

673. _____, "The Representation of Things and
People," in Gombrich, Hochberg and Black, Art,
Representation and Reality, (Baltimore: Johns
Hopkins University Press, 1972), 47-94.

674. Hocutt, Max, "What We Perceive: An Examination of the
Paradox of Perception and of the Sense-Datum
Philosophy As Its Solution," APQ 5 (1968), 43-53.
The paradox of perception is generated by cases in which
something is seen that does not exist, or is seen as
something it is not, or is both seen and heard. Author
argues that sense-datum theories are not acceptable

77

solutions to this paradox, since such theories rest on a confusion between two sorts of ways in which one can talk about what it is that we perceive.

675. Hodges, M. and Carter, W. R., "Nelson on Dreaming Pain," Phil Studies 20 (1969), 43-46.

676. Holborrow, L. C., "Against Projecting Pains," A 29 (1969), 105-08.
Discussion of logical differences between pains and other types of sensations.

677. _____, "Sensations and Sensible Properties," AJP 48 (1970), 17-30.
There is a logical distinction to be drawn between perceiving and having sensations, yet having bodily sensations play an important role in some kinds of perception. Rejects Wittgenstein's suggestion that it is only a matter of grammar that we do not speak of pain-patches on plants.

678. _____, "Materialism and Phenomenal Qualities: Part I," ASSP 47 (1973), 87-105.
Author discusses and criticizes three recent attempts (Armstrong, Locke and Cornman) to give a materialistic account of sensory experience. Sketches the outlines of an alternative to materialism.

679. Holland, Harry C., The Spiral After-Illusion, International Series of Monographs in Experimental Psychology, (Oxford: Pergamon, 1965).
The after effect is an illusory movement in a direction opposite to that of the stimulus. Summary of earlier research efforts and statement of the present attempts at explanation.

680. Hollis, Martin, "Monadologue," A 30 (1970), 145-47.
Unusual discussion of the problem of induction.

681. _____, "Reason and Reality," PAS 68 (1968), 271-86.

682. Hooker, C. A., "Empiricism, Perception and Conceptual Change," Can J Phil 3 (1973), 59-74.
Attack on Feyerabend's relativism.

683. Hoor, Marten Ten, "Awareness and Inference: An Approach to Realism," JP 33 (1936), 589-96.
Defends realism: the character of one's experience justifies inference to real, independently existing external objects.

684. Hope, V., "Speaking of Sensations," M 82 (1973), 183-90.

We can describe private sensations by means of a public vocabulary. Such descriptions are not verifiable, but they are intelligible.

685. Hopkins, James, "Visual Geometry," PR 82 (1973), 3-34.
Phenomenal space cannot be shown to be either Euclidean or non-Euclidean. Our devices are too crude to determine either.

686. Howell, Robert, "Seeing As," S 23 (1972), 400-22.
An attempt to give a formal representation (truth-conditions) of "seeing-as" statements by using techniques of semantic interpretation developed by Jaako Hintikka in [#653]. Interpretation of such statements given in terms of doxastic alternatives to the actual world. A valuable extension of Hintikka's work.

687. Hubel, David H., "Tungsten Microelectrode for Recording from Single Units," Science 123 (1957), 549-50.

688. _____, and Wiesel, T. N., "Receptive Fields of Single Neurones in the Cat's Striate Cortex," J Physiol 148 (1959), 574-91.
Mapping of receptive fields (restricted retinal areas) shows them to be composed of flanking areas of excitatory and inhibitory regions. Stimuli specific in form, size, position and orientation were more effective than diffuse illumination of the whole retina. Strength of response to a spot of light depended on direction of movement of the spot.

689. _____, and Wiesel, T. N., "Receptive Fields of Optic Nerve Fibers in the Spider Monkey," J Physiol 154 (1960), 572-80.
Receptive fields of retinal ganglion cells are of two main types, excitatory and inhibitatory, and are arranged in concentric figures. Smallest receptive field centers found near the fovea; increasing distance from the fovea corresponds to increasing size of receptive field centres. Specific response to colored light discussed.

690. _____, and Wiesel, T. N., "Integrative Action in the Cat's Lateral Geniculate Body," J Physiol 155 (1961), 385-99.
Comparison of receptive fields in the retina, lateral geniculate body, and striate cortex. Increasing receptive field complexity is found, with corresponding increased variety in cell types and interconnections in the cortex. The lateral geniculate body was found to modify incoming signals from the optic-tract, resulting in increased peripheral suppression at the geniculate level.

691. _____, and Wiesel, T. N., "Receptive Fields,

Binocular Interaction and Funcational Architecture in the Cat's Visual Cortex," J Physiol 160 (1962), 106-54.
Receptive fields of cells in the visual cortex fall into two categories--simple and complex. Simple receptive fields differ in axis orientation. Complex receptive fields differ from simple ones in that in complex fields response to light could not be predicted from the arrangement of excitatory and inhibitory regions. The most effective stimuli from activating cells with simple fields (slits, edges and dark bars) also are the most effective in activating complex fields. Authors suggest relevance of findings to form perception in mammals.

692.   _____, and Wiesel, T. N., "Receptive Fields and Functional Architecture of Monkey Striate Cortex," J Physiol 195 (1967), 215-43.
Studies show that specific small areas of the striate cortex respond to a corresponding small area of the visual field in terms of direction of light-dark contours, type of contour, and change in direction (curvature) of contour.

693.   Hudson, H., "Achievement Expressions," A 16 (1955), 127-30.
Discusses the logic of these expressions without relating them explicitly to verbs of perception. (Ryle has suggested that 'perceive' is an achievement expression.)

694.   Hull, Richard T., "Evidence, Incorrigibility and Acquaintance," (abstract) JP 70 (1973), 657.
Color words can be regarded in such a way that judgments involving them may be incorrigible.

695.   Hunter, John, "Some Questions About Dreaming," M 80 (1971), 70-92.
States and comments on a number of central philosohpical questions about dreaming, e.g., whether it makes sense to ask whether a person has remembered a dream correctly or not.

696.   Hurvich, Leo M., and Jameson, Dorothea, The Perception of Brightness and Darkness, (Boston: Allyn and Bacon, 1966).
Discussion of threshold data and adaptation levels; an undergraduate text on the experimental literature.

697.   Hutten, Ernest, H., "Perception and Knowledge," JP 44 (1947), 85-97.
Attempts to reconcile the public nature of the language of objects with the alleged privacy of the language of percepts.

698.   Huxley, Aldous, The Door's of Perception, (London: Chatto and Windus, 1954; 2nd ed., New York: Harper and Row, 1963).

A remarkable account of the author's experience with mescaline. Includes detailed description of subjective perceptual changes. Suggests some theories as to how mescaline affects the CNS and argues that the use of mescaline should be encouraged as it provides unique opportuni-
ties for spiritual insight, by means of direct, immediate
and heightened awareness of senses.

699. Ihde, Don, "Parmenidean Meditations," The Jour of the Brit
        Soc for Phenomenol 1 (1970), 16-23.
      A discussion of the phenomenology of auditory experience.
      We are surrounded by a field of sound, this field has a
      shape and at the boundary of this there is silence. He
      inserts quotes from Parmenides as parallels to his claims
      about sound.

700. _____, and Slaughter, Thomas F., "Studies in the
        Phenomenology of Sound: I. Listening," IPQ 10
        (1970), 232-39.
      Contrast between "Husserlian" and "Heideggerian" pheno-
      menologies as applied to the task of attending to music.
      The latter technique is more appropriate for listening
      to music, as the former seems to be infested with con-
      cepts derived from visual experience.

701. _____, "Studies in the Phenomenology of Sound: II.
        On Perceiving Persons," IPQ 10 (1970), 240-46.
      Discusses the perception of other persons from an auditory
      standpoint, and maintains that, though we usually se
      persons before we hear them, the Other is most manifestly
      present through the auditory contact.

702. _____, "Studies in the Phenomenology of Sound: III.
        God and Sound," IPQ 10 (1970), 247-51.
      There are parallels (invisibility, spatiality, temporal-
      ity) between auditory phenomena and the nature of God
      (the Hebrew God)--considered as a cultural idea.

703. Imlay, Robert A., "Immediate Awareness," Dialogue (Canada)
        8 (1969-70), 228-42.
      There is no such thing as immediate awareness since there
      is no satisfactory notion of 'incorrigible' available to
      those who use the term.

704. Ingram-Pearson, C. W., "The Reality of Appearances," RM 9
        (1955), 200-06.
      Appearances are real, and this leads to interesting con-
      clusions about the distinction between reality and truth.

705. Isenberg, Arnold, "Perception, Meaning and the Subject-
        Matter of Art," JP 41 (1944), 561-75.

706. Ishiguro, Hide, "Imagination," ASSP 41 (1967), 37-56.
        Reply to I. Dilman [Same vol., 19-36].

707. Isaacs, Nathan, _The Foundations of Common Sense_, (London: Routledge and Kegan Paul, 1949).

708. Ittelson, W. H., and Kilpatrick, F. P., "Experiments in Perception," _Sci Amer 185_ (August, 1951), 50-55. Studies of perception of apparent motion, distorted rooms and the rotating trapezoidal window used to support claim that what we see is a personal construction based on past experience. Perception is a form of prediction.

709. _____, _The Ames Demonstrations in Perception: A Guide to Their Construction and Use_, (Princeton: Princeton University Press, 1952).

710. _____, and Cantrill, Hadley, _Perception: A Transactional Approach_, (Garden City, New York: Doubleday, 1954). A concise statement of the transactionalist theory of perception. All perception is active transaction with the environment. Transaction is constructive from the perceiver's point of view.

711. _____, _Visual Space Perception_, (New York: Springer, 1960). Perception is transaction; thus, the gap is bridged between phenomenological theories and behavioral theories. The perceiver adds to the cues he receives.

712. _____, "Perception and Transactional Psychology," in S. Koch, ed., _Psychology: A Study of A Science_, (New York: McGraw-Hill, 1962), vol. 4, 660-704. Introduction outlines perception from common-sense versus psychological viewpoint. Discussion of how approaches to problems of perception differ as between phenomenological description and S-R theorists (including learning theory and psychophysical concerns). Transactional approach contrasted with these and the issues deriving from this methodology discussed. Describes experiments (size-distant relationships, rotating trapezoid, aniseikonic lenses and perception of social and complex processes) which derive from transactional approach. Includes chapter on patient-therapist interaction as based on transactional theory of perceptual change.

713. Ivins, William M., _Art and Geometry: A Study in Spatial Intuitions_, (Cambridge, Massachusetts, 1946).

714. _____, _Prints and Visual Communication_, (London: Routledge and Kegan Paul, 1953).

715. Jackson, Frank, "Review of Dretske's _Seeing and Knowing_," _AJP 48_ (1970), 148-50.

716. _____, and Pinkerton, R. J., "On An Argument

Against Sensory Items," M 82 (1973), 269-72.
Defends against D. M. Armstrong's attack on non-physical
sensory items. Rejects argument from the transitivity
of 'exactly similar in colour-appearance'.

717.   Jacobs, Norman, "Physicalism and Sensation Sentences,"
       JP 34 (1937), 602-11.
       Attempts to reconcile certain alleged conflicts between
       physicalism and the ordinary use of sensation words.

718.   Jameson, Dorothea and Hurvich, Leo M., eds., Visual
       Psychophysics, (New York: Springer-Verlag, 1972).
       Meant to document, through numerous chapters, the current
       state of psychophysical research on vision.

719.   Johansson, Gunnar, "On Theories for Visual Space Percep-
       tion: A Letter to Gibson," Scandinavian J Psychol
       11 (1970). 67-74.
       Critique of Gibson [#492]. Analyzes Gibson's construct of
       ecological optics and argues tridimensionality must be
       assumed as the visual apparatus decodes data. Reply by
       Gibson, p. 75-79.

720.   Johnson, David, "A Formulation Model of Perceptual Know-
       ledge," APQ 8 (1971), 54-62.
       Suggests an alternative model to those offered by sense-
       datum theories. Identifies perceptual data with uncon-
       scious thoughts which perceivers are caused to have by
       sense experience. Such data are not to be construed as
       entities.

721.   _____, "Another Perspective on the Speckled Hen,"
       Can J Phil 1 (1971), 235-44.

722.   _____, "The Temporal Dimension of Perceptual
       Experience: A Non-traditional Empiricism," APQ 11
       (1974), 71-76.
       Distinguishes between what he calls the "form" and the
       "content" of perceptual experience. "Form" includes
       shape, texture and size of an object; "content" includes
       color, felt resistance, felt temperature, etc. He claims
       that empiricists currently favor content over form for
       the role of what is "real" in perception, and that this
       emphasis is misguided.

723.   Jonas, Hans, "Causality and Perception," JP 47 (1950),
       319-24.
       Our notion of causality is not derived from perceptual
       experience, but from the force associated with bodily
       movement.

724.   _____, "The Nobility of Sight: A Study in the
       Phenomenology of the Senses," PPR 14 (1953), 507-19.

83

725. Jones, D. Caradog, "Visual and Tactual Sensations: A
      Case Study," The Jour of the Brit Soc for Phenom 1
      (1970), 68-71.
      Draws on a distinction between two types of nervous sys-
      tems--the epicritic and protopathic (proposed by Sir Henry
      Head) and describes a case in which a man loses tactual
      sensations associated with the epicritic system while
      retaining those associated with the protopathic.

726. Jones, J. R., "The Self in Sensory Cognition," M 58
      (1949), 40-61.
      Attempt to provide an account of the self that will allow
      for the analysis of sensory events in terms of a relation
      between the sensed object and something else without
      supposing there is a subject of awareness.

727. _____, "Dr. Moore's Revised Directions for Picking
      Out Visual Sense-Data," PQ 1 (1950), 433-38.

728. _____, "Sense-Data: A Suggested Source of the
      Fallacy," M 63 (1954), 180-202.
      Offers an analysis of perception which generates a proof
      of the claim that appearances of things cannot be regarded
      as objects (sense-data).

729. Jones, O. R., "Reason and Certainty," P 45 (1970), 55-58.
      Chisholm has made unnecessary concessions to the sceptic
      in his accounts of the fallibility of memory and percep-
      tion.

730. _____, "After-Images," APQ 9 (1972), 150-58.
      Argues against N. Malcolm [#880]. The ideas of numerical
      diversity and numerical identity do make sense as applied
      to after-images; reports of after-images are corrigible
      in a way that, e.g., reports of pains, are not.

731. Johnstone, Henry W., "A Postscript on Sense-Data," JP 48
      (1951), 908-14.

732. Joske, W. D., "Inferring and Perceiving," PR 72 (1963),
      433-45.
      The question whether or not perceptual judgments are infer-
      ential indicates a need for a clearer notion of inference.
      Knowledge of ourselves as creatures with past experience
      and judgments about physical objects we recognize are non-
      inferential.

733. Julesz, Bela, Foundations of Cyclopean Perception, (Chi-
      cago, University of Chicago, 1971).
      Investigation of perception by using stimuli that bring
      about formation of a perception at some central location in
      the visual system, where it could not be formed earlier in
      the system.

734. Kaal, Hans, "Senses of 'perceive' or senses of 'senses of perceive'," A 24 (1963), 6-11.

735. Kadish, Mortimer, "A Note on the Grounds of Evidence," JP 46 (1949), 229-42.
Discussion of the "immediacy" theory: the claim that data of immediate experience provide the evidence for empirical statements.

736. Kagan, Jerome, "Attention and Psychological Change in the Young Child," Science 170 (1970), 826-31.
Attempts to ascertain determinants of attention by varying schema thought to be paradigmatic.

737. Kahl, R. ed., Selected Writings of Herman von Helmholtz, (Middletown: Wesleyan University Press, 1971).

738. Kantor, Jay, "Pinching and Dreaming," Phil Studies 21 (1970), 28-32.
Argues against the claim that ability to feel pain is a sufficient condition of knowing that one is awake.

739. Kates, Carol A., "Perception and Temporality in Husserl's Phenomenology," Phil Today 14 (1970), 89-100.

740. Kattsoff, Louis O., "Physics nad Reality," PPR 5 (1944), 108-20, 125-26. Comments by Riezler.
Indirectly a commentary on Riezler's Physics and Reality in the form of a dialogue between modern reincarnations of Aristotle and Newton.

741. Katz, David, The World of Color, (London: Routledge and Kegan Paul, 1935). Translated R. B. MacLeod and L. W. Fox.

742. Kaufman, E. L., Lord, M. W., Reese, T. W., and Volkman, J., "The Discrimination of Visual Number," American Jour of Psych 62 (1949), 498-525.

743. Kaufman, Lloyd and Rock, Irvin, "The Moon Illusion," Sci Amer 207 (1962), 129-30.
The moon illusion depends on the presence and distance effect of the terrain. Color, apparent brightness and eye elevation have no evident influence on the phenomenon.

744. Kennedy, John M., A Psychology of Picture Perception, (San Francisco: Jossey-Bass, 1974).
Pictures convey information and thus communicate. Data is drawn from many fields. Theory is of a Gibson type in origin.

745. Kenny, Anthony, "The Argument From Illusion in Aristotle's Metaphysics Gamma (1009-10)," M 76 (1967), 184-97.

746.   _____, "Critical Realism," Encyclopedia of Philo-
                sophy, Vol. 2, 261.

747.   Khatchadourian, Haig, "Aboug Imaginary Objects," R 8
                (1966), 77-89.
            Ordinary uses of 'about' in statements about imaginary
            objects analyzed.

748.   _____, "Objects and Qualities," APQ 6
                (1969), 103-15.
            Discussion of the logical grammar of 'object', 'quality'
            and 'property'.

749.   Kidd, Aline H., and Jeanne L. Rivoire, eds., Perceptual
                Development in Children, (New York: International
                University Press, 1966).
            Anthology, works by: W. C. Halstead and P. M. Rennick,
            G. E. Ellman, N. H. Pronko, R. Ebert, and G. Greenberg,
            J. L. Rivoire and A. H. Kidd, R. M. Kidd, R. L. Fantz,
            L. B. Ames, David Elkind, L. K. Frank, J. H. Flavell,
            C. M. Solley, D. McCarthy, J. E. Garai, M. D. Vernon,
            K. Lovell, S. Goldstone, and Joyce L. Goldfarb, J. Kagan.

750.   Kielkopf, Charles, "The Pictures in the Head of a Man
                Born Blind," PPR 28 (1968), 501-13.
            If we can conceive of a congenitally blind person des-
            cribing what he images in sentences containing color-
            words, it follows that visual images are not pictures in
            the mind.

751.   Kilpatrick, Franklin P., "Two Processes in Perceptual
                Learning," Jour of Exper Psych 47 (1954), 362-70.
            Alterations in visual space perception can be learned as
            shown by experiments with the Ames distorted rooms. Two
            processes are discussed: (1) reweighting of visual cues
            that tend to give away the distortion, and (2) a process
            whereby there is an actual change in the way a given
            stimulus pattern is perceived. Author suggests both
            processes function in all perceptual learning.

752.   _____, ed., Explorations in Transact-
                ional Psychology, (New York: New York University,
                1961).
            Anthology, works by: H. Cantrill, A. Ames, Jr., Albert
            H. Hastorf, W. H. Ittelson, F. P. Kilpatrick, W. Wittreich,
            M. Grace, K. B. Radcliffe, Jr., E. Engel, H. H. Toch.

753.   King-Farlow, John, "Senses and Sensibilia," A 23 (1962),
                37-40.

754.   Kiteley, M., "The Argument from Illusion: Objects and
                Objections," M 81 (1972), 191-207.
            Gives neat standard statement of the argument from

illusion: (1) that it introduces puzzling entities; (2) that perceptual verbs are not primarily used to report immediately apprehended sensible appearances, but (3) are used to allude to evidence, quality assertive force or express doubt. Kitely concentrates, in his substantive remarks, on the premise in the argument which goes: 'the stick looks bent to me; therefore what I see is bent'. He compares this to 'he failed to become angry; therefore what he failed to become was angry'. In both cases the consequent embodied an existential generalization of a complex substantive term not occurring in the antecedent.

755. Klausner, N. W., "The Epistemology of C. A. Strong," <u>JP</u> <u>42</u> (1945), 683-94.
Discussion of Strong's critical realism.

756. Klein, George S., <u>Perception, Motives and Personality</u>, (New York: Knopf, 1970).
A psychoanalytically oriented theory of perception as directed by active motives of the perceiver. The unity of perceptual objects is an experienced unity--a coded event and not a property. What we experience depends to some extent upon our motives.

757. Klein, Peter D., "<u>The</u> Private Language Argument and <u>The</u> Sense-Datum Theory," <u>AJP</u> <u>47</u> (1969), 325-43.
Attacks the private language argument and thereby clears the way for a renewed defense of the sense-datum theory. (The author seems to accept the claim that a sense-datum theory does involve the possibility of some private langauge.)

758. Kmieck, George A., S. J., La Drier, M. La Verne, and Zegers, Richard T., S. J., "The Role of the Sensible Species in St. Thomas' Epistemology: A Comparison with Contemporary Perception Theory," <u>IPQ</u> <u>14</u> (1974), 455-74.
The authors argue that the concept of the sensible species in St. Thomas is identical with that of the neurological relational representation of stimulus information in modern psychology. They base this claim on five points of convergence between the two.

759. Kneale, William C., <u>Probability and Induction</u>, (Oxford: Oxford University Press, 1949).
Argues that perception involves going beyond what is immediately given in sensation and thus serves as a basis for natural necessity (natural laws).

760. _____, "Sensation and the Physical World," <u>PQ</u> <u>1</u> (1950), 109-26.
Locke's distinction between primary and secondary qualities is in need of, and is here given, a reformulation which

bears on certain sorts of mistakes about perception.

761. _____, "Experience and Introspection," PAS 50 (1950), 1-28.
Discussion of the empiricist thesis that the source of all knowledge is experience and that one of the sources of experience is introspection. Criticizes theory of introspection that rests on an analogy between perception and introspection.

762. _____, "What Can We See?" in S. Korner, ed., Observation and Interpretation: A Symposium of Philosophers and Physicists, (New York, Academic Press, 1957).

763. _____, "An Analysis of Perceiving in Terms of the Causation of Beliefs," in F. N. Sibley, [(ed.,) #1227].
A reply to Cox, same volume.

764. Knox, John, Jr., "Concerning the Argument From Perspectival Variation," RM 15 (1961), 518-21.
Discussion of the question whether a table really does appear to grow larger as I walk toward it.

765. _____, "On Mr. Nelson's Refutation of Sense-Data," Ratio 8 (1966), 90.

766. _____, "The Logic of Appearing," I 10 (1967), 245-50.

767. _____, "Can A Valid Argument Be Based on Differential Certainty?" M 79 (1970), 275-77.

768. _____, "Speaking of Appearances," Personalist 51 (1970), 387-92.
Argues that some non-comparative statements about how things appear entail the existence of appearances.

769. _____, "Do Appearances Exist?" APQ Monograph Series, No. 4, (1970), 79-101.
Appearances exist as entities distinct from the objects that appear so the question how an object is related to its appearance is one that must remain open. How something appears is not to be analyzed in terms of physical objects and their properties.

770. _____, "Don Locke and 'Appearance-Determined Qualities'," M 81 (1972), 267-70.
Argues against Locke's claim that we can distinguish primary from secondary qualities on the grounds that secondary qualities are appearance-determined whereas primary qualities are not. Distinguishes two senses of 'perceive' and 'appears' and holds that it is never the

case that what quality I perceive is determined by how
what I perceive appears.

771. Koch, Sigmund, ed., Psychology: A Study of Science, Vol.
        1, Sensory, Perceptual and Physiological Formulations,
        (New York, McGraw Hill, 1959).
      Anthology, works by: Dael Wolfle, Sigmund Koch, J. C. R.
      Licklider, C. H. Grahamer, M. H. Pirenne and F. H. C.
      Marriott, Kenneth N. Ogle, Albert A. Blank, W. C. H.
      Prentice, James J. Gibson, Leo Postman and Edward C.
      Tolman, Harry Helson, D. O. Hebb, Clifford T. Morgan.

772. Koffka, K., Principles of Gestalt Psychology, (New York:
        Harcourt Brace, 1935).
      A classic statement of Gestalt principles that defines
      the task of psychology as that of theorizing about pure
      descriptions of behavior. This can be best done through
      the notion of a field, a system of stresses and strain.

773. Kohler, Ivo, "Experiments with Goggles," Sci Amer 206
        (1962), 62-72.
      Experiments with prisms and tinted goggles show that the
      visual system can correct for most types of induced
      distortions, although not for the "color-stereo" effect
      in which blue is seen as closer to the perceiver than red.

774. Köhler, Wolfgang, Dynamics in Psychology, (New York:
        Grove Press, 1940).

775. _____, The Task of Gestalt Psychology, (Prince-
        ton University, 1969).
      A classic restatement of the general Gestalt position.

776. Kolers, P. A., "Some Differences Between Real and Apparent
        Visual Movement," Visual Research 3 (1963), 191-206.

777. _____, "The Illusion of Movement," Sci Amer 211
        (1964), 98-106.
      Studies in the perception of apparent motion tend to
      support an "assembly line" model of visual perceptions as
      constructions from numerous operations occurring at
      different times and places in the nervous system.

778. Konorski, J., Integrative Activity of the Brain, (Chicago:
        University of Chicago, 1967).
      An interdisciplinary approach. Uses concept of gnostic
      units and areas to discuss the brain's functioning. Uses
      this theory to present interesting and neurophysiological
      data concerning perception.

779. Kordig, Carl R., "Theory-Ladenness of Observation," RM 24
        (1971), 448-84.
      Critical discussion of the claims (Hanson, Feyerabend,

Kuhn, Toulmin) concerning the role of observation in
scientific theory-change, concentrating on relationship
between seeing, seeing-that, knowing-that and believing-
that.

780. Kotarbinska, Janina, "On Ostensive Definitions," PS 27
(1960), 1-22.
Ostensive definitions inform the hearer about the criteria
of applicability of a certain term, but only partially.
Author discusses the informational value of ostensive
definitions and the characteristics of terms introduced by
means of them.

781. Kuehl, James, "Perceiving and Imaging," PPR 31 (1970),
212-24.
A phenomenologically-based distinction between the object
as perceived and as imagined. The image-object cannot
meet the requirements for a perceived object as established by phenomenological analysis.

782. Kuhlenbeck, Hartwig, Brain and Consciousness, Some Prole-
gommena to an Approach to the Problem, Supplement to
Vol. 17, Confinia Neurologica, (Basel: Karger, 1957).

783. Kullman, Michael and C. Taylor, "The Pre-Objective World,"
RM 12 (1958), 108-32.
Discussion of Merleau-Ponty's notion of the pre-objective
world and its relation to his solutions to certain
traditional problems in perception, in particular the
argument from illusion.

784. Kultgen, John, "Intentionality and the Publicity of the
Perceptual World," PPR 33 (1973), 503-13.
The public/private distinction can be drawn by noting
that in perception our experience is public.

785. Kurtz, Richard M., "A Conceptual Investigation of Witkin's
Notion of Perceptual Style," M 78 (1969), 522-33.
There can be no such thing as a perceptual style. Con-
fusions in Witkin's psychological theory are said to be
instances of the kind of confusion engendered by inadequate attention to the ordinary senses of words like
'perceive', 'field', 'style', and 'experience'.

786. Kuspit, Donald Burton, The Philosophical Life of the
Senses, New York, (Philosophical Library, 1969).

787. Lafleur, Laurence J., "The Object of Observation and the
Object of Knowledge," P 18 (1973), 195-203.
Argues for a functionalist account of the object of
observation.

788. Lahey, John L., "The Primacy of Perception," Dianoia
(1970), 1-12.

789. Laird, John, "Things and Appearances, M 46 (1937), 302-19.

790. _____, "Hume's Account of Sensitive Belief," M 48 (1939), 427-45.

791. _____, "On Certain of Russell's Views Concerning the Human Mind," in P. Schilpp, ed., The Philosophy of Bertrand Russell, (Evanston, Illinois: Northwestern University Press, 1944).

792. Langer, Susanne K., Mind: An Essay on Human Feeling, Vol. 1 and 2 (Baltimore: John Hopkins Press, 1967). A biological model for human cognition.

793. Langford, C. H., and Marion, "Appearance and Reality in Perception," PPR 20 (1959), 532-34. The logical subject of a perceptual report is a sense-datum, not a physical object.

794. Langtry, Bruce, "Perception and Corrigibility," AJP 48 (1970), 369-72. Criticizes two arguments purporting to show the logical impossibility of having experiences with characteristics that logically guarantee the existence of some external state of affairs. It is argued that such experiences have not been shown to be logically impossible.

795. Lawrence, D. H., and Coles, G. R., "Accuracy of Recognition with Alternatives Before and After the Stimulus," J Exp Psych 47 (1954), 208-14. Examines the hypothesis that advance information about the nature of the alternatives allows an observer to become set to perceive the features that are distinctive for that set of alternatives. Results show no difference for before or after conditions and did not support the hypothesis.

796. _____, "The Nature of a Stimulus: Some Relationships Between Learning and Perception," in S. Koch, ed., Psychology: A Study of a Science, (New York: McGraw-Hill, 1963),vol. 5, 179-212. Restatement of traditional problems of perception in concepts derived from learning theory; emphasis on factors typically assigned to the influence of set, instructions, and attitudes. Fundamental assumptions underlying psycho-physical method are discussed and previous attempts by learning theorists to handle these factors are outlined.

797. Lawrie, Reynold, "The Existence of Mental Images," PQ 20 (1970), 253-57.

798. Lazerowitz, Morris, "(Review of) Austin's Sense and

Sensibilia," <u>P 38</u> (1963), 242-52.

799.   _____, <u>Philosophy and Illusion</u>, (London: Allen and Unwin, 1968).
A Wittgensteinian approach to appearance and reality.

800. Lazlo, Ervin, <u>System, Structure and Experience</u>, (New York: Gordon and Breach, 1969).
A not very clear attempt to provide a systems model for traditional philosophical problems.

801. Leaky, M. P. T., "Seeing and What We See," <u>M 82</u> (1973), 426-32.
Augments the conditions offered by Warnock [#1385] for the truth of the proposition "A sees x at time t" by adding: (a) $\underline{A}$ knows what an x is. (b) The object x is such that $\underline{A}$'s eyes are acute enough to pick out x's. These additional requirements are introduced to rule out the possibility of infants and animals being said to see objects.

802. Lean, Martin, <u>Sense-Perception and Matter</u>. A Critical Analysis of C. D. Broad's Theory of Perception. (London: Routledge and Kegan Paul, 1953).

803. Lee, Donald S., "The Construction of Empirical Concepts," <u>PPR 27</u> (1966), 183-98.

804. Lee, Harold Newton, <u>Perception and Aesthetic Vision</u>, (New York: Prentice-Hall, 1938).

805. Lefebre, Henri, "Reply to Professor Chisholm and Comments," <u>PPR 30</u> (1969), 22-30.

806. LeGrand, Y., <u>Light, Color and Vision</u>, (London: Chapman and Hall, 1957).
Chapter 19 contains an argument against naive realism based on the facts of color-vision.

807. Leibowitz, Herschel W., ed., <u>Visual Perception</u>, (New York: Macmillan, 1964).
Anthology, works by: E. G. Boring, H. P. Zeigler and H. W. Leibowitz, R. Held and M. Schlank, C. Leuba and C. Lucas, W. J. Wittreich, I. Rock and L. Kaufman, S. S. Stevens, E. von Holst.

808.   _____, and Pick, Herbert A., Jr., "Cross-cultural and Educational Aspects of the Ponzo Perspective Illusion," <u>Perception and Psychophysics 12</u> (1972), 430-32.
Experiments with college-trained and rural Ugandans show that the latter group do not perceive the illusory variation in length of two horizontal lines embedded in converging vertical lines. Authors hypothesize that this

is due to the fact that rural subjects respond to flat-
ness cues, whereas educated subjects respond to depth
cues in two-dimensional stimulus situations.

809. Lemos, Ramon M., "Sensation, Perception and the Given,"
          R 6 (1964), 63-80.
      A defense of the distinction between a "given" and an
      inferential element in perception. Argues that we do
      not need a sense-datum language in which to describe the
      given, but maintains that such a language is at least
      theoretically possible.

810. _____, "Immediacy, Privacy and Ineffability,"
          PPR 25 (1964), 500-15.
      Disembodied minds are possible; the privacy of our
      immediate experience is not necessarily a reflection of
      the fact that we each have our own bodies.

811. Lenneberg, Eric H., "The Relationship of Language to the
          Formation of Concepts," S 14 (1962), 103-09.
      Discusses acquisition of concepts--concept-acquisition
      is a result of man's basic constitution. No explicit
      reference to perceptual concepts, although this problem
      is relevant for, e.g., the analysis of perceiving in
      terms of the acquisition of beliefs.

812. Lenzen, Victor F., "Interaction Between Subject and
          Object," Erkenntis Band 6 Heft 5/6 (1936), 326-35.

813. _____, "The Concepts of Reality in Physical
          Theory," PR 54 (1945), 321-44.
      Discussion of relationship between concepts and obser-
      vations in physical theory.

814. _____, "Concepts and Reality in Quantum
          Mechanics," PS 16 (1949), 279-86.
      The concept of a physical object in quantum mechanics
      involves the qualities of discontinuity, complementarity
      and relativity.

815. _____, "Verification in Science," RIP 5
          (1951), 323-46.

816. Lettvin, J. Y., Maturana, H. R., Pitts, W. H., and
          McCulloch, W. S., "Two Remarks on the Visual System
          of the Frog," in W. A. Rosenblith, ed., Sensory
          Communication, (New York: Wiley, 1961).

817. Levensky, Mark, ed., Human Factual Knowledge, (Englewood
          Cliffs, New Jersey: Prentice Hall, 1971).
      Anthology: Part three on perception includes articles by
      Ayer, Hirst, and Whitely.

818. Levinas, Emmanuel, "Intentionalité et Sensation," RIP 19
     (1955), 34-54.

819. Levy, Erwin, "On the Possibility of a Perceptual World-
     in-Common," PPR 28 (1967), 48-57.
     "I see what you see" is true if construed as a claim
     about structural isomorphism of percepts.

820. Lewis, Carroll, "On Undetectable Differences in Sensa-
     tions," A 33 (1973), 193-94.
     Differences between pain-sensations can be detectable
     only by inference, not by sensing.

821. Lewis, C. I., An Analysis of Knowledge and Valuation,
     (LaSalle, Illinois: Open Court, 1946).
     Argues that empirical knowledge is gained only through
     presentation of sense, ultimately by direct perception.
     The theory of knowledge into which this fits is
     elaborately and interestingly laid out in great detail.

822. _____, "Professor Chisholm and Empiricism," JP 45
     (1948), 517-24. Reprinted in Swartz [#1301].
     Reply to Chisholm's review of Lewis' An Analysis of
     Knowledge and Valuation, [#257].

823. _____, "The Given Element in Empirical Knowledge,"
     PR 61 (1952), 168-75. Symposium with Reichenbach
     and Goodman.

824. _____, "Realism or Phenomenalism," PR 64 (1955),
     233-47.
     Sketches an account of our knowledge of things according
     to which we have knowledge of things via their properties
     and wonders whether such an account is realistic or
     phenomenalistic.

825. Lewis, David K., "Percepts and Color Mosaics in Visual
     Experience," PR 75 (1966), 357-68.
     Discussion of Firth's "Sense-Data and the Percept-
     Theory." Argues that the Exposure Hypothesis does not
     conflict with the percept-theory as Firth had claimed.

826. Lewis, Douglas, "Some Problems of Perceptions," PS 37
     (1970), 100-13.
     Argues that Pritchard and others who hold that secondary
     qualities are private mental entities have confused a
     scientific account of perception (the causal theory)
     with the (separable) philosophical thesis that secondary
     qualities are particular. Lewis argues that, without
     this assumption, secondary qualities need not be construed
     as private.

827. Lewis, H. D., "Naive Realism and a Passage in the

Theaetetus," <u>M 47</u> (1938), 351-56.

828. _____, "Private and Public Space," <u>PAS 53</u> (1953), 79-94.
Attacks traditional distinction between private and public spaces and argues that, in some sense, the multitudinous character of private space can be useful in accounting for illusions and hallucinations.

829. Lewy, Casimir, "The Terminology of Sense-Data " <u>M 55</u> (1946), 166-69.
A defense of Moore as against A. J. Ayer [#77]. Lewy defends the claim that on Moore's characterization of sense-data it is still an open question whether some sense-data are identical with the surfaces of physical objects.

830. Liberman, Alvin M., Harris, Katherine Safford, Hoffman, Howard S., Griffith, Belver C., "The Discrimination of Speech Bounds Within and Across Phoneme Boundaries," <u>J Exp Psychol 54</u> (1957), 358-68.
Learning and past experience seem to have an effect of the auditory discrimination of <u>d</u>, <u>g</u>, and <u>b</u> as different letters.

831. Ligis, Alphonso F., "The Perception of Others," <u>Res Phenomenol 2</u> (1972), 47-62.

832. Lindberg, David C., ed., <u>John Peckam and the Science of Optics</u> (Madison: University of Wisconsin Press, 1970).
Translation and critical edition of a classic Medieval optics text. Very useful introduction.

833. Lindsky, Leonard, "Illusions and Dreams," <u>M 71</u> (1962), 364-71.
Discussion of Malcolm and Ayer on dreams.

834. Lloyd, A. C., "Empiricism, Sense-Data and Scientific Language," <u>M 59</u> (1950), 57-70.
Argues that basic, experiential or sense-datum statements are incorrigible only relative to the language in which they are formulated--i.e., that no other statements in the language could be invoked as corrections for the original.

835. _____, "The Visual Field and Perception," <u>ASSP 31</u> (1957), 125-44.

836. _____, "Skepticism," <u>Encyclopedia of Philosophy</u>, Vol. 7, 450.

837. Locke, Don, "Appearance-Determined Qualities," <u>A 28</u> (1967), 39-42.

A reply to Mundle [#958]. Defends his original distinction between primary and secondary qualities along the
lines that secondary qualities are, while primary qualities are not, "appearance-determined." Argues that "This
colour looks blue but is white" is self-contradictory.

838. _____, Perception and Our Knowledge of the External
      World, (London: George Allen and Unwin, 1967).
      Critical review of the recent literature--defends a
      belief-theory of perception.

839. _____, "Perceiving and Thinking," ASSP 42 (1968),
      173-90.
      What is it to perceive that something is a so-and-so, or
      to take it that what one perceives is a so-and-so? Dis-
      cussion of what it is to believe something; distinguishes
      between thinking about and thinking that as well as seeing
      as and seeing that. Symposium with A. Quinton.

840. _____, "Can a Materialist See What Isn't There?"
      PQ 22 (1972), 55-56.
      Argues against Flew [#433] that distinction between two
      senses of 'see' is useful.

841. Logique et Perception, Etudes D'Epistemologie Genetique,
      V and VI (Presses Universitaires de France, 1958).

842. Lorenz, K., "Gestalt Perception as Fundamental to
      Scientific Knowledge," in L. V. Bertalanffy and A.
      Rapaport, eds., General Systems VII (Ann Arbor:
      Society for General Systems Research, 1962), 37-56.

843. Luce, Arthur A., "The Berkelian Idea of Sense," ASSP 27
      (1953), 1-20.

844. _____, Sense Without Matter or Direct Percep-
      tion, (London: T. Nelson, 1954).
      A theory of perception dispensing with both physical
      objects and material things on the grounds that they
      are merely names for aspects or sensible appearances.

845. Luckiesh, M., Visual Illusions: Their Causes, Character-
      istics and Applications, (New York: Dover, 1965;
      originally 1922).

846. Luneburg, R. K., Mathematical Analysis of Binocular
      Vision, (Ann Arbor: Edwards Brothers, Inc., 1948).

847. Lycan, William G., "Gombrich, Wittgenstein, and the
      Duck-Rabbit," J Aes Art Crit 30 (1971), 229-37.
      On the notion of 'seeing-as'.

848. _____, "Inverted Spectrum," Ratio 15 (1973),
      315-19.

96

An inverted spectrum is conceptually possible. Behavioristic arguments against such a possibility fail. A case is presented which shows that someone's having an inverted spectrum is possible.

849. Lycos, K., "Aristotle and Plato on 'Appearing'," M 73 (1964), 496-514.
      Relates arguments from Plato and Aristotle to the view of sense-impressions held by D. M. Armstrong [#41].

850. _____, "Images and the Imaginary," AJP 43 (1965), 321-38.
      Criticizes Ryle's arguments against mental images.

851. Lynn, R., Attention, Arousal and the Orientation Reaction, (Oxford: Pergamon Press, 1966).
      A physiological study, primarily, of Pavlov's orientation reaction and related concepts.

852. MacIver, A. M., "Knowledge," ASSP 32 (1958), 1-24.

853. MacLeod, Robert B., and Pick, Herbert L., Perception: Essays in Honor of James J. Gibson, (Ithaca: Cornell University Press, 1974).
      Articles by Hochberg, Henle, Metzger, von Fieandt, Gombrich, Metelli, Johansson, Bower, Pick, Beck, Flock, Kennedy, Gippenreiter and Romanov, Lee, Hay and Shaw, McIntyre and Mace.

854. MacKinnon, Edward, "Epistemological Problems in the Philosophy of Science I and II," RM 22 (1968), 113-37, 327-58.
      Critical study of Israel Scheffler's The Anatomy of Inquiry, S. Körner's Experience and Theory and Errol Harris' The Foundations of Metaphysics in Science.

855. McAlister, Linda L., "Franz Brentano and Intentional Inexistence," JHP 8 (1970), 423-30.

856. McClatchey, John G., "Some Uses of 'Appearance'," SJ Phil 10 (1972).
      Distinguishes two uses of 'appearance' and argues that Chisholm's theory of appearing is based on a confusion between them.

857. McCleary, Robert A., ed., Genetics and Experimental Factors in Perception: Research and Commentary, (Glenview, Illinois: Scott, Foresman and Co., 1970).

858. McClintock, Thomas, "'Real' and Excluders," A 30 (1969), 16-22.
      Continuation and refinement of a point made by Austin

about 'real' in connection with the argument from illusion.

859. McCurdy, John D., "The Sensory Media," The Jour of the
     Brit Soc for Phenomenol 3 (1972), 165-86.
     A discussion of Merleau-Ponty and perception.

860. McDaniel, S. V., "A Note on the Percept Theory," M 72
     (1963), 409-13.
     Argues against Firth et al that qualities belonging to the
     objects of direct awareness are much more limited than the
     percept theory wants to allow.

861. McGill, U. J., "Epistemological Dualism and the Parti-
     tion," PPR 23 (1962), 511-26.
     A discussion of Lovejoy's Revolt Against Dualism.

862. McKee, Patrick L., "Perception and Physiology," M 80
     (1971), 594-96.
     The physiologist's account of perception, that we see
     from behind the optic nerve and relevant portions of the
     brain, cannot compete with the common-sense account (we
     see with our eyes) without producing nonsense.

863. _____, "Non-Conscious Seeing," APQ 9 (1972),
     319-26.
     Non-conscious seeing takes place when someone becomes
     aware, shortly after an object disappears from his visual
     field, that they have been visually aware of that object.
     Author argues that Dretske's account of this phenomenon
     [#357] is inadequate.

864. _____, "A. J. Ayer on the Argument from Illu-
     sion," Can J Phil 3 (1974), 275-80.

865. _____, "Malcolm on After-Images," PQ 24
     (1974), 132-39.
     Criticizes the view that seeing an after-image is a case
     of seeing some special (non-physical) sort of thing;
     argues that seeing an after-image is seeing a physical
     object, on the grounds that seeing an after-image is
     seeing the object that transmitted the operative stimulus
     energy that continues to activate the visual receptors.

866. McKenzie, J. C., "The Externalization of Pains," A 28
     (1968), 189-93.

867. McKim, Robert H., Experiences in Visual Thinking, (Bel-
     mont: Brooks-Cole, 1972).
     A workbook for those who wish to improve their ability to
     visualize. Suggests visualization techniques for prob-
     lem solving.

868. McKinney, J. P., "Phenomenalism: A Survey and Reassess-
     ment," AJP 37 (1959), 221-33.

Argues that the failure of phenomenalism (and of empiricism in general) can be traced to the assumption that knowledge is an individual, rather than communal, matter.

869.   McLendon, Hiram J., "Has Russell Proved Naive Realism Self-Contradictory?" JP 53 (1956), 299-302.
        Answers that he has not.

870.   McNabb, D. G. C., "Phenomenalism," PAS 41 (1941), 67-90.

871.   _____, "The Causal Argument for Physical Objects," ASSP 19 (1945), 77-91. Symposium with Ewing and Aaron.
        Criticizes the notion of unsensed sensibilia.

872.   Macdonald, Margaret, "Linguistic Philosophy and Perception," P 28 (1953), 311-24.
        Metaphilosophical essay on the comparison of four philosophical theories of perception and the claim made by linguistic philosophers that rival theories are, in effect, rival languages.

873.   _____, ed., Philosophy and Analysis, (New York: Philosophical Library, 1954).

874.   Machamer, Peter K., "Recent Work on Perception," APQ 7 (1970), 1-22.
        Bibliography and discussion of works on philosophy of perception from 1955-1970.

875.   _____, "A Recent Drawing of the Theory/ Observation Distinction," PS 38 (1971), 413-14.
        Reply to J. Cornman [#292].

876.   Mackie, J. L., "What's Really Wrong with Phenomenalism?" Proceedings of the British Academy 60 (1969), 113-27.
        Phenomenalists confuse two senses of 'mind-dependence' and thus conflate an ontological issue with a linguistic one about the status of perceived entities.

877.   Madden, Edward H., "E. C. Boring's Philosophy of Science," PS 32 (1965), 194-201.
        Discussion of Boring's essays (published in History, Psychology and Science: Selected Papers, ed. by Robert I. Watson and Donald T. Campbell, New York, John Wiley and Sons, 1963) with special attention to those on operationalism and psychological theory.

878.   Makous, W. L., "Cutaneous Color Sensitivity: Explanation and Demonstration," Psych Rev 73 (1966), 280-94.
        Thermodynamics used to explain how subjects can

discriminate colors in the dark using their fingers only.
Repeatable experiment described.

879. Malcolm, Norman, "The Verification Argument," in Max
       Black, ed., Philosophical Analysis, (Ithaca, New
       York: Cornell University Press, 1950).
    A discussion of the claim that no empirical statement is
    ever completely verifiable since the observations needed
    to do so would be, in principle, infinite. Malcolm
    analyzes the argument for this claim in detail and offers
    counterarguments to several versions of it. The claim is
    one that has been used by Ayer and others to support the
    contention that no finite number of sense-datum statements
    can ever be equivalent to a physical-object statement
    since the latter implicitly involves predictions about the
    future.

880. _____, "Direct Perception," PQ 3 (1953), 301-16.
       Reprinted in Malcolm, Knowledge and Certainty,
       (Englewood Cliffs, New Jersey: Prentice-Hall, 1963),
       73-95.
    Argues that in Moore's sense of 'directly perceive' the
    sort of thing that is directly perceived is an after-
    image, and in this sense it is never the case that a
    physical object is directly perceived. Offers a tenta-
    tive explanation of Moore's tendency to hold the contrary
    view.

881. _____, "Certainty and Empirical Statements,"
       M 51 (1942), 8-46. Discussion by M. Black, 361-67.
    Analysis of the grounds on which some philosophers have
    claimed that no empirical proposition can be known with
    certainty. Malcolm argues that this position is mistaken
    due to a confusion of two senses of 'possibility.'

882. _____, "Dreaming and Skepticism," P 65 (1956),
       14-37.
    One who is asleep cannot have thoughts, impressions or
    sensations, so that dreaming could never be mistaken for
    waking experience.

883. Malinovich, S., "Perception: An Experience of An Achieve-
       ment?" PPR 25 (1964), 161-68.
    A defense of Ryle's analysis of perceptual verbs as
    against criticisms raised by A. J. Ayer.

884. Malmgren, Helge "Moore's Concept of "Indirect Appre-
       hension"," Theoria 37 (1971), 185-208.

885. Malpas, R. M. P., "The Location of Sound," in Butler,
       R. J., ed., Analytical Philosophy, 2nd Series
       (Oxford, 1965), 131-44.
    Locating a sound is not the same as locating the source
    or cause of a sound. What occurs when we locate sounds

by ear is crucial to understanding the notion of where
sounds come from. Spatial characteristics are not
intrinsic to sounds; there is no experience of hearing
where a sound comes from.

886. Mandelbaum, Maurice, Philosophy, Science and Sense-Percep-
          tion, (Baltimore: Johns Hopkins University Press,
          1964).
     Essays on Locke's Realism, Newton and Boyle, Sensible
     Scepticism and Critical Realism.

887. _____, "Definiteness and Coherence in Sense-
          Perception," N 1 (1967), 123-38.

888. Mann, Ida, and Antoinette Pirie, The Science of Seeing,
          (Harmondsworth, Middlesex: Penguin, 1946 and 1950).
     A discussion of various kinds of eyes and how they work,
     and of various medical facets relating to vision and
     visual defects.

889. Marc-Wogau, Konrad, "On C. D. Broad's Theory of Sensa,"
          in Schilpp, ed., The Philosophy of C. D. Broad,
          (New York: Tudor, 1959).

890. _____, "Gilbert Ryle on Sensation," in
          Philosophical Essays Dedicated to Gunnar Aspelin,
          (Lund: C. W. K. Gleerup Bokforlag, 1963).

891. Margolis, Joseph, "If I Carefully Examine a Visual After-
          Image, What am I Looking at and Where is it?" A 19
          (1958), 97-99.

892. _____, "Nothing Can Be Heard But Sound," A 20
          (1959), 82-87.

893. _____, "How do we Know that Anything Continues
          to Exist when it is Unperceived?" A 21 (1960), 105-
          08.

894. _____, "Fourteen Points on the Senses and Their
          Objects," Theoria 28 (1962), 303-08.

895. _____, "The Privacy of Sensations," R 6
          (1964), 147-53.

896. _____, "Certainty About Sensations," PPR 25
          (1964), 242-47.
     The only way pain reports can be mistaken is by choosing
     the wrong word in making them.

897. _____, "After-Images and Pains," P 41 (1966),
          333-40.
     Discussion of the conceptual link between first-person
     reports of the having of after-images and the occurrences

of after-images.

898. _____, "Awawreness of Sensations and of the
          Location of Sensations," A 27 (1966), 29-32.
      Rejects an argument from G. N. A. Vesey [#1359] for the
      "Local Sign" theory regarding sensations. In parti-
      cular, the claim that children can be aware of sensa-
      tions before they are aware that they have bodies.
      Having a location is a defining characteristic of sensa-
      tions and no one can locate a sensation without aware-
      ness of having a body.

899. _____, "Esse est Percipi Once Again," Dialogue
          5 (1967), 516-24.

900. _____, "Perception, Inference and Meditation,"
          JP 64 (1967), 119-23.
      Argues against G. N. A. Vesey [#1359] that there can be
      no "non-proper-object immediate perception."

901. _____, "Locke and Scientific Realism," RM 22
          (1968), 359-70.
      Discussion of Locke's distinction between primary and
      secondary qualities and Berkeley's attack on it. Relates
      this dispute to current issues raised by scientific
      realists.

902. _____, "Existential Import and Perceptual
          Judgments " JP 66 (1969), 403-08.
      Argues (against D. Locke) that to say that someone per-
      ceives something is to say (entails) that that thing
      .exists.

903. _____, "Anscombe on Knowledge Without Obser-
          vation," Personalist 51 (1970). 46-57.

904. _____, "Scientific Realism, Ontology and the
          Sensory Modes," PS 37 (1970), 114-20.
      Attack on scientific realism (Sellars) for failure to
      adequately analyze sensory modes. Argues that in order
      to handle sensory modes the scientific realist must also
      provide for the existence of persons and thus of physical
      objects.

905. _____, "Transitive and Intransitive Modes of
          Sentience," PPR 32 (1972), 478-87.
      Intransitive modes of sentience (in which what is veri-
      dically discriminated does exist independently of such
      discrimination) should not be called perceiving. In an
      hallucination, therefore, one is veridically aware of
      something (intransitive mode) but is perceiving nothing.
      All instances of nonveridical perception will be cases of
      misidentification of the (independently existing) object
      perceived.

906. Marhenke, Paul, "Moore's Analysis of Sense-Perception," in
       P. Schilpp, ed., The Philosophy of G. E. Moore,
       (Evanston, Illinois: Northwestern University Press,
       1942).

907. _____, "Phenomenalism," in M. Black, ed., Philo-
       sophical Analysis, (Englewood Cliffs, New Jersey:
       Prentice-Hall, 1950).

908. Markus, R. A., "Illusions," Encyclopedia of Philosophy,
       Vol. 4, 130.

909. Marshall, C. R., "A Factor in Hypnagogic Images," M 45
       (1936), 67-70.
       Argues that visual experiences that occur in the hypna-
       gogic state and under the influence of mescaline are due
       to the chorio-capillary circulation in the eye.

910. Martin, Oliver, "The Given and the Interpretive Element
       in Perception," JP 35 (1938), 337-45.
       Proposes a three-part analysis of perception which is
       designed to account for perceptual error while overcoming
       the problems in both idealism and realism.

911. Martos, Joseph, "The Cartesian Constellation," Kinesis 3
       (1971), 63-80.

912. Mascall, E. L., "Perception and Sensation," PAS 64 (1964),
       259-72.
       Discusses the historical role of sensation in perception
       and puts forth an alternative theory concerning the func-
       tion of the non-sensory element in perception. This is
       said to be apprehension rather than interpretation or
       inference.

913. Mates, Benson, "Sense-Data," I 10 (1967), 225-44.
       Reasons typically given for rejecting sense-data are in-
       conclusive, incoherent or false. When philosophers
       introduce 'sense-datum' to refer to what is immediately
       perceived they are not giving the sense of the term, but
       its denotation. Thus arguments against sense-data that
       are based on the complaint that the notion of being
       "immediately perceived" is not clear are ill-founded.

914. Matthews, Gareth B., "Modes of Polysemy," JP 71 (1974),
       711-21. Symposium with Zeno Vendler and Charles
       Raff.
       There is no sense of 'see' in which it means 'sees part
       of the surface of'.

915. Matthews, H. E., "Locke, Malebranche and the Represen-
       tative Theory," Locke News 2 (1971), 12-21.

916. Maxwell, Grover, "The Ontological Status of Theoretical

Entities," in Feigl and Maxwell, Minnesota Studies in the Philosophy of Science, III, (Minneapolis, Minnesota: University of Minnesota Press, 1958). Argues for a continuity between kinds of things that are observed; and, on this basis, against a rigid distinction between theoretical and observational terms.

917. Maxwell, Nicholas, "Understanding Sensations," AJP 46 (1968), 127-45.
Defense of a non-Smartian version of the identity theory. Even though sensations are held to be contingently identical with brain processes, there are facts about sensations that cannot be understood or described in terms of any physical theory.

918. Maynard, Patrick, "Depiction, Vision, and Convention," APQ 9 (1972), 243-50.
Attempt to define what an accurate or faithful pictorial representation of something is. A picture is held to be realistic or naturalistic insofar as it employs devices which convey strong sensations of the physical properties it represents the object as possessing.

919. Mays, W., "The Epistemology of Professor Piaget," PAS 54 (1954), 49-76.

920. Mead, George Herbert, The Philosophy of the Act, (Chicago: University of Chicago, 1938).
Part II deals with perceptual theory in greatest detail. Perception is defined as a relation between organism and environment; uses selection (natural) model to talk about the organisms adjusting to that environment. An interesting pragmatic account that stresses manipulation of perceptual and scientific objects.

921. Meager, R., "Seeing Paintings," ASSP 40 (1966), 63-84.
Symposium with E. Bedford.

922. Melchert, Norman, "A Note on the Belief Theory of Perception," Phil Studies 24 (1973), 427-29.
Author calls D. M. Armstrong and G. Pitcher to task for having neglected consideration of the critical realist position (as defended by R. W. Sellars, Chisholm and W. Sellars) that an alternative to the belief theorists' form of Direct Realism in which sensory contents plays no role. Sensory contents can be reinstated in a direct realism but they will not be the direct objects of perception.

923. Mellor, David, "Materialism and Phenomenal Qualities: Part II," ASSP 47 (1973), 107-18.
Materialists have not been able to produce a coherent account of the crucial term 'physical property'. Unless and until this can be done materialism is too vague to

be of interest.

924. Mellor, W.W., "The Incorrigibles," PQ 15 (1965), 35-42.
There is no class of incorrigible empirical statements.
To suppose that there is rests on a mis-use of the principle that to know the meaning of an expression is to
know how to use it correctly.

925. Melzack, Ronald, "The Perception of Pain," Sci Amer 204
(February, 1961), 41-49.
Pain is not a single sensation produced by a single
stimulus; it is a category of complex experiences, the
nature of which is, to some extent, by the individual's
unique past experience, the meaning he gives to the pain-
producing situation and his "state of mind."

926. Merleau-Ponty, Maurice, La Structure du Comportement,
(Paris: Presses Universitaires de France, 1942)
(translated by A. Fisher, Methuen, 1965).
Attack on stimulus-response theories of psychology. The
organism changes as it responds to the stimulus and is
no longer as it was prior to stimulus.

927. _____, Phenomenologie de la Perception,
(Paris: Librarie Gallimard, 1945) (translated by
C. Smith, Routledge, 1962).
An inventory of various aspects of the perceived world.
A phenomenological attack on traditional psychology and,
more generally, on the Cartesian-mechanical approach to
perception, the body, and our perceptual knowledge.

928. _____, The Primacy of Perception and
other Essays, ed., J. M. Edie, (Evanston, Illinois:
Northwestern University Press, 1964).
A collection of papers. The central theme of interest
is that perception is not an act performed by an interpreting, organization consciousness. It is an original
experience; the perceived world is fundamental.

929. _____, Le Visible et l'invisible, C.
Lefort, ed., (Paris: Gallimard, 1964) (translated
by A. Lingis, Northwestern University Press, 1968).

930. Metcalf, M. V., "The Reality of the Unobservables," PS 7
(1940), 337-41.
The causal theory of perception provides grounds for
rejecting the meaninglessness of unobservables.

931. Metzger, Arnold, "Perception, Recollection and Death," RM
4 (1950), 13-30.
Phenomenological approach to the relation between perceptual experience and death.

932. Meyers, R. C., "A Note on Sense-Data and Depth Perception,"

M 80 (1971), 437-40.
Sense-data cannot be three-dimensional as C. D. Broad and
H. H. Price hold. Sense-data need to be two-dimensional
if certain geometrical descriptions of objects are correct. Likewise sense-datum theorists' analysis of certain illusions require that they are treated as projec-
tions on a flat plane. Depth perception remains a problem
for sense-datum theorists.

933. Michotte, A., La Perception de la Causalite, (Louvain, S.
A. Standard Boekhandel, 1954; originally 1946),
(translated Methuen: 1963).
Causality is perceived directly. Interesting experimental
data is an important part of this book.

934. Miller, G. A., "The Magical Number Seven, Plus or Minus
Two: Some Limits on our Capacity for Processing
Information," Psych Rev 63 (1956), 81-97.

935. Miller, Harlan B., "'Is Red' and 'Looks red'," M 76
(1967); 439-40.

936. Miller, Richard W., "On the Privacy of Colour," A 30
(1969), 60-61.
The sceptic cannot consistently claim not to know whether
what he experiences when he says 'This is red' is similar
to what others experience when they say 'This is red'.

937. Milmed, B. K., "Lewis' Concept of Expressive Statements,"
JP 51 (1954), 200-13.

938. Mischel, Theodore, "Wundt and the Conceptual Foundations
of Psychology," PPR 31 (1970), 1-26.
Good historical article on a founder of psychology.

939. Moles, Abraham, Information Theory and Esthetic Perception, (University of Illinois, 1966).

940. Montcrieff, M. M., The Clairvoyant Theory of Perception,
(London: Faber and Faber, 1951).

941. Moncrieff, R. W., Odour Preferences, (New York: Wiley,
1966).

942. Moore, Asher, "Verifiability and Phenomenalism," JP 47
(1950), 169-77.
Presents a version of phenomenalism according to which
material-object sentences are empirically meaningful.

943. _____, "Chisholm on Intentionality," PPR 21 (1960),
248-54.
Discussion of Chisholm's Perceiving.

944. Moore, George Edward, Some Main Problems of Philosophy,

(London: Allen and Unwin, 1953).
One of the classic statements of the sense-data position.
The lectures were originally given in 1910-11.

945. _____, "Visual Sense-Data," in C. A. Mace,
ed., British Philosophy in Med-Century, (London:
Allen and Unwin, 1957). Reprinted in Swartz [#1301].

946. _____, Philosophical Papers, (London:
Allen and Unwin, 1959).
Inclues "Certainty," "A Defense of Common Sense," "Proof
of an External World," "Four Forms of Scepticism."

947. _____, Commonplace Books, C. Lewy, ed.,
(London: Allen and Unwin, 1962).
I: 9, 10, 25, 27, 29, 30, 32, 34,35.
II: 2, 4, 10, 11, 13, 15, 17-20.
IV: 1, 2, 4, 10, 14, 16.
V: 4, 8, 11, 12, 17, 20, 21, 23, 25.
VII: 11
IX: 17.

948. _____, Lectures on Philosophy, C. Lewy,
ed., (London: Allen and Unwin, 1966). Especially
Part I.
More detailed account of Moore's views on sense data and
epistemology.

949. Moray, Neville, Attention: Selective Processes in Vision
and Hearing, (New York: Academic Press, 1970).
Attempts to use information theory and machine models to
construct an operationally viable theory of attention. A
positive theory is put forward.

950. Moreau, Joseph, L'horizon des esprits: essai critique sur
la Phenomenologie de la Perception, (Paris: Presses
Universitaires de France, 1960).

951. Morgenbesser, Sydney, "Perception: Cause and Achievement,"
Summary in M. Wartofsky, ed., Boston Studies in the
Philosophy of Science I, (Dordrecht - Holland: D.
Reidel, 1963).

952. Morrison, James C., "Husserl and Brentano on Intentionality," PPR 31 (1970), 27-46.

953. Moseley, Jeannine, "Peirce and Perceptual Judgments,"
Dialogue (Phi Sigma Tau) 7 (1965), 1-12.
An examination of Peirce's claim that there is no intuition and that perceptual judgments have the form of
hypotheses.

954. Mostofsky, David I., Attention: Contemporary Theory and

Analysis, (New York: Appleton-Century-Crofts, 1970).
Relevant chapters by Boring, Mostofsky, Berlyne, Broadbent, Silverman, Hochberg, Jerison, Lindsay, Mackintosh, Honig, Jenkins and Sainsbury, Warren, Derdzinski, Hirayoshi and Mumma.

955. Mourelàtos, Alexander, "The Real, Appearances and Human Error in Early Greek Philosophy," RM 19 (1965), 346-65.

956. Mundle, C. W. K., "Mr. Hirst's Theory of Perception," M 61 (1952), 386-90.

957. _____, "Common Sense Versus Mr. Hirst's Theory of Perception," PAS 60 (1960), 61-78. Reply by Hirst, 78 i-vi.
Discussion of R. J. Hirst [#662] with special attention to his rejection of the Immediacy Assumption.

958. _____, "Primary and Secondary Qualities," A 28 (1967), 33-38.
Criticism of Don Locke's claim [#838] that secondary, but not primary, qualities are "appearance-determined." Mundle argues that there is symmetry as between what color a thing looks and what color it is and what shape a thing looks and what shape it is. Critical of the conventionalist thesis that what color a thing is is to be defined in terms of what color it appears to be to a normal perceiver under standard conditions.

959. Murch, Gerald M., Visual and Auditory Perception, (Indianapolis: Bobbs-Merrill, 1973).
A text with a strong physiological slant.

960. Murphy, John P., "Another Note on a Misreading of Wittgenstein," A 29 (1968), 62-64.

961. Murray, A. R. M., "Is There a Problem About Sense-Data?" ASSP 15 (1936), 88-101. Symposium with G. A. Paul and G. M. Smith.
Reply to G. A. Paul's paper, same volume, 61-87.

962. Myers, Charles Mason, "On Actually Seeing," Phil Studies 7 (1956), 28-32.
It is false that we see only surfaces of objects.

963. _____, "Phenomenological Idiom and Perceptual Mode," PS 25 (1958), 71-81.
Contrasts several pairs of sentences which might be used in phenomenological perceptual descriptions and argues that one of the sentences in each pair is more basic and less idiomatic that the other.

964. _____, "The Determinate and Determinable

Modes of Appearing," M 67 (1958), 32-49.
An account of the given that is compatible with both the
sense-datum and the percept theory.

965. _____, "Phenomenal Organization and Perceptual Mode," P 34 (1959), 331-37.

966. _____, "Perceptual Events, States and Processes," PS 29 (1962), 825-91.

967. Myers, G. E., "Perception and the 'Time-lag' Arguments,"
A 17 (1956), 97-192.

968. _____, "Perception and the Sentience Hypothesis,"
M 72 (1963), 111-120.
Discussion of R. J. Hirst's "Sentience Hypothesis,"
[#662] according to which perceiving is the modifying of
a basic sentience by attitude, set and beliefs.

969. Naess, Arne and Siri, "Psychological Research and Humean
Problems," PS 27 (1960), 134-46.
Passages from Hume's Treatise of Human Nature are shown
to contain predominantly sentences that are declarative,
synthetic, and therefore open to empirical testing. Contemporary psychology has contributed to the testing of
some of Hume's hypotheses.

970. Nagel, Thomas, "The Boundaries of Inner Space," JP 66
(1958), 452-48.
A commentary on J. Fodor's "The Appeal to Tacit Knowledge
in Psychological Explanation," [#438] Nagel focuses on
the question how much of the neurophysiological compo-
nents of an intentional action can legitimately be
ascribed to a person as something he does in performing
the action.

971. _____, "Brain Dissection and Unity of Consciousness," S 22 (1971), 396-413.
Review of research on persons whose brains have been
bisected into left and right hemispheres; argues that
the notion of a single, countable mind cannot be coher-
ently applied in such cases. It follows that the attri-
bution of mental activity does not require the existence
of a single mental subject. Thus unity of consciousness,
based on a model of functional integration, conflicts
with neurophysiological data.

972. Nakhinikian, George, "Plato's Theory of Sensation," RM 9
(1955), 129-48, 306-27.
Detailed exposition of Plato's theory of sensation in the
Theaetetus.

973. _____, "A Note on Plato's Theory of

Sensation," RM 10 (1956), 355-56.
Clarification of [#972].

974. Natsoulas, Thomas, 'What Are Perceptual Reports About?"
Psych Bull 67 (1967), 247-272.
Defines report, as opposed to response, behavior. Contrasts philosophical treatments of "aboutness" of perceptual reports with psychological discussions in which a
"reporting response" is said to be about the discrimina-
tive stimulus that controls it.

975. _____, "Interpreting Perceptual Reports,"
Psych Bull 70 (1968), 575-91.
Follows earlier piece, distinguishes causally between
phenomenal or cognitive aspects of perception, and shows
this relates to interpretation of experience.

976. Nayak, G. C., "Can There Be Any Indeterminate Perception?"
Darshana Int 10 (1970), 41-49.
Whether there can be unconceptualized knowledge depends on
what we mean by "knowledge."

977. Needleman, J., "Experience," Encyclopedia of Philosophy,
Vol. 3, 157.

978. Neisser, Hans P., "Are Space and Time Real?" PPR 31 (1970-
71), 421-25.

979. Neisser, Ulric, "Visual Search," Sci Amer 210 (1964), 94-
103.
Experiments with scanning procedures used to visually
locate one item among many show that our perceptual systems are capable of carrying out many such procedures
simultaneously.

980. _____, Cognitive Psychology, (New York: Appleton-
Century-Crofts, 1966).
Argues for the cognitive approach that whatever we know
about reality is mediated by the interpretation of information by our processing systems. Part II is on Visual
Cognition and Part III on Auditory Cognition. Through a
review of the literature Neisser attempts to account for
it all in terms of his cognitive processing theory.

981. _____, "The Process of Vision," Sci Amer 219
(1968), 204-14.
Argues against the camera-model of vision. There is no
copying of visual input either in perceiving or remembering. Perceiving involves extraction of complex patterns from sensory input and these patterns are processed
constructively so that the experience of perceiver is
brought into correspondence with perceived environment.
Sensory input is simply raw material for essentially constructive activity of vision.

982.   Nelson, Everett, "Categorical Interpretation of Exper-
            ience," PPR 13 (1952), 84-95.
        Argues that a satisfactory account of induction presup-
        poses certain nonempirical concepts.

983.   Nelson, John O., "On the Impossibility of Sense-Data,"
            R 6 (1964), 145-60.
        When sense-data are equated with appearances so that they
        cannot appear other than as they are, they cannot
        consistently be held to exist.

984.   _____, "An Exmination of D. M. Armstrong's
            Theory of Perception," APQ 1 (1964), 154-60.
        Examines Armstrong's claim that perception is the
        acquiring of beliefs by means of the senses.

985.   _____, "Tastes," PPR 26 (1966), 537-45.
        Presents four theories about the nature of tastes.

986.   _____, "Can Systems of Imperceptible Particles
            Appear to Perceivers?" M 82 (1973), 253-57.

987.   Norman, Donald A., Memory and Attention: An Introduction
            to Human Information Processing, (New York: Wiley,
            1969).
        An elementary text on memory, especially visual memory.

988.   Nunn, William A., "Margolis and Vesey on Sensations,"
            M 80 (1971), 583-88.
        Criticism of Margolis [#898]. Rejects claim that non-
        verbal behavior necessarily implies an awareness of the
        location of sensations on the part of those who have them.

989.   Oakley, H. D., "Perception and Historicity (with Special
            Attention to Professor H. H. Price's Perception,)"
            PAS 38 (1938), 21-46.

990.   Odegard, Douglas, "Sensations as Qualities," PQ 17 (1967),
            308-16.

991.   _____, "Qualities and Owners," PQ 20 (1970),
            248-52.
        Discussion of an unsatisfactory argument against the
        bundle-theory of qualities.

992.   _____, "Images," M 80 (1971), 262-65.
        Argues that mental images are not "things in their own
        right" on the grounds that images cannot be said to be
        numerically identical, since they are not of particulars,
        but only of kinds of things.

993.   _____, "Berkeley and the Perception of Ideas,"
            Can. J. Phil. 1 (1971), 155-71.
        Suggests four possible interpretations of what it is to

perceive an idea and argues that Berkeley favored one of
them.

994. Olafson, Frederick A., "A Note on Perceptual Illusion,"
        JP 50 (1953), 274-78.

995. Oldfield, R. C., "Memory Mechanisms and the Theory of
        Schemata," Brit J of Psychol 45 (1954), 14-23.
        What is stored in memory are schemata, or precis of the
        original material.

996. Olding, A., "Armstrong, Smart and the "Ontological Status
        of Secondary Qualities"," AJP 46 (1968), 52-64.

997. Oliver, James W., "The Problem of Epistemology," JP 57
        (1960), 297-304.
        Formulates in theoretically neutral terms a proposed
        question which should be taken as the fundamental issue
        of epistemology. The question is, basically, "What
        statements ought to be believed?"

998. Oliver, W. Donald, "The Logic of Perspective Realism," JP
        35 (1938), 197-208.
        Argues against a dispositional analysis of sensations.

999. O'Neil, John, Perception, Expression and History, (Evans-
        ton, Illinois: Northwestern University Press, 1970).

1000. Osgood, Charles E., Method and Theory in Experimental
        Psychology, (New York: Oxford University Press,
        1953).
        Classic text. First two parts concern sensory processes
        and perceptual processes. 'Perception' refers to a set
        of variables that intervene between sensory stimulation
        and awareness, as the later state is indexed by verbal or
        other modes of response.

1001. O'Shaughnessy, Brian, "The Location of Sound," M 66
        (1957), 471-90.

1002. _____, "An Impossible Auditory Exper-
        ience," PAS 57 (1957), 53-82.

1003. _____, "Material Objects and Perceptual
        Standpoints," PAS 65 (1965), 77-98.
        Our relation to an object's surface and color is dif-
        ferent from our relation to its sides.

1004. _____, "The Temporal Ordering of Percep-
        tions and Reactions," in F. N. Sibley, ed., [#1227].

1005. Over, Ray, "Explanations of Geometrical Illusions,"

112

Psych Bull 70 (1968), 545-62.
Explanations of geometrical illusions in terms of
deformed field of retinal induction, cortical satiation,
directional eye movements and inappropriate constancy
scaling are inadequate. Such theories of illusions tend
to yield inaccurate predictions. Author suggests that
geometrical illusions are not solely visual, but may also
be haptic (tactual-kinesthetic).

1006.   Pailthorp, Clark, "Is Immediate Knowledge Reason Based,"
        M 78 (1969), 550-70.
        Argues that there is no incompatibility between knowing
        something directly and having reasons for what is known.
        Examples of direct knowing drawn from perception, and
        reasons for what is thus known are argued to be causes
        rather than inferential warrants for what is known. An
        attempt is made to provide general justification for
        regarding perceptual beliefs about colors to be true.

1007.   Pallaid, Jaques, La Pensee et la Vie: recherche sur la
        logique de la perception, (Paris: Presses Univer-
        sitaires de France, 1951).

1008.   Pantle, A., and Sekuler, R. W., "Size Detecting Mechan-
        isms in Human Vision," Science 162 (1968), 1146-48.

1009.   _____, "Velocity-sensitive
        Elements in Human Vision: Initial Psychophysical
        Evidence," Vision Research 8 (1968), 445-50.

1010.   Pap, Arthur, Elements of Analytical Philosophy, (New
        York: Macmillan, 1949).
        Chapter Two contains a defense of phenomenalism.

1011.   _____, "Semantic Analysis and Psycho-Physical
        Dualism," M 61 (1952), 209-21.
        Criticism of Ryle's arguments against the privacy theory
        of sensations; accuses Ryle of having misused facts about
        ordinary language in attacking philosophical theories.

1012.   Parker, DeWitt H., "Esse est Percipi, with Particular
        Reference to Numbers," JP 42 (1945), 280-91.
        Numbers are on a par with other qualities of things;
        neither they nor other qualities can exist unperceived.

1013.   Pastore, Nicholas, "Condillac's Phenomenological Rejec-
        tion of Locke and Berkeley," PPR 27 (1967), 29-31.

1014.   _____, Selective History of Theories of
        Visual Perception: 1650-1950, (Oxford: Oxford
        University Press, 1971).
        Starting with Descartes and ending with the functionalism
        of Ames and Murphy, Pastore reviews theories of vision
        by concentrating on treatments of the "constancy

hypothesis"; viz., that the retinal image and the original perception are in conformity or correspondence
regarding their spatial attributes.

1015.   Paul, G. A., "The Analysis of Sense-Data," A 3 (1935),
           12-20. (Reply by Wisdom)
        An attack on J. O. Wisdom.

1016.   _____, "Is There a Problem About Sense-Data?"
           ASSP 15 (1936), 61-77.
        Reprinted in Swartz [#1301]. An influential attack on
        the claim that it is necessary to speak of any elements
        in perception corresponding to sense-data in giving a
        full account of a perceptual situation. Cautions
        against certain ways of introducing the term 'sense-
        datum' into philosophical theories and argues that an
        examination of the chosen role for this term is
        philosophically prior to the epistemological questions
        that motivate its use.

1017.   _____, "Lenin's Theory of Perception," A 5 (1938),
           65-73. (Reprinted in Macdonald, ed., [Philosophy
           and Analysis, (New York: Philosophical Library,
           1954, 278-286.)]
        Examination of the claims on which Lenin basis his
        defense of a representative theory of perception. His
        dialectical motivations are mentioned.

1018.   Paul, L., Persons and Perception, (London: Faber and
           Faber, 1961).
        Contains an historical review of the impasse over per-
        ception (from Locke to Russell). Offers an analysis of
        percepts in terms of concepts of a mystical energy.

1019.   Paul, Robert, "Appearances and Expectations," M 78
           (1969), 342-53.
        Hume's formulation of the problem of induction is
        confused.

1020.   Pearl, Leon, "Is Theaetetus Dreaming?" PPR 31 (1970-
           1971), 108-13.
        Discussion of the dream-problem. Defends a non-
        sceptical position; viz., that if a man is awake and
        believes he is, this constitutes a sufficient condition
        for his knowing that he is awake.

1021.   Peeples, David R., and Teller, David Y., "Color Vision
           and Brightness Discrimination in Two-Month-Old
           Human Infants," Science 189 (1975), 1102-03.
        Concludes that infants have some form of color vision;
        these infants stared at all intensities of a red bar and
        not of a white bar.

1022.   Peetz, Vera, "Note on Armstrong's 'Absolute and Relative

Motion'," M 79 (1971), 427-30.

1023. Penelhum, Terence, Survival and Disembodied Existence,
        (London: Routledge and Kegan Paul, 1970).
        Discusses what it is like to perceive without a body.

1024. Pennycuick, John, In Contact With the Physical World,
        (London: Allen and Unwin, 1972).
        Evolution endows us with the ability to interpret visual
        sense data and, thus, to acquire correct information
        about the world.

1025. Pepper, Stephen C., "A Dynamic View of Perception,"
        PPR 32 (1971), 42-46.
        Defense of a causal theory of perception. Visual per-
        ception must be understood as a case of purposive
        action. Distinguishes proximate and ultimate objects
        of perception, the former are immediate sensory objects,
        the latter are the causal sources of our visual impres-
        sions.

1026. Perkins, Moreland, "Intersubjectivity and Gestalt
        Psychology," PPR 13 (1952), 437-51.
        Argues that certain statements about perceptual exper-
        ience are such that they are intersubjectively confirmed
        and cannot be translated into statements about physical
        objects. This poses a problem for positivist programs.

1027. _____,"The Knowing in Seeing," A 30 (1970),
        125-31.
        Proposes a minimal form of epistemic seeing called visual
        "knowledge-by-acquaintance." It is a non-propositional
        form of knowing according to which if S sees D (in this
        sense) S gains some knowledge about D, but not that S
        knows that what he sees is a D. Seeing involves gaining
        (or refreshing previous) knowledge of a thing.

1028. _____, "The Picturing in Seeing," JP 67
        (1970), 321-39.
        There is a picturing in seeing that consists in a
        structural isomorphism between the spatial arrangement
        of visible information of surfaces of a perceived scene
        and the distribution of information within the brain of
        the perceiver--a neurophysical "picture" of what is
        seen in the brain. Rejects the notion of a phenomenal
        picture (visual impression) of what is seen.

1029. _____, "Sentience," JP 68 (1971), 329-37.
        The existence of "occurrent colors" (colors which are
        not dispositions of things nor mere resemblance between
        seen things) is logically separable from the existence
        of visually sentient beings.

1030. _____, "Matter, Sensation and Understanding,"

115

APQ 8 (1971), 1-12.
Discussion of the role played in theoretical physical
understanding by the sensuous element in experience.
Argues that the sensuousness in experience is a quality
of our noticing, and not of objects of sense-organs.

1031. Peters, R., "Observationalism in Psychology," M 60
       (1951), 43-51.
       Supports Popper's attack on observationalism (the view
       that all laws describe inductively-based correlations
       among series of sensations) by arguing that it has had
       detrimental effects in psychology.

1032. Phillips, Robert L., "Austin and Berkeley on Percep-
       tion," P 39 (1964), 161-63.

1033. Piaget, Jean, Introduction a l'Epistemologie Genetique,
       (Paris: Presses Universitaires de France, 1950).
       (Especially Tome I, Sections 2-4)
       The classic statement of Piaget's epistemology. Argues
       at length that developmental considerations are
       essential for understanding the human and his under-
       standing. This view gets refined and clarified in later
       works.

1034. _____, The Mechanisms of Perception, (translated
       G. N. Seagrim) (New York: Basic Books, 1969;
       originally 1961).
       Attempts to find laws for illusions; it is argued that
       veridical seeing is just an equilibrium between two
       possible types of illusions. Some illusions do not
       change with age or development, others do.

1035. _____, Biology and Knowledge: An Essay on the
       Relations Between Organic Regulations and Cognitive
       Processes, (translated by B. Walsh) (Chicago:
       University of Chicago Press, 1971; originally 1967).
       Argues that cognitive processes, including perceptual
       learning, are based upon elementary form of biological
       organization and develop from these by the "bursting of
       instincts."

1036. Pialt, Donald A., "That Will-o'-the-Wisp, The Innocent
       Inscrutable Given," JP 32 (1935), 337-50.

1037. Pick, Anne D., "Improvement of Visual and Tactual Form
       Discrimination," J of Exp Psychol 69 (1965), 331-
       39.
       Sets up a discrimination learning paradigm and transfer
       tests to argue that the distinctive feature hypothesis
       as a theory of form perception is superior to the
       schema hypothesis.

116

1038. Pickering, F. R., "A Refutation of an Objection to the
      Causal Theory of Perception," A 34 (1974), 129-32.
      Criticizes J. M. Hinton [#656 and #659]. Defends the
      causal theory of perception takes the form of defending
      the existence of an event called psi-ing which is said
      to necessarily occur in visual illusions and hallucina-
      tions, and often, or almost always occur in standard
      visual perception.

1039. _____, "Is Light the Proper Object of
      Vision?" M 84 (1975), 119-21.
      Argues against a claim made by Bede Rundle [#1154] that
      light is the proper object of sight as opposed to color.
      Light cannot be the proper object of sight because it is
      not usually the case that when we see things we see
      light; thus light fails to meet one of Rundle's own
      criteria for a proper object of a sense.

1040. Pickford, R. W., Psychology and Visual Aesthetics, (New
      York: Crane, 1972).

1041. _____, "A Colour Vision Defective Artist,"
      Brit J Aes 13 (1973), 384-87.
      A report concerning a red-green color-blind artist and a
      discussion of how he handles color in his painting.

1042. Pieron, Henri, La Connaissance sensorielle et les
      problemes de la vision, (Paris: Hermann, 1936).

1043. Pike, Alfred, "The Phenomenological Approach to Musical
      Perception," PPR 27 (1966), 247-54.

1044. _____, "Foundational Aspects of Musical Percep-
      tion: A Phenomenological Analysis," PPR 34 (1974),
      429-34.
      A phenomenologist listens to a musical theme and hears
      notes, their relationships, rhythmic patterns, etc.
      Author argues that phenomenological "inspection" of
      music is a necessary precondition of "cognitive
      analysis."

1045. Pirenne, M. H., Vision and the Eye, (London: Chapman
      and Hall, 1948).

1046. _____, "The Scientific Basis of Leonardo Da
      Vinci's Theory of Perception," BJPS 3 (1952), 169-
      216.
      Renaissance perspective represents a natural system of
      perspective corresponding to the way we see. The theory
      of linear perspective used to support this claim is held
      not to depend in any way upon structure of eye, brain or
      on psychological facts about the perceiver; it is also
      valid for animals.

1047. _____, "Physiological Mechanisms in the Per-
          ception of Distance by Sight and Berkeley's Theory
          of Vision," BJPS 4 (1953), 13-21.
          Discussion of recent discoveries in physiological
          optics, their relation to Berkeley's claims about visual
          perception of distance, and Berkeley's influence on later
          empirical scientists.

1048. Pitcher, George, "McKenzie on Pains," A 29 (1969), 103-
          05.
          Reply to McKenzie [#866].

1049. _____, "Minds and Ideas in Berkeley," APQ 6
          (1969), 198-207.

1050. _____, "Pain Perception," PR 79 (1970), 368-93.
          Defense of the claim that to feel a pain is to perceive
          something, and that this perception is a form of direct
          awareness of an objective physical state of affairs.

1051. _____, "The Awfulness of Pain," JP 67 (1970),
          481-92.

1052. _____, A Theory of Perception, (Princeton, New
          Jersey: Princeton University Press, 1971).
          A well argued attempt to provide a behaviorist theory of
          perception. Begins with a very clear statement and
          attack on sense-data theories. Has a good section on
          the relation between psychological studies and philoso-
          phical concerns, though it fails to support the central
          claim that they are unrelated.

1053. _____, "Thomson's Problem," (abstract) JP 71
          (1974), 651-52.
          Reply to J. J. Thomson [#1313].

1054. Place, U. T., "Consciousness and Perception in Psycho-
          logy," ASSP 40 (1966), 101-24. Symposium with A.
          Watson.
          Argues against Watson that the notion of consciousness
          can consistently be integrated into a materialistic
          psychology.

1055. _____, "Sensations and Processes--A Reply to
          Munsat," M 81 (1972), 106-12.
          Continuation in the literature about identity-theory.
          Author re-asserts his view that sensations are processes
          in the brain, on the grounds that sensations meet all the
          previously agreed-upon criteria for being processes save
          one, which he rejects.

1056. Platt, J., "Two Faces of Perception," in B. Rothblatt,
          ed., Changing Perspectives on Man, (Chicago:
          University Press, 1968), 63-116.

1057. Platt, H. C., "Empiricism, Solipsism, and Realism,"
       BJPS 13 (1962), 216-28.
       Constructs a solipsistic model of the world from two
       assumptions and then introduces "the axiom of absolute
       symmetry" by means of which a logical justification for
       the belief in other persons and in a real world can be
       made.

1058. Pleydell-Pearce, A. G., "Perceptual Illusion, Symbolic
       Constructs and Stimulus-Response Psychology,"
       The Jour of the Brit Soc for Phenomenol 2 (1971), 41-
       48.
       Treatment of optical illusions (including Müller-Lyer
       lines, Zollner illusion and refraction) indicate a cer-
       tain prejudice on the part of many psychologists,
       especially behaviorists. We need not take the appear-
       ances to be distinct from the object--rather the object
       is the totality of its appearances and so is "funda-
       mentally ambiguous" by presenting different appearances
       under different conditions.

1059. _____, "Imagination and Perception,"
       The Jour of the Brit Soc for Phenomenol 5 (1974),
       37-40.

1060. Pollen, Daniel A., and Lee, James R., "How Does the
       Striate Cortex Begin the Reconstruction of the
       Visual World?" Science 173 (1971), 74-77.
       Transformations occurring in the visual system at the
       complex cell stage express a conservation of informa-
       tion. The topographical representation of visual space
       is transformed by the striate cortex into a Fourier
       transform at the complex cell level. Each of the stages
       in the transformation contains the same amount of infor-
       mation, but the form of presentation is changed.

1061. Pollock, John L., "Criteria and Our Knowledge of the
       Material World," PR 76 (1967), 28-60.
       Criteria are to be regarded as determined by their jus-
       tification conditions rather than by their truth con-
       ditions. Once this is done we can explain how a cri-
       terion functions is grounding knowledge of the material
       world.

1062. _____, "Chisholm's Definition of Knowledge,"
       Phil Studies 19 (1968), 72-76.

1063. _____, "The Structure of Epistemic Justifica-
       tion," Studies in the Theory of Knowledge: American
       Phil Quarterly Monograph, 4-6 (1970-1972), 62-78.
       Includes discussion of the logical connection between 'x
       looks red' and 'x is red'.

1064. _____, "Perceptual Knowledge," PR 80 (1971),

287-319.
Proposes a modification of Chisholm's distinction between the comparative and non-comparative uses of words used to describe how we are being appeared to. In the phenomenological use beliefs about how we are appeared to are incorrigible and provide <u>prima facie</u> justifica-tion for our beliefs about how things are. It is a consequence of this claim that descriptivism, naive realism and direct realism give equivalent accounts of perceptual knowledge.

1065. _____, <u>Knowledge and Justification</u>, (Prince-ton: Princeton University Press, 1974).
Chapter 3 critically reviews various theories of perceptual knowledge, arguing for a descriptivist account. Chapter 5 has an interesting treatment of perceptual attributes.

1066. Poppel, Ernst, "Oscillations as Possible Basis of Time Perception," <u>Studium Generale 24</u> (1971), 85-107.

1067. Popper, Karl, <u>Logik der Forschung</u>, (Vienna: Springer, 1935), (English translation, London: Hutchinson, 1958).
Discusses the empirical basis of science and basic statements. Argues against sense data and other theories that propose an incorrigible empirical basis for knowledge.

1068. _____, "A Note on Berkeley as a Precursor of Mach," <u>BJPS 4</u> (1953), 26-36.

1069. Popsel, Howard, "Scepticism and Modal Logic," <u>Log Anal 15</u> (1972), 653-64.
Modal arguments for perceptual scepticism examined and refuted.

1070. Posner, M. I., and Mitchell, R. F., "Chronometric Analysis of Classification," <u>Psych Rev 74</u> (1967), 392-409.
Discrimination performance based upon visual characteristics is more rapid and more accurate than that based on associative characteristics.

1071. _____, Goldsmith, R., and Welton, K. E., Jr., "Perceived Distance and the Classification of Distorted Patterns," <u>J of Exper Psychol 75</u> (1967), 28-38.

1072. _____, and Keele, S. W., "On the Genesis of Abstract Ideas," <u>J of Exper Psychol 77</u> (1968), 353-63.

1073.   _____, "Abstraction and the Process of Recog-
              nition," in Bower, Gordon H., and Spence, Janet
              Taylor, eds., The Psychology of Learning and Moti-
              vation; Advances in Research and Theory, Vol. 3
              (New York: Academic Press, 1969), 43-96.
         Argues for a schema theory in perception, memory and
         abstraction.

1074.   _____, and Keele, S. W., "Retention of Abstract
              Ideas," J of Exper Psychol 83 (1970), 304-08.

1075.   _____, Cognition: An Introduction, (Glenview,
              Illinois: Scott, Foresman and Company, 1973).
         Interesting survey of data concerning memory, abstrac-
         tion, mental operations and consciousness.

1076.   Postman, L., "Association Theory and Perceptual
              Learning," Psychol Rev 62 (1955), 438-46. Reply
              by J. J. and E. J. Gibson.
         A defense of associationism and criticism of the
         specificity hypothesis put forth by Gibson and Gibson.
         Criticizes the latter on the grounds that it cannot
         account for improvement in discrimination and does not
         entail a workable theory of perceptual learning.

1077.   _____, and Tolman, E. C., "Brunswik's Probabilistic
              Functionalism," in S. Koch, ed., Psychology: A
              Study of a Science, (New York: McGraw-Hill, 1963),
              vol. 1, 502-564.
         Authors summarize Brunswik's position on the place of
         psychology in the movement of unified science and the
         rise of functionalism. Discussion of Brunswik's prob-
         abilistic functionalism and his method of representative
         design. A final section is devoted to Brunswik's
         evaluation of some of the criticisms that have been
         directed against his views.

1078.   Prado, C. G., "Fragmenting Subjects," M 81 (1972), 123-
              24.
         A criticism of D. M. Armstrong [#46]. If Armstrong's
         notion of an intention is taken literally it follows
         that it is discrete mental states which perceive, have
         goals and introspect, rather than minds.

1079.   Prall, D. W., Aesthetic Analysis, (New York: Crowell,
              1936).
         Analyzes aesthetics in terms of the data of sense per-
         ception. Attempts to synthesize these data into
         patterns of order and relation.

1080.   Presson, Virginia, "G. E. Moore's Theory of Sense-Data,"
              JP 48 (1951), 34-42.
         Moore's claim that sense-data are the ultimate subjects

of perceptual experience is incompatible with his defense
of naive realism.

1081.   Pribram, Karl H., Spinelli, D. M., and Reitz, S. L.,
        "Effects of Radical Disconnection of Occipital and
        Temporal Cortex on Visual Behavior in Monkeys,"
        Brain 92 (1959), 301-12.

1082.   _____, ed., Perception and Action, (Balti-
        more: Penguin Books, 1969).
        Volume 2 of Pribram's set of readings, Brain and Behavior.
        Includes selections from papers dealing with the
        physiological aspects of perception (parts one and two).

1083.   _____, "The Brain," Psych Today, (Sept.,
        1971), 44-48, 88-90.
        A popular description of the author's holographic
        approach to modeling brain processes, including per-
        ceptual processes.

1084.   _____, "The Realization of Mind," Synthese
        22 (1971), 313-22.
        Attack on Cartesian dualism, in favor of the biologist's
        view. The biologist's position is derived from des-
        criptive science.

1085.   _____, Languages of the Brain: Experimental
        Paradoxes and Principles in Neuropsychology,
        (Englewood Cliffs, New Jersey: Prentice-Hall,
        1971).

1086.   _____, Nuwer, M., and Baron, R., "The Holo-
        graphic Hypothesis of Memory Structure in Brain
        Function and Perception," in R. C. Atkinson, D. H.
        Krantz, R. C. Luce, and P. Suppes, eds., Contem-
        porary Developments in Mathematical Psychology,
        (San Francisco: W. H. Freeman and Co., 1974).
        Summarizes neurological evidence that makes plausible a
        holographic hypothesis; presents a mathematical network
        model for holographic processes; and assesses evidence
        for the neurological assumptions.

1087.   Price, H. H., "Some Philosophical Questions About Tele-
        pathy and Clairvoyance," P 15 (1940), 363-85.

1088.   _____, "Review of The Foundations of Empirical
        Knowledge," M 50 (1941), 280-93.

1089.   _____, "Touch and Organic Sensation," PAS 44
        (1944), i-xxx.
        Philosophers can be distinguished into those who regard
        touch, as opposed to vision, as the primary source of
        contact with the material world.

1090.   _____, "The Causal Argument for Physical Objects,"
         ASSP 19 (1945), 92-100.

1091.   _____, "Seeming," _ASSP 26_ (1952), 215-34.
         Symposium with Britton and Quinton.

1092.   _____, _Thinking and Experience_, (London:
         Hutchinson, 1953).
         Recognition is a conceptual action. A discussion of
         concepts and how they function.

1093.   _____, "The Argument From Illusion," in H. D.
         Lewis, ed., _Contemporary British Philosophy III_,
         (London: Allen and Unwin, 1956).

1094.   _____, "Professor Ayer on the Problem of Know-
         ledge," _M 67_ (1958), 433-64.
         An extensive, detailed critical discussion of Ayer [#81].

1095.   _____, "Comment on Burgener," _RM 12_ (1958), 481-
         85.

1096.   _____, "The Nature and Status of Sense-Data in
         Broad's Epistemology," in P. Schilpp, ed., _The
         Philosophy of C. D. Broad_, (New York: Tudor, 1959).

1097.   _____, "Appearing and Appearances," _APQ 1_ (1964),
         3-19.
         Relates the decline of sense-datum theory to a decline
         in event metaphysics and suggests that a sense-datum
         philosopher's concern with appearances is legitimate.

1098.   Prior, A. N., "Self-Perception and Contingency," _A 30_
         (1969), 46-49.
         A criticism of an argument given by Sydney Shoemaker
         [#1219]. Shoemaker argues that no one can possible per-
         ceive himself perceiving anything, on the grounds that
         if it is possible to do that it should also be possible
         to perceive onself _not_ perceiving something, and this is
         clearly impossible. Prior criticizes the form of the
         argument.

1099.   Pritchard, H. A., "The Sense-Datum Fallacy," _ASSP 17_
         (1938), 1-18. Reprinted in _Knowledge and Percep-
         tion_.
         Argues that certain questions raised about sense-data
         (which are actually Berkelian questions about the
         perception of secondary qualities) are fallacious in
         that they are based on the idea that perception is a
         form of knowing.

1100.   _____, _Knowledge and Perception_, Sir David
         Ross, ed., (Oxford: Oxford University Press,
         1950).

1101.   Pritchard, Roy M., "Stabilized Images on the Retina,"
        Sci Amer 204 (June, 1961), 72-78.
        Results of experiments on stabilized retinal images
        show that the images fade and reappear. These findings
        suggest new approaches to problems of color vision and
        reconciling Gestalt theory with a cell-assembly
        approach.

1102.   Pucetti, Roland, "The Sensations of Pleasure," BJPS 20
        (1969), 239-45.
        Argues against Ryle's view that pleasure is not a sen-
        sation by appealing to recent experiments that seem to
        indicate several areas of the rat's brain which, when
        stimulated, produce pleasure.

1103.   Pustilnik, Jack, "Austin's Epistemology and His Critics,"
        P 39 (1964), 163-64.

1104.   Putnam, Ruth Anna, "Seeing and Observing," M 78 (1969),
        493-500.
        Argues against Hanson that seeing is not intentional,
        and does not involve believing, knowing or identifying
        what is seen. These negative claims are consistent
        with the views that 'seeing' is an achievement-word and
        that seeing is at times theory-laden. Defends distinc-
        tion between seeing and observing.

1105.   Quine, W. V. O., "Epistemology Naturalized," in
                Ontological Relativity and Other Essays, (New York:
                Columbia University Press, 1969), 69-90.
        Argues against the empiricist's tenets that all meanings
        of words rest on sensory evidence, and that all evidence
        for science is sensory evidence. Provides good counter
        move to arguments which purport to show that appeals to
        psychological facts in philosophical arguments are
        illegitimate.

1106.   _____, "Grades of Theoriticity," L. Foster and
                J. W. Swanson, eds., Experience and Theory,
                (Amhurst: University of Massachusetts Press, 1970),
                1-17.
        Begins with some remarks on what counts as data, dis-
        tance from which is the measure of degree of theoriticity
        of an object. Observation sentences defined behaviorally,
        and these replace data as the basic notion. Generality
        is introduced through induction and attributive com-
        pounds of observation terms. Distinction between sub-
        stitutional and objectual quantification drawn--latter
        points to a higher grade of theoriticity than the former.

1107.   Quinton, Anthony M., "Seeming," ASSP 26 (1952), 235-52.
                Symposium with K. Britton and H. H. Price.

1108.   , "The Problem of Perception," M 64
       (1955), 28-51. Reprinted in Swartz, [#1301] and
       Warnock, [#1386].
An attack on the claim that we are never directly aware
of material objects. Argues that a statement about what
appears to be the case is only rarely a description of
our sense-experience; usually it is a guarded claim about
what we are inclined to believe is the case. Such statements are not expressions of a special, direct, indubitable form of knowledge. Extensive and thorough critique of the argument from illusion. Suggests that the
search for perfect standard conditions for the basis of
empirical claims about material objects is misguided.

1109.   , "Matter and Space," M 73 (1964),
       332-52.
Examination of Descartes' principle that the essential
attribute of matter is extension. Quinton considers
two possible counterexamples to this principle: sense-
data, which appear to occupy space and yet are not
material things, and lines of points which are material
but do not occupy space. He concludes that neither is a
genuine counterexample to the principle. Defends the
claim that sense-data are either material or else not
really occupants of public space. Argues that there
are necessary truths about non-primary qualities of
things, and that 'scarlet is darker than pink' is one
of them.

1110.   , "The Foundations of Knowledge," in
       Williams, B., and Montefiore, A., eds., British
       Analytical Philosophy, (New York: Humanities
       Press, 1966), 55-86.
A lucid and thorough discussion of arguments for and
against the thesis that knowledge must be logically
derivable from basic statements, which may be intuitive,
ostensive or phenomenal, but whose truth is said to be
certain and incorrigible. Several interpretations of
the notion of basic statements discussed. The alternative to the thesis of foundationalism is a coherence
theory of truth and knowledge. Quinton examines
several versions, concentrating particularly on the work
of Popper.

1111.   , "Perceiving and Thinking," ASSP 42
       (1968), 191-208.
Comments on Don Locke.

1112.   , "Review of Aune's Knowledge, Mind
       and Nature," M 78 (1969), 442-53.

1113. Rader, Melvin, "The Imaginative Mode of Awareness," Jour
       Aes and Art Crit 33 (1974), 131-37.

Difference between "normal" and aesthetic modes of
awareness of things. Latter said to be a function of
aspect perception: in aesthetic awareness object is
seen as it appears, and not as it is.

1114. Raff, Charles, "Moore on 'See'," JP 71 (1974), 722-23.
On Gareth Matthews [#914].

1115. Ralston, Howard L., "Kinesthetic Sensations Revisited,"
JP 62 (1965), 96-100.
Defense of Anscombe's claims regarding knowing the
position of one's bodily parts without perceptual
evidence.

1116. Ramsperger, A. G., "What is Scientific Knowledge?" PS 6
(1939), 390-403.
Scientific knowledge differs only in degree of abstraction from other knowledge.

1117. _____, "Objects Perceived and Objects
Known," JP 37 (1940), 291-97.
Defense of direct realism and a direct realist explana-
tion of visual hallucinations.

1118. Ramussen, E. Tranekjaer, "Berkeley and Modern Psychology," BJPS 4 (1953), 2-12.

1119. Rankin, K. W., "Ayer's Anti-Phenomenalism," AJP 36
(1958), 109-19.
Critical discussion of Ayer's rejection of phenomenalism
in The Problem of Knowledge.

1120. Rankin, Nani L., "A Note on Ducasse's Perceivable Causation," PPR 28 (1967), 269-70.

1121. Rapaport, David, ed., Organization and Pathology of
Thought, (New York: Columbia University Press,
1965).
Anthology, contains works by: Narciss, Karl Buehler, E.
Claparede, Kurt Lewin, J. Varendonck, Ernst Kris, Paul
Schilder, Hans Buerger-Prinz and Martti Kaila, and David
Rapaport, Jean Piaget, Herbert Silberer, Karl Schroetter,
Gaston Roffenstein, M. Nachmansohn, Stefan Betlheim and
Heinz Hartmann, Wilhelm Stekel, Sigmund Freud, Otto
Fenichel.

1122. Ratliff, F., Mach Bands: Quantitative Studies on Neural
Networks in the Retina, (San Francisco: Holden-Day,
1965).
Considers and develops mathematical models for neural
networks. Includes translations of some of Ernst Mach's
papers.

1123.   _____, "Contour and Contrast," Proc of the Amer Philosophical Society 115 (1971), 150-63.

1124.   _____, "Illusions in Man and His Instruments," JP 68 (1971), 591-97.
Elaborates on A. Shimony [#1218]. Sense organs systematically select the information they transmit to the brain because all information processing devices (from computers to nervous systems) dissipate some of the energy of the original input.

1125.   Ratner, Joseph, "Scientific Objects and Empirical Things," JP 32 (1935), 393-408.
Science, not philosophy, establishes the reality of empirical things, and this makes it mandatory that philosophers separate metaphysics from reality.

1126.   Reale, Miguel, "Realism," Encyclopedia of Philosophy, Vol. 7, p. 77.

1127.   Reck, Andrew J., "The Realism of Roy Wood Sellars," The New Scholasticism 14 (1971), 209-44.

1128.   Reed, S. K., "Pattern Recognition and Categorization," Cognitive Psychology 3 (1972), 382-407.

1129.   Reese, Hayne W., The Perception of Stimulus Relations: Discriminatory Learning and Transposition, (New York: Academic Press, 1968).
A study of transposition phenomena and a review of the various theories.

1130.   Reese, T. W., "The Application of the Theory of Physical Measurement to the Measurement of Psychological Magnitudes," Psych Monograph 55 (1943).

1131.   Reichenbach, Hans, "On Observing and Perceiving," Phil Studies 2 (1951), 92-93.
Reply to Chisholm [#259].

1132.   _____, "Are Phenomenal Reports Absolutely Certain?" PR 61 (1952), 147-59. Symposium with Lewis and Goodman.

1133.   Rescher, N., and Oppenheim, Paul, "Logical Analysis of Gestalt Concepts," BJPS 6 (1955), 89-106.
Discussion of the concept of whole as it is used in Gestalt theory.

1134.   _____, "Presuppositions of Knowledge," RIP 13 (1959), 418-29.

1135.   Resnick, Lawrence, "Empiricism and Natural Kinds," JP 57

(1960), 555-59.
Critical review of H. H. Price's Thinking and Experience.

1136. Revesz, G., Introduction to the Psychology of Music,
(London: Longmans, Green, 1952) (Originally 1946,
translated G. I. C. de Courcy).

1137. Richards, Norvin, "Depicting and Visualizing," M 82
(1973), 218-25.
Analogous sets of criteria determine what an artist has
depicted in a painting and what someone has visualized
on a certain occasion. These criteria include inten-
tions, content, biographical facts and (sometimes)
appropriateness of conventions used. Disanalogy between
depicting and visualizing is due to the fact that in
visualizing rules are neither taught nor consciously
followed.

1138. Richards, Robert J., "The Whereabouts of Percepts," JP
55 (1958), 344-48.
Attacks an argument based on the relation of contiguity
between cause and effect which had been used to show
that percepts are in the brain.

1139. Riesen, Austin H., "Arrested Vision," Sci Amer 183 (July,
1950), 16-19.
Chimpanzees raised in darkness exhibit visual responses
when first exposed to the light. Visual pursuit of
moving objects, however, requires several weeks of practice as does the automatic blinking in response to
objects moving across the visual field.

1140. _____, "Problems in Correlating Behavioral
and Physiological Development," Chapter Four of
Sterman, M. B., McGentry, Dennis J., and Adinolfi,
Anthony M., eds., Brain Development and Behavior,
(New York: Academic Press, 1971),59-70.
Proposes guidelines for distinguishing correlations
between physiological and behavioral processes from
causal relationships between them.

1141. Riley, Donald A., Discrimination Learning, (Boston:
Allyn and Bacon, 1968).
Discusses stimulus generalization, transposition and
stimulus value reversal.

1142. Ritchie, D. A., "A Defense of Sense-Data," PQ 2 (1952),
240-45.
Disagreements in application of color-terms shows that
such terms cannot be grounded solely in mathematical
or geometrical relationships.

1143. Ritchie, R. M., "Can Animals See? A Cartesian Query,"
PAS 64 (1964), 221-42.

Critical discussion of Descartes' views concerning the difference between men and animals.

1144.   Roberts, Fred S., and Suppes, Patrick, "Some Problems in the Geometry of Visual Perception," S 17 (1967), 173-201.
Primitive visual space is non-Euclidean. Discussion of modifications produced by learning, focusing on perception of size and shape constancies.

1145.   Robinson, Helier J., "The Two Head Hypothesis and the Paradoxes of Perception," Int Log Rev 3 (1972), 99-123.
All philosophic problems of perception are reducible to the problem that subjectively known perceptual experience is incompatible with the causal theory.

1146.   Robinson, H. M., "Professor Armstrong on 'Non-Physical Sensory Items'," M 81 (1972), 84-86.
Defense of sense-data against two arguments from D. M. Armstrong [#46].

1147.   _____, "The Irrelevance of Intentionality to Perception," PQ 24 (1974), 300-15.
Intentionalist accounts of sense-experience are not adequate. He rejects Anscombe's claim that the question of the ontological status of direct objects (and so of intentional objects) cannot be raised. Whenever S seems to see something F he is aware of the quality F ("or an F quality-pattern"); this awareness is not intentional.

1148.   Robinson, William S., "Dennett's Analysis of Awareness," Phil Studies 23 (1972), 147-52.
Suggests a third sense of 'aware' which is like Dennett's 'aware$_1$' save that the creature who has awareness$_3$ lacks a speech-center. This third sense of 'aware' cannot be subsumed under either of Dennett's senses.

1149.   Rock, Irvin, The Nature of Perceptual Adaptation, (New York: Basic Books, 1966).
A study of the effects of the optical transformation of retinal images produced by various types of distorting prisms, lenses and mirrors. The types of distortion discussed include displacement, altered size of retinal image, disorientation, and distortion of form. Extensive discussion of how perceivers adapt to such distortion and how the nervous system changes to the resulting alterations in perceptual information.

1150.   _____, and Harris, Charles S., "Vision and Touch," Sci Amer 26 (1967), 96-104.
Experiments designed to test the relative dominance of visual and tactile perception show that vision dominates.

1151. Rommetreit, Ragnar, "Epistemological Notes on Recent Studies of Social Perception," I 1 (1958), 213-31.
Survey and discussion of theories of social perception.

1152. Ronchi, Vasco, Optics: The Science of Vision, (New York: New York University Press, 1957). Translated by Edward Rosen.
This is an influential book.

1153. Rorty, R., "Mind-Body Identity, Privacy and Categories," RM 19 (1965), 24-54.
The elimination of sensations is possible for a materialistic theory.

1154. _____, "Strawson's Objectivity Argument," RM 24 (1970), 207-44.
Exegesis and clarification of Strawson's restatement of Transcendental Deduction (in The Bounds of Sense).

1155. _____, "Verificationism and Transcendental Arguments," N 5 (1971), 3-14.
APA Symposium with Judith J. Thomson and Kai Nielson.

1156. _____, "Dennett on Awareness," Phil Studies 23 (1972), 153-62.
Dennett's notion of a "speech-center" is inadequate for explaining incorrigible knowledge. The functional sense of 'speech-center' is too abstract and loose a notion to help in explaining the nature of human awareness.

1157. Rosch, Eleanor H., "Natural Categories," Cognitive Psychol 4 (1973), 328-50.
Domains of color and form are structured into non-arbitrary semantics categories. Stimuli in these categories are more easily learned than "distorted" categories. Discusses cross-cultural studies.

1158. Rose, Guenter H., "Relationship of Electrophysiological and Behavioral Indices of Visual Development in Mammals," in Sterman, McGentry and Adinolfi, eds., Brain Development and Behavior, (New York: Academic Press, 1971), chapter 9.
Reports findings from experiments on the correlation between electrophysiological, anatomical and behavior indices in immature kittens and rats.

1159. Rosenthal, Sandra, "Peirce's Theory of the Perceptual Judgment," JHP 7 (1969), 303-14.

1160. Rosenzweig, Mark R., "Auditory Localization," Sci Amer 205 (1961), 132-42.
Discussion of the physiological basis for our ability to detect the source of a sound.

1161. Ross, J. J., "The Reification of Appearance," P 40
          (1965), 113-28.
          Argues that delusive appearances of objects cannot be
          adequately explained by treating an appearance as an
          entity of some sort, and insofar as the sense-datum
          theory rests on some such treatment of delusive exper-
          iences it, too, must be rejected.

1162. _____, The Appeal to the Given, (London: Allen
          and Unwin, 1970).
          A critical survey of recent theories which make use of
          a concept of the given in perception and knowledge.

1163. Rundle, Bede, Perception, Sensation and Verification,
          (Oxford: Clarendon Press, 1972).
          Argues from a modified stimulus-response model that
          knowledge is involved in perception, even in cases of
          animal perception. Perception is disanalogous to sen-
          sation in some respects, e.g., the self-aware character
          of the latter. Discusses many of the traditional
          problems concerning mental events, behaviorism and
          other minds.

1164. Russell, Bertrand, Our Knowledge of the External World,
          (London: Allen and Unwin, 1929).
          Discusses the relation between physics and senses; the
          latter is used to verify the former.

1165. _____, An Inquiry Into Meaning and Truth,
          (London: Allen and Unwin, 1940).
          We fill out our sensations into perceptual experiences;
          these are bundles of sensations; see especially sections
          4, 6, 8, 9, 10 for a defense of analytical phenomenalism.

1166. _____, "Reply to Criticisms," in P. Schilpp,
          ed., The Philosophy of Bertrand Russell, (Evanston,
          Illinois: Northwestern University Press, 1944).

1167. _____, "On the Nature of Acquaintance," in
          Logic and Knowledge, R. C. Marsh, ed., (Allen and
          Unwin, 1956).

1168. _____, "The Philosophy of Logical Atomism,"
          Logic and Knowledge, R. C. Marsh, ed., (Allen and
          Unwin, 1956).
          Particulars are sense-data, and physical objects are
          constructions out of them.

1169. _____, Human Knowledge, Its Scope and Limits,
          (New York: Simon and Schuster, 1948).

1170. Ryle, Gilbert, The Concept of Mind, (London: Hutchinson,
          1949).

131

The sense-datum theory rests on the howler of assimilating the concept of sensation to the concept of observation. Perception is an achievement, an observational success.

1171.   _____, "Feelings," PQ 1 (1950), 193-205.
Distinguishes seven uses of the verb 'to feel' and argues against assimilating some to others of them.

1172.   _____, "Perception," in [#1174].

1173.   _____, "Sensation," in H. D. Lewis, ed., Contemporary British Philosophy, (London: Allen and Unwin, 1956). (Reprinted in Swartz [#1301].

1174.   _____, Dilemmas, (Cambridge University Press, 1954).
The Tarner lectures; two lectures are relevant: "The World of Science and the Everyday World" and "Perception". In both it is argued that the conflict between common sense and science is only apparent, with common sense being basic. Perception is not a process bodily or psychological but rather the scoring of an investigational success.

1175.   Sabra, A. I., Theories of Light from Descartes to Newton, (London: Oldbourne Press, 1967).
A useful history of the role that light plays in the scientific theories of many seventeenth century thinkers.

1176.   Saiyidain, Zehra, The Realm of Perception, (Simla, India: Indian Institute of Advanced Study, 1970).

1177.   Sanford, David H,, "Volume and Solidity," AJP 45 (1967), 329-40.
Proposes definitions and examples which might make it true that a material thing might not occupy space, and that two material things, both of which occupy space, might occupy the same space at the same time.

1178.   Santayana, George, "On Synthesis and Memory," JP 67 (1970), 5-17.
Consists of two author-rejected chapters from Realms of Being. Further remarks on his concept of Spirit.

1179.   Sartorius, Rolf, "A Neglected Aspect of the Relationship Between Berkeley's Theory of Vision and His Immaterialism," APQ 6 (1969), 318-23.
Berkeley's New Theory of Vision contains an important defense of his immaterialism; there Berkeley argues that there are no sensible ideas common to both sight and touch. This, the author argues, is in effect a rejection of Locke's distinction between primary and

secondary qualities, which is crucial in Berkeley's defense of immaterialism.

1180. Savage, C. Wade, The Measurement of Sensation, (Berkeley: University of California Press, 1970).
A somewhat dated examination of psycho-physical theories and their nature.

1181. Sayce, L. A., et. al., Visual Problems of Colour,(London: Her Majesty's Stationary Office, 1958). Two volumes.
Contains papers on color vision read at a symposium held at the National Physical Laboratory, September, 1957.

1182. Sayre, Kenneth M., "On Disagreements About Perception," I 7 (1964), 143-62.
An examination of various forms of arguments used in disagreements about perception--examples drawn from phenomenalism, against Aristotle's identification of sensing faculty and sensed object and against Berkeley's account of observation by means of instruments.

1183. _____, Recognition: A Study in the Philoso- phy of Artifical Intelligence, (Notre Dame, Indiana: University of Notre Dame Press, 1965).
Failure to appreciate a conceptual distinction between classification and recognition has hampered simulation studies with digital computers. In part one the author summarizes the results of such studies and articulates the confusion between recognition and classification. In parts two and three the concept of recognition is discussed in connection with the acts of sensation and perception. In part four the conceptual apparatus is used to develop a new model for mechanical pattern-recognition in which recognition is equated with recep- tion of information.

1184. _____, Consciousness: A Philosophic Study of Minds and Machines, (New York: Random House, 1969).
An attempt to analyze consciousness by comparing it to other mechanisms, e.g., homing devices.

1185. Scheffler, Israel, Science and Subjectivity, (Indianapo- lis: Bobbs-Merrill, 1967).
Attempts to adjudicate between a foundationalist view of perception, e.g., C. I. Lewis, and the theory laden position of Hanson.

1186. _____, "Vision and Revolutions: A Postscript on Kuhn," PS 39 (1972), 366-74.
First part contains author's earlier ("Science and Sub- jectivity") criticisms of Kuhn and replies to Kuhn's replies. In the second part author argues that Kuhn's metaphors of vision and revolution are "incongruous".

133

1187. Schilder, Paul, Mind: Perception and Thought in Their
          Constructive Aspects, (New York: Columbia Univer-
          sity Press, 1938).

1188. Schlagel, Richard H., "Language and Perception," PPR 23
          (1962), 192-204.
          Reviews arguments for saying that we perceive physical
          objects and for saying we perceive sense-data and sug-
          gests that ordinary language will not provide the
          grounds for choosing one or the other.

1189. Schmitt, Richard, "Maurice Merleau-Ponty I and II," RM
          19 (1965), 492-516, 728-741.

1190. Schultz, Arnold, A Theory of Consciousness, (New York:
          Philosophical Library, 1973).

1191. Schultzer, Bert, Observation and Protocol Statement,
          (London: Williams and Northgate, 1939).

1192. Scriven, Michael, "Modern Experiments in Telepathy," PR
          65 (1956), 231-53.
          Includes discussion of whether we should count ESP as
          perceptual phenomena.

1193. Scruton, Roger, "Objectivity and the Will," M 82 (1973),
          381-400.
          Phenomenalism is either true or nonsense. Considers
          whether we need to have knowledge of physical objects
          in order to have knowledge of our sensations, which are,
          according to phenomenalism, what we experience.

1194. Segell, Marshall, Donald T. Campbell and Melville J.
          Herskovits, The Influence of Culture on Visual
          Perception, (New York: Bobbs-Merrill, 1966).
          Describes the authors' tests with illusions and other
          perceptual stimuli from some fifteen different cultures.
          There are differences they claim, for example, in the
          perception of the Mueller-Lyer illusion.

1195. Sekuler, R. W., Rubin, E. L., and Cushman, W. H.,
          "Selectivities of Human Visual Mechanisms for
          Direction of Movement and Contour Orientation,"
          Journal of the Optical Society of America 58
          (1968), 1146-50.

1196. Self, Donnie J., "Sense-Data and the Argument from Illu-
          sion," Dialogue (PST) 16 (1974), 53-56.
          Discussion of the premisses and assumptions of argument
          from illusion as presented by A. J. Ayer. Author rejects
          the argument for Austinian reasons.

1197. Seligman, David, "Sensations: Perceived Sensible

Qualities?" PPR 32 (1972), 447-64.
Criticism of the view that sensations are perceived
sensible qualities that qualify parts of our bodies.
Argues that sensations are not perceived--pain is not
felt. Rather sensations are ways of perceiving dis-
turbances, states or qualities of the body.

1198. _____, "A Note on Odegard's Sensations," PQ 19
(1968), 71-72.

1199. Sellars, Roy Wood, "Critical Realism and the Independence
of the Object," JP 34 (1937), 541-50.
Articulates main differences in the analysis of perceiving between himself and C. I. Lewis.

1200. _____, "A Statement of Critical Realism,"
RIP 1 (1938), Reprinted in Hirst [#666].

1201. _____, "Philosophy of Organism and Physical
Realism," in P. Schilpp, ed., The Philosophy of
Alfred North Whitehead, (Evanston, Illinois:
Northwestern University Press, 1941).

1202. _____, "Causation and Perception," PR 53
(1944), 534-38.
Carefully distinguishing between sensing and perceiving
can aid in grounding a realistic, rather than phenomen-
alistic, empiricism.

1203. _____, "Sensations as Guides to Perceiving,"
M 68 (1959), 2-15.
Presents a brief history of critical realism in its two
main varieties and outlines his theory in relation to
modern biology and psychology.

1204. Sellars, Wilfrid, "Physical Realism," PPR 15 (1954), 13-
32.
Comparison and discussion of points of agreement between
the author's physical realism and Roy Wood Sellars'
critical realism.

1205. _____, "Intentionality and the Mental," in
Feigl, Scriven and Maxwell, Minnesota Studies in
the Philosophy of Science II, (University of Minnesota Press, 1958). Correspondence with R. Chisholm.
Criticism of Chisholm's account of intentionality.

1206. _____, "The Language of Theories," in Feigl
and Maxwell, eds., Current Issues in the Philosophy
of Science, (New York: Holt, 1961). Reprinted in
Science, Perception and Reality, 1962.

1207. _____, "Empiricism and the Philosophy of

135

Mind," in Feigl and Scriven, eds., <u>Minnesota Studies in the Philosophy of Science I</u>, (University of Minnesota Press, 1958). Reprinted in <u>Science, Perception and Reality</u>, 1962.

1208.   , "The Refutation of Phenomenalism: Prolegomena to a Defense of Scientific Realism," in Feyerabend, P. and Maxwell, G., eds., <u>Mind, Matter and Method: Essays in Honor of Herbert Feigl</u>, (Minneapolis: University of Minnesota Press, 1966),198-214. Also in <u>Science, Perception and Reality</u>, 76-90.
Attack on the notion, essential to the phenomenalist position, of a "possible sense content." Presuppositions of phenomenalism contrasted with those of scientific realism.

1209.   , "Some Reflections on Thoughts and Things," <u>N 1</u> (1967), 97-121.

1210.   , <u>Science and Metaphysics: Variations on Kantian Themes</u>, (London: Routledge and Kegan Paul, 1968).

1211.   , "Toward A Theory of the Categories," in L. L. Foster and J. W. Swanson, eds., <u>Experience and Theory</u>, (Amherst: University of Massachusetts Press, 1970), 55-78.
Attempts to sketch a theory of categories in terms of the functioning of predicates. He allies it with a Kantian-type theory of categorization.

1212.   , "Science, Sense Impressions, and Sensa: A Reply to Cornman," <u>RM 24</u> (1971), 391-447.
A reply to Cornman [#293].

1213.   , "Givenness and Explanatory Coherence," <u>JP 70</u> (1970), 612-24.
An excerpt from a longer paper given at an APA Symposium, December 28, 1973. A discussion of issues raised by Firth [#423]. Comments by Peter Unger and Arthur Smullyan-abstracts in same journal.

1214. Severens, Richard, "Seeing," <u>PPR 28</u> (1967), 213-21.
Examination of the logic of 'see' in its visual propositional occurrences—e.g., 'Johnny sees that the man is bald.' Argues against construing all visual occurrences of 'see' as implicitly propositional.

1215. Shanab, Robert E. A., "Locke on Knowledge and Perception," <u>J Crit Anal 2</u> (1971), 16-23.
An analysis of Locke's use of the term 'proposition.'

136

1216. Shearn, Martin, "Other People's Sense-Data," PAS 50
(1950), 15-26.
Argues that the fact that other people have experiences
can be justified only by an appeal to their observable
behavior.

1217. Sheridan, Gregory, "The Electroencephalogram Argument
Against Incorrigibility," APQ 6 (1969), 62-70.
Defends with qualifications the Wittgensteinian argument
for the incorrigibility of first-person-sensation-
reports against the EEG argument (the claim that there
are circumstances in which the evidence of EEG reports
would tend to override an honest first person report).

1218. Shimony, Abner, "Perception From an Evolutionary Point
of View," JP 68 (1971), 571-83.
Defense of the causal theory of perception. Human perception is adaptive and that evolutionary considerations
override quasi-teleological explanations of perceptual
features within the framework of the causal theory.

1219. Shoemaker, Sidney, Self-Knowledge and Self-Identity,
(Ithaca, New York: Cornell University Press, 1963).
A neo-Wittgensteinian attempt to provide criteria for
first person psychological states. Self knowledge is
unlike our knowledge of objects. A good discussion of
the claim and implications of all seeing is from a point
of view.

1220. _____, "Self-Reference and Self-Awareness,"
JP 65 (1968), 555-67. Comments by Michael Woods.

1221. _____, "A Critical Study of "Myself and
Others" by Don Locke," PQ 19 (1969), 272-79.

1222. Shope, Robert K., "The Neutrality of Experiential Statements," PPR 32 (1972), 377-83.
Attempts by Firth and Ayer to defend the claim that
experiential statements (e.g., "It looks to me as if I
am seeing a pig") are neutral (in several senses) are
inadequate.

1223. Shwayder, D. S., "The Varieties and Objects of Visual
Phenomena," M 70 (1961), 307-30.
Visual phenomena are defined as those whose description
requires the use of 'see' or its cognates. Distinguishes
five categories of visual phenomena, and discusses the
correct descriptions pertaining to abnormalities in each.
Discusses the question whether there is one particular
kind of object of all types of visual experience.

1224. Sibley, F. N., "Seeking, Scrutinizing and Seeing," M 64
(1955), 455-78. Reprinted in Warnock, [#1386].

Argues as against Ryle that 'see' and 'hear' are not achievement-verbs. Begins by separating the concepts of 'looking for' and 'looking at'. This leads to a more general distinction between the concepts of quests and scrutinies, as well as a corresponding distinction of some of the uses of 'see' in which it is not an achievement-verb; e.g., the sense of 'see' which is equivalent to 'keeping in sight.'

1225. _____, "Colours," PAS 68 (1968), 145-66.
Discussion of the question what must be the case for it to be true that the statement that something is green is unchallengeable. Gives an account of how colour-terms might have been introduced, and discusses several hypothetical situations in which sudden and either complete or incomplete reversal in color-perception occurs, and considers how such shifts might affect verbal agreement on the application of color-terms.

1226. _____, "Analysing Seeing," in F. N. Sibley, ed.,
         [#1227].
Defends claim that an epistemic use of 'see' is more fundamental than the non-epistemic use. Argues that epistemic use of 'see' is not restricted to 'seeing-that' constructions; rather there are two uses of 'see' with a direct object, and one of them (the more basic) is epistemic. Thorough discussion of positions defended by Armstrong and Dretske, though without much explicit citation of their specific claims.

1227. _____, ed., Perception: A Philosophical Sympo-
         sium, (London: Methuen; New York: Barnes and
         Noble, 1971).
Includes the following articles: Warnock, J. J., "On What Is Seen"; Taylor, D. M., "On What Is Seen"; Cox, J. W. Roxbee, "An Analysis of Perceiving in Terms of the Causation of Beliefs"; Kneale, William, "An Analysis of Perceiving in Terms of the Causation of Beliefs"; Sibley, F. N., "Analysing Seeing"; Vesey, G. N. A., "Analysing Seeing"; O'Shaughnessy, Brian, "The Temporal Ordering of Perceptions and Reactions"; Williams, Bernard, "The Temporal Ordering of Perceptions and Reactions".

1228. Siegler, F. A., "Probability, Certainty and Illusions,"
         I 5 (1962), 91-115.
Those who argue that no empirical statements are certain employ a form of reasoning that also casts doubt on the certainty of calculations in mathematics and logic. Author criticizes this reasoning (said to be a version of the argument from illusion).

1229. Sinha, L. P. N., "Berkeley's Learning Theory of Percep-
         tion," Darshana Int 10 (1970), 12-21.

We perceive signs by means of our senses and learn to associate signs with signified objects. Berkeley is an immaterialist with respect to signs.

1230. _____, "Bertrand Russell and the Problem of Perception," Indian Phil Cult 17 (1972), 5-13. Uses Berkeley to "help" Russell.

1231. Sircello, G., "Perceptual Acts and Pictorial Arts: a defense of the expression theory," JP 62 (1965), 669-77.

1232. Slakely, Thomas, "Aristotle on Sense-Perception," PR 70 (1961), 470-84.

1233. Sleinis, E. E., "Hanson on Observation and Explanation," Phil Papers 2 (1973), 73-83.

1234. Slomann, Aage, "Primary and Secondary Qualities," M 73 (1964), 413-16. That there is a difference between primary and secondary qualities can be shown in the fact that an illusory visual experience of a primary quality is detectable by the perceiver, whereas in the case of secondary qualities it may be indetectable.

1235. _____, "Perception of Size: Some Remarks on Size as a Primary Quality and 'Size Constancy'," I 11 (1968), 101-13. Presents an expanded, modified version of the theory defended in previous article [#1234]. The perceived size of an object can be shown to decrease with increasing distance of the object from the perceiver, and this decrease is less rapid than that of the size of the retinal image of the object. Purports to show by means of diagrams that in theory it is possible that perceived size may vary among perceivers and that this variance could be discovered. Objects that one can see the decreased perceived size when smaller than medium-sized physical objects are considered. Draws a distinction between three kinds of 'object' to be considered in analysis of size: 1) the percept (in private space) 2) the "objective" object (in physical space) 3) the "physical" or "real" object (a thing-in-itself, unobservable, cause of percept).

1236. Smart, J. J. C., "Colours," P 36 (1961), 128-42. Argues against Objectivist and Subjectivist (Lockean) theories of color-qualities. Puts forward an alternative to both according to which color concepts are relational. Proposes to analyze color concepts in terms of the notion 'discriminates with respect to color'. Argues that a blind person can know the meanings of color-terms.

1237. _____, Philosophy and Scientific Realism,
       (London: Routledge and Kegan Paul, 1963).
The theme of the book (or series of connected essays)
reflected Smart's own shift in stance from thinking of
philosophy as conceptual analysis to thinking of it as
being nearer to science. The motivation in the work is
an attack on "anthropocentric" strains of thought in
philosophy. These include phenomenalist and subjectivist
theories of mind, matter, space and time.

1238. _____, "Physical Objects and Physical
       Theories," in Philosophy and Scientific Realism,
       (London: Routledge and Kegan Paul, 1963), 16-49.
An attack on the view that to say electrons are real is
to say only that the word 'electron' plays a useful role
in certain physical theories that enable us to predict
and control events on the macroscopic level. Smart
argues that such a view about physics is similar in some
respects to phenomenalism--matter is a "permanent possibility of sensation" and electrons are "permanent possibilities of observations of physical objects." Argues
that electrons are not "logical fictions." Long internal critique of phenomenalism on both the macroscopic
and sub-microscopic levels.

1239. _____, "The Secondary Qualities," in Philosophy
       and Scientific Realism, (London: Routledge and
       Kegan Paul, 1963), 64-87.
Attempts to set out a view concerning the secondary
qualities (especially color) according to which they are
to be understood in terms of reactions of organisms to
stimuli. Such a view can explain both why scientists
regard secondary qualities as superfluous and how they
can be encompassed in a physicalistic world-view.

1240. _____, "Reports of Immediate Experience," S 22
       (1971), 346-59.
Proposes modifications and revisions in his previous
views concerning the correct analysis of statements like
'I have a yellow sense-datum.' These were held to be
analysable by means of reference to a stimulus which
typically causes experiences of the same sort; e.g.,
'This is like what goes on in me when I see a lemon'.
Also rejects his former Lockean view that colors are
powers in objects to cause certain effects in perceivers
in favor of the claim that colors are objective physical
qualities, to be regarded by materialists   as quasi-
theoretical primitives.

1241. _____, "Time, Consciousness of," Encyclopedia
       of Philosophy, Vol. 8, 135.

1242. Smith, H. M., "Is There A Problem About Sense-Data,"
       ASSP 15 (1936), 78-87. Symposium with G. A. Paul
       and Murray.

1243. Smith, Karl V., and Smith, William M., Perception and
       Motion: An Analysis of Space-Structured Behavior,
       (Philadelphia: W. B. Saunders, 1962).
       Deals with perceptual-motor organization. Some ingenious
       experiments done with television.

1244. Smith, R. J., "Comments on Ichheiser's Theory of Social
       Perception," PPR 30 (1969), 457-61.
       Reviews findings in the field of social perception and
       suggests that these may have some relevance in the area
       of ethics.

1245. Smullyan, Arthur, "Aspects," PR 64 (1955), 33-42.
       Sensa are aspects of physical objects.

1246. _____, "Sense Content and Perceptual Assur-
       ance," (abstract) JP 70 (1973), 625-28.
       Commentary on Sellars [#1213].
       Smullyan gives a "different" account of some aspects of
       perceptual assurance, e.g., the sense in which the sub-
       ject of sense experience has perceptual assurance that
       certain objective states of affairs obtain. He holds
       that experience of sense contents themselves is not an
       example of perceptual assurance. What we have perceptual
       assurance of is that a state of affairs obtains and not,
       for example, of the sensory experience by which we have
       assurance.

1247. Smythies, J. R., "The Mescaline Phenomena," BJPS 3
       (1952), 339-47.
       Gives account of the effects of mescaline on visual
       perception, and suggests that these may have philosophi-
       cal implications, especially in the area of hallucina-
       tions.

1248. _____, "Analysis of Projection," BJPS 5 (1954),
       120-33.
       Argues that the notion of projection as employed in
       current neurophysiological accounts of perception is
       incoherent, although it is useful in psycho-analysis and
       in neuro-anatomy.

1249. _____, "A Note on Mr. Hirst's Recent Paper in
       Mind," M 63 (1954), 388-89.
       Comment on Hirst [#664]. Mescaline produces hallucina-
       tions without loss of subject's powers of discrimination,
       contrary to Hirst.

1250. _____, "The Stroboscope as Providing Empirical
       Confirmation of the Representative Theory of

Perception," BJPS 6 (1955), 332-35.
The phenomena of lines and patterns produced in the
visual field of someone looking at a rapidly flashing
light 'suggest that in normal perception, the visual
field is constructed by representative mechanisms like
those that operate in the stroboscopic experience.

1251. _____, "A Note on Martin Lean's Sense Perception and Matter," Phil Studies 6 (1955), 4-8.

1252. _____, "On Some Properties and Relations of
Images," PR 67 (1958), 359-94.
Images are spatial entities that may stand in causal
and spatial relations to material things.

1253. _____, "On the Space and Time of Images," BJPS
9 (1958), 40-52. Reply to Chari, [#252].
Hallucinatory images do have the geometrical properties
they appear to have.

1254. _____, "'Philosophical' and 'Scientific' Sense-
Data," BJPS 9 (1958), 224-25. Reply to Tucker
[#1335].

1255. _____, "The Problem of Perception," BJPS 11
(1960), 224-38. Critical and detailed review of
R. J. Hirst, The Problem of Perception.

1256. _____, The Analysis of Perception, (London:
Routledge and Kegan Paul, 1956).
Argues for the television theory of perception that
sense data are like images on a television screen.
Attempts to argue that we can know that sense-data are
like the physical objects that caused them.

1257. _____, "Some Recent Theories of Mind," in I. T.
Ramsey, ed., Biology and Purpose, (Oxford: Black-
well, 1965).
Comments by H. H. Price and A. M. Quinton.

1258. _____, "The Representative Theory of Percep-
tion," in Smythies, ed., Brain and Mind, (London:
Routledge and Kegan Paul, 1965).
Comments by Brain and Price.

1259. Solley, Charles M., and Murphy, Gardner, Development of
the Perceptual World, (New York: Basic Books,
1960).
A psychology of perception implies a theory of learning.
Learning is dependent upon motivation. The authors
review numerous works in an attempt to fit them into the
concepts sketched above.

1260. Soltis, Jonas F., Seeing, Knowing and Believing: A

Study of the Language of Visual Perception, (London: George Allen and Unwin, 1966).
Part I contains discussion and criticism of Ryle, War-nock, Chisholm, Hanson and Price. Problems involved in their views can be traced to ambiguity in 'see'. This ambiguity leads to controversy concerning the possibility of unconscious seeing and seeing things that don't exist. Introduces a three-part distinction to resolve this ambiguity: successful and unsucessful seeing are said to involve acquisition of knowledge or beliefs whereas "simple seeing" involves mere discrimination. Discussion of knowledge in seeing--holds that since not all know-ledge involves expectations, not all visual knowledge can be cast into conditional claims. Non-verbal know-ledge acquired by vision introduced via the notion of a "perception-recipe"--the knowledge we possess of the looks of a thing. In Part III he examines failures in seeing--these are cases where we acquire false beliefs. Special attention to illusions.

1261. Sorabji, Richard, "Aristotle on Demarcating the Five Senses," PR 80 (1971), 55-79.
Discussion of Aristotle's De Anima. Argues that one cannot be successful in attempting to define the senses by reference solely to their respective objects, and in this Aristotle is vindicated. Discusses problems with Aristotle's use of the contact criteria for defining the sense of touch.

1262. _____, Aristotle on Memory, (London: Duck-worth, 1972).

1263. Sosa, Ernst, "Propositional Knowledge," Phil Studies 20 (1969), 33-43.
Reply to Gettier-type counterexamples to analysis of knowledge in terms of justified true belief.

1264. Spector, Marshall, "Theory and Observation, I and II," BJPS 17 (1965), 1-20, 89-109.
An attack on the theoretical term/observation term dis-tinction and on the claim that theoretical terms are given only an indirect and partial interpretation through their roles in the framework of a given theory.

1265. Sperling, G., Budiansky, J., Spivak, J. G., and Johnson, M. C., "Extremely Rapid Visual Search: The Maximum Rate of Scanning Letters for the Presence of a Numeral," Science 174 (1971), 307-11.
When observers were required to detect the presence of a numeral in a rapid sequence of alphabetic displays, a reliable but small advantage occurred when the observer knew in advance which numeral was the target.

1266. Spiegel, Irwin M., ed., Readings in the Study of Visually

Perceived Movement, (New York: Harper and Row, 1965).
Articles on real movement by Brown, Ekman and Dahlback, Mandriota, Mintz and Notterman, Gibson, Ludvigh, Smith and Gulick, Johannson. On apparent movement by Gengerelli, Spigel, Sekuler and Ganz, Scott, Jordan and Powell, Weiskrantz, Crutchfield and Edwards. On physiological bases by Smith, Motokawa, Hubel and Wiesel, Grusser-Cornehls, Grusser and Bullock.

1267.   Spiegelberg, Herbert, "Toward a Phenomenology of Exper- ience," APQ 1 (1964), 325-32.
Formulates eight theses regarding the nature of exper- ience.

1268.   Sprague, Elmer, "Beauty," Encyclopedia of Philosophy, Vol. 1, 264.

1269.   Sprigge, Timothy L. S., "The Common-sense View of Physical Objects," I 9 (1966), 339-73.
Using 'sense-datum' in Moore's sense Sprigge argues that the common man takes himself to be aware of sense-data when perceiving a physical object, and that the sense- data are normally thought to be identical with the physical object. Suggests that this is not the logi- cian's senses of 'identity'. Offers an analysis of relational properties and argues that "looks pink to me" is not a relational property.

1270.   _____, "The Privacy of Experience," M 78 (1969), 512-21.
Argues for the possibility of private experiences and private language.

1271.   _____, Facts, Words and Beliefs, (London: Routledge and Kegan Paul, 1970).
Defends a "harmless" version of the sense-datum theory and offers a theory of belief.

1272.   Squires, J. E. Roger, "Visualizing," M 77 (1968), 58-67.
Defends a Rylean position on the status of mental images. Questions the alleged connection between the faculty of visualising and seeing, and argues that the relation between a person and his mental images is not like that between a person and the objects of his senses.
Squires dissents from Ryle's positive analysis of vis- ualising as "mock-seeing" and proposes that visualising is seeming to see something when there is nothing of the sort there to be seen and when we do not believe that we are actually seeing.

1273.   _____, "Depicting," P 44 (1969), 193-204.
A discussion of the question "What makes a painting of

McX a painting of McX?" He rejects several possibilities and concludes that there is no analyzable single relation designated by the 'of' in 'painting of McX'.

1274.   _____, "The Problem of Dreams," P 48 (1973),
         245-59.
         Argues that we are not aware of the events that we dream
         about, and that we do not "remember" but only seem to
         remember, our dreams when we wake.

1275.   Staack, George J., "Berkeley's Phenomenalism," P 50
         (1969), 335-59.

1276.   _____, "Berkeley's New Theory of Vision,"
         Personalist 51 (1970), 106-38.
         Outlines Berkeley's argument in New Theory of Vision.

1277.   _____, "Berkeley and Phenomenalism," MS 47
         (1970), 391-422.
         Spells out the details of the oft-made charge that cur-
         rent phenomenalism is simply Berkeley without God.

1278.   _____, Berkeley's Analysis of Perception,
         (The Hague: Mouton, 1970).

1279.   Stace, W. T., The Nature of the World: An Essay in
         Phenomenalist Metaphysics, (Princeton: Princeton
         University Press, 1940).

1280.   _____, "Are All Empirical Statements Merely
         Hypotheses?" JP 44 (1947), 29-38.
         There is a theoretical sense in which empirical state-
         ments are certain, and another (practical) sense in
         which they are only probable.

1281.   Stadler, Ingrid H., "On 'Seeing As'," PR 67 (1958), 91-
         94.
         A reply to Noel Fleming [#427]. It is not a necessary
         condition of recognizing x as y by sight that one sees
         x as y.

1282.   Stainsby, H. V., "Sight and Sense-data," M 79 (1970),
         170-87.
         Criticizes two aspects of the argument from illusion.
         There are two senses of 'see'--one in which the
         hallucinated persons see a physical object (i.e., the
         sense in which it is correct to say that what Macbeth
         saw was a dagger), and the other in which there is
         nothing to see. It does not follow from cases of varia-
         tion in appearance that what is seen is not a physical
         object. Same sort of objection raised against the
         time-gap argument. Attempts to clarify confusions in
         the notion of perceived size.

1283.   _____, "Austin on Ryle on Seeing and "Seeing","
         M 82 (1973), 608.

1284. Steiner, Mark, "Platonism and the Causal Theory of Know-
         ledge," JP 70 (1973), 57-66.
       Discussion of how the causal theory bears on the know-
       ability of mathematical truths.

1285. Stevens, S. S., and Volkmann, J., "The Quantum of Sensory
         Discrimination," Science 20 (1940), 583-85.
       An argument for the quantal theory of discrimination,
       according to which noticeable differences occur only when
       a certain level of increase in stimulus occurs.

1286.   _____, "The Surprising Simplicity of Sensory
         Metrics," American Psychologist 17 (1962), 29-39.
       Introduces the psychological "power law" which gives the
       relationship between input and output of sensory systems
       in terms of a power function.

1287.   _____, "Quantifying Sensory Experience," in
         Feyerabend and Maxwell, eds., Mind, Matter and
         Method, Essays in Philosophy and Science in Honor
         of Herbert Feigl, (Minneapolis, Minnesota: Univer-
         sity of Minnesota Press, 1966).

1288. Stiles, W. S., "Color Vision: The Approach Through
         Increment Threshold Sensitivity," Proceedings of the
         National Academy of Sciences 45 (1959), 100-14.

1289. Stough, Charlotte L., Greek Scepticism: A Study in
         Epistemology (Berkeley: University of California
         Press, 1969).

1290. Stout, G. F., "Phenomenalism," PAS 39 (1939), 1-18.
       Criticism of phenomenalism on the grounds that it is un-
       verifiable, contradictory to the evidence of sense-per-
       ception and tends to misconstrue the relation between
       what is actual and what is possible.

1291. Strang, Colin, "The Perception of Heat," PAS 61 (1961),
         239-52.
       Discussion of physiological notion of heat sensations
       and the relation of these to heat and coldness in
       objects. Takes up questions as to how the notion of
       temperature arises.

1292. Straus, Erwin, The Primary World of Senses: A Vindica-
         tion of Sensory Experience, (New York: Free Press,
         1963). (translation J. Needleman)

1293. Strawson, P. F., "Professor Ayer's The Problem of Know-
         ledge," P 32 (1957), 302-14.

1294. _____, "Perception and Identification," <u>ASSP</u>
       <u>15</u> (1961), 97-120. Symposium with S. Hampshire.

1295. _____, <u>Individuals</u>, (London: Methuen, 1959).
       Argues that material bodies are basic particulars. The
       personal body has a unique position in perceptual ex-
       periences. Also includes a fascinating chapter des-
       cribing a purely auditory world.

1296. _____, <u>The Bounds of Sense: An Essay on Kant's</u>
       <u>Critique of Pure Reason</u>, (London: Methuen, 1966).
       A Kantian metaphysical examination; the attempt is to
       define the limits of thinking about experience and
       reality.

1297. _____, "Imagination and Perception," in L. L.
       Foster and J. W. Swanson, eds., <u>Experience and</u>
       <u>Theory</u>, (Amherst: University of Massachusetts
       Press, 1970), 31-54.
       A discussion of the role of the imagination (in a cer-
       tain technical sense) in perception as conceived by Kant
       and Hume. Wittgenstein (<u>Investigations</u>) also said to be
       concerned with imagination in this technical sense in his
       treatment of <u>seeing as</u> and aspects. The affinities and
       differences between Kantian and Wittgensteinian accounts
       explored.

1298. Streams, Isabel, "The Grounds of Knowledge," <u>PPR 2</u>
       (1941), 359-75.
       Phenomenologist's account of perception as a synthesis
       between experience and experienced.

1299. Strong, C. A., "The Sensori-Motor Theory of Awareness,"
       <u>JP 36</u> (1939), 393-405.

1300. Suchting, W. A., "Perception and the Time-Gap Argument,"
       <u>PQ 19</u> (1969), 46-56.
       Defends the view that what is seen in the case of an
       exploded star is some past state of the star which exists
       when perceived (though the star itself does not).

1301. Swartz, Robert J., ed., <u>Perceiving, Sensing and Knowing</u>,"
       (Garden City, New York: Anchor, 1956).
       Anthology, includes classic articles by Moore, Broad,
       Warnock, Vesey, Barnes, Chisholm, Ryle, Firth, Paul,
       Lewis, Berlin, Price, Grice, and Quinton.

1302. _____, "Color Concepts and Dispositions," <u>S</u>
       <u>17</u> (1967), 202-22.
       Color-predicates cannot be analysed as purely disposi-
       tional; it is a contingent, not a necessary, truth that
       if x is red and y (a normal perceiver) sees x under
       normal conditions, then x would look red to y.

1303.   _____, "Seeing and Substitutivity," <u>JP 70</u>
           (1973), 526-36.
           Substituting descriptions of what is seen in apparently
           opaque contexts can be accomplished by rewriting such
           sentences so as to include reference to the object of
           sight outside the scope of the perceptual verb.

1304. Swets, John A., Tanner, Wilson P., Jr., and Birdsall,
           Theodore G., "Decision Processes in Perception,"
           <u>Psych Rev 68</u> (1961), 301-40.
           Techniques of statistical decision theory as applied to
           signal detection are held to show quantitative relation-
           ships between sensory stimulus and perceiver's goals and
           previously acquired information.

1305. Tagiuri, Renato, and Petrullo, Luigi, eds., <u>Person Per-
           ception and Interpersonal Behavior</u>, (Stanford:
           Stanford University Press, 1958).

1306. Taube, Mortimer, "A Re-examination of Some Arguments for
           Realism," <u>PS 5</u> (1938), 410-20.
           Examination of two main arguments in defense of naive
           realism--both held to be fallacious.

1307. Taylor, Charles, and Kullman, M., "The Pre-Objective
           World," <u>RM 2</u> (1958), 108-32.
           A study of Merleau-Ponty.

1308.   _____, <u>The Explanation of Behavior</u>, (London:
           Routledge and Kegan Paul, 1964).
           A non-behavioristic theory of behavior with crucial
           sections on intentionality, data language and spatial
           orientation.

1309. Taylor, D. M., "On What Is Seen," in F. N. Sibley, ed.,
           [1227].
           A reply to Warnock.

1310. Taylor, James G., <u>The Behavioral Basis of Perception</u>,
           (New Haven: Yale University Press, 1962).
           Perception is a necessary and predictable consequence of
           the properties of the living organism. Includes a review
           of literature supporting this and an interesting account
           of the inverted spectacles cases. Mathemtical formula-
           tion in Appendix by Seymour Papert.

1311. Taylor, Richard, "Knowledge and Certainty," <u>RM 7</u> (1953),
           679-680.
           Comments by Brandt, Hempel, Firth and Wolhout.

1312.   _____, and Duggan, L. P., "On Seeing Double,"
           <u>PQ 8</u> (1958), 171-74.
           Discussion of the implications of a claim made by Thomas

Reid to the effect that we always see objects doubled
when they are between our eyes and a more distant object
on which our eyes are focused. The authors suggest this
shows that we can be mistaken about how things appear to
us.

1313. Taylor, William, The Relationship Between Psychology and
     Science (Somerset: Martigan, 1964).

1314. Teichmann, Jenny, "Perception and Causation," PAS 70
     (1970-71), 29-41.
     A causal theory of perception represents a physiologi-
     cally-based concern with perception and that some
     objects of sight (e.g., the sky) cannot be regarded as
     originating visual processes and for that reason cannot
     be regarded as causing our seeing them.

1315. Thalberg, Irving, "Looks, Impressions and Incorrigibil-
     ity," PPR 25 (1964), 365-74.
     Statements about the appearances or looks of things, if
     possible at all, can be wrong. However, it is a mistake
     to conclude that what we are wrong about in such cases is
     "the look of a look."

1316. _____, "Ingredients of Perception," A 33
     (1971), 145-55.
     Author attempts to relate three components in seeing--
     (1) neural events, (2) sense-data and (3) objects and
     events that we perceive by sight--in such a way as to
     avoid certain problems. These components are not
     identifiable nor completely separable. Proposes a
     "component analysis" according to which each is a com-
     ponent of an event of visual activity.

1317. Theobald, D. W., "Observation and Reality," M 76 (1957),
     198-207.
     Problem of the "reality" of theoretical entities.

1318. Thomas, George B., "Wittgenstein on Sensations," Phil
     Studies 20 (1969), 19-23.

1319. Thomas, L. E., "Looking," PQ 7 (1957), 109-15.
     Argues against inference from "x looks f" to "x (or
     something) is really f."

1320. Thomas, William J., "Communication Without Sensory
     Overlap," JP 72 (1975), 256-57.
     A critical comment on N. Grossman [#542]. Thomas con-
     tends that the questions raised by Grossman are easily
     answerable. (1) If there were a being with no sensory
     input and no means of manipulating its environment then
     communication would be impossible between such beings
     and humans. (2) For communication to be possible it is

not required that a being share a sense with humans; all
that is required is that the being be able to sense, by
whatever means, gestures made by humans.

1321. Thomason, Richmond H., "Perception and Individuation," in
         Munitz, Milton K., ed , Identity and Existence, (New
         York: New York University Press, 1972),261-85.
       On Hintikka [#653].

1322. Thompson, Judith Harvis, "Molyneux's Problem," JP 71
         (1974), 637-50.
       Attempts to apply possible worlds jargon to the outcome
       of Molyneux's man-born-blind problem. Perhaps, the con-
       clusion is that Molyneux was wrong.

1323. Thornton, M. T., "Ostensive Terms and Materialism,"
         Monist 56 (1972), 193-214.
       Criticism of materialist analysis of color and sensation
       which are held to be dispositions to produce sense
       impressions in sentient beings.

1324. Tibbetts, Paul, "John Dewey and Contemporary Phenomeno-
         logy on Experience and the Subject-Object Relation,"
         Phil Today 15 (1971), 250-75.
       John Dewey's views regarding 'experience' and the 'sub-
       ject-object relation' related to corresponding themes
       in the writings of Merleau-Ponty and Erwin Strauss. The
       'primacy of perception' and the role of the body in
       perception are shown to have important parallels in
       Dewey's thought.

1325. _____, "Phenomenological and Empirical Inade-
         quacies of Russell's Theory of Perception," Phil
         Stud (Ireland) 20 (1972), 98-108.

1326. _____, ed., Perception: Selected Readings in
         Science and Phenomenology, (Chicago: Quadrangle
         Books, 1969).
       Anthology, contains classic papers of neurophysiology
       (Mueller, Brain, Lashley, Sperry, Van Holst, Penfield),
       psychological selections (Hochberg, Gregory, Gibson,
       Piaget, Pritchard Heron and Gebb, Seagall, Campbell,
       and Herskovits, Gregory and Wallace, Heron, Doane and
       Scott) and phenomenological studies (Husserl, Merleau-
       Ponty, Gurwitch, Straus, Cassirer).

1327. _____, "Mead's Theory of the Act and Percep-
         tion: Some Empirical Confirmations," Personalist
         55 (1974), 115-38.
       Includes reports of experiments on relation between vis-
       ual and tactual perception.

1328. Tighe, L. S., and Tighe, T. J., "Discrimination

Learning: Two Views in Historical Perspective,"
Psych Bull 66 (1966), 353-70.
Two major views of nature of discrimination learning:
the mediation view (as held by associationists) and the
differentiation view (primarily developed by J. J. and
E. J. Gibson). These are shown to differ primarily in
the role accorded to the stimulus in learning.

1329. Tilghman, B. R., "Aesthetic Perception and the Problem of
the 'Aesthetic Object'," M 75 (1966), 351-67.
Examination of S. C. Pepper's theory of contextualism,
whereby perception is explained as the result of interaction between an object and a sentient organism that
produces a third thing (not called a sense-datum).

1330. Todd, D. D., "Direct Perception," PPR 35 (1975), 352-62.
A defense, following N. Malcolm, of the direct/indirect
distinction. Todd argues that sense-data should be
regarded as sensible qualities, and can be described
independently of identifying things that have those
qualities.

1331. Tomas, Vincent, "Aesthetic Vision," PR 68 (1959), 52-67.
Distinguishes between the "ordinary" and the "aesthetic"
way of seeing things. Characterizes the latter as
attending to the appearance of a thing rather than to
the thing itself.

1332. Tormey, Alan, The Concept of Expression: A Study in
Philosophical Psychology and Aesthetics, (Princeton: Princeton University Press, 1971).

1333. _____, "Access, Incorrigibility and Identity,"
JP 70 (1973), 115-28.
Discussion of an argument that purports to show that
another person may have incorrigible knowledge of my
being in pain. Considers the question whether knowledge
of the position of our limbs and bodies or states of
visceral organs is perceptual or not, or whether there
is logically privileged access to states of which I (and
no one else) is non-perceptually aware.

1334. Trebicot, Joyce, "Dr. Kenny's Perceptions," M 79 (1970),
142-43.

1335. Tucker, John, "The Television Theory of Perception,"
BJPS 9 (1958), 51-57.
A critical review of J. R. Smythies' Analysis of Percep-
tion.

1336. Uhr, Leonard, ed., Pattern Recognition: Theory, Experiment, Computer Simulations, and Dynamic Models of
Form Perception and Discovery, (New York: Wiley,

1966).
A good collection of classic papers on the items
mentioned in the subtitle.

1337.   _____, Pattern Recognition, Learning and Thought:
Computer-programmed Models of Higher Mental Processes, (Englewood Cliffs: Prentice-Hall, 1973).

1338. Unger, Peter, "Our Knowledge of the Material World," APQ
Monograph Series, No. 4-6 (1970-1972), 40-61.
Argues against scepticism of the Cartesian variety.
A person knows something (p) if and only if it is "not
accidental" that he is right about its being the case
that p. When one consciously (as opposed to sublimin-
ally) perceives a material thing one cannot help
believing that it exists. Our consciously perceiving a
material thing may "directly bring it about that" we
cannot help but be right about its being the case that
the material thing is there before us.

1339. Urmson, J. O., "Recognition," PAS 56 (1956), 259-80.

1340.   _____, The Objects of the Five Senses, (London:
Oxford University Press, 1968).

1341.   _____, "Memory and Imagination," M 80 (1971),
607.
Urmson restates his denial that we have a case of
imagination only when a mental image is "lifelike and
interesting."

1342. Ushenko, Andrew, "A Theory of Perception," JP 37 (1940),
141-51.
Contrasts representative and direct realism and objects
to both.

1343.   _____, "A Note on the 'Argument from Illusion,'," M 54 (1945), 159-60.

1344.   _____, "A Note on Russell and Naive Realism,"
JP 53 (1956), 819-20.

1345. Uttal, William R., "The Psychobiological Silly Season--
or--What happens when Neurophysiological Data
Become Psychological Theories," J of Gen Psychol 84
(1971), 151-66.
Argues there is no straightforward way to use physiological data to draw psychological conclusions; many such
arguments equivocate on terms such as 'coding'.

1346. Van Iten, Richard J., "Berkeley's Realism and His Alleged
Solipsism Re-examined," RIP 22 (1962),   413-22.

152

1347. Vander Veer, Garrett L., "Austin on Perception," RM 17
(1963), 557-67.
Argues against Austin [#72] that although we do not
ordinarily speak of inferring the existence of an
object from seeing it we might, plausibly and usefully,
do so. There is, the author contends, an important
similarity that Austin overlooks between perception and
discursive inference.

1348. Vendler, Zeno, "Verbs and Times," PR 66 (1957), 143-60.
Distinguishes between activities, achievements, accom-
plishments and states on the basis of whether the time
at which each takes place must be definite and unique
or not. Proceeds to consideration of some special problems that arise when we try to classify verbs like 'see'
and 'hear' as belonging to one or another of these
categories.

1349. _____, "Seeing More," JP 71 (1974), 721-22.
Comment on Gareth Matthews [#914].

1350. Ver Eecke, Wilfried, "Interpretation and Perception:
From Phenomenology through Psychoanalysis to
Hermeneutics," IPQ 11 (1971), 372-84.
We can learn more about things-in-themselves by changing
our way of perceiving the world--we cannot know all there
is to know about them all at once though. A partial
rejection of Kant's claim that we can't know things in
themselves.

1351. Vernon, Magdalen Dorthea, A Further Study in Visual Perception, (Cambridge: Cambridge University Press,
1954).

1352. _____, The Psychology of Perception,
(Harmondsworth, Middlesex: Penguin Books, 1962).
An overview of the problems and literature in the
psychology of perception. A good review but little
positive theory is argued.

1353. _____, Perception Through Experience,
(New York: Barnes and Noble, 1970).
A survey of the literature of the last twenty years.
Argues that the processes of identification and classi-
fication depend to a large extent on learning, memory,
attention, reasoning and language.

1354. _____, Experiments in Visual Percep-
tion, (Penguin, 1966).
Anthology, works by: Koffka, Gottschaldt, Fantz, Ghent,
Anderson and Leonard, Julesz, Walk and Gibson, Gibson,
Bergman, and Purdy, Kilpatrick, Smith and Smith, Witkin
and Asch, Thouless, Ittelson, Borresen and Lichte, Jenkin

153

and Hyman, Zeigler and Leibowitz, Brown, Shipley, Kenney
and King, Jones and Bruner, Michotte, Olum, Houssiades,
Bruner and Minturn, Evans and Piggins, Cohen, Zubek,
Pushkar, Sansom and Gowing, Tajfel, Pettigrew, Allport
and Barnett, Bruner and Postman, McGinnies, Lazarus and
McCleary, Rosen, Gardner and Long, Piaget.

1355.   Vesey, G. N. A., "Seeing and Seeing As," PAS 56 (1956),
         109-24. Reprinted in Swartz [#1301].
         All seeing is seeing as, though seeing as does not
         necessarily involve a judgment either about an object or
         about something non-material.

1356.   _____, "Berkeley and Sensations of Heat," PR
         69 (1960), 201-10.
         Discusses three of the arguments Berkeley uses in the
         Dialogues to show that heat and pain cannot exist without
         the mind.

1357.   _____, "Unconscious Perception," ASSP 34
         (1960), 67-78. Symposium with J. P. Day.

1358.   _____, "Berkeley and the Man Born Blind," PAS
         61 (1961), 189-206.
         Examination of arguments used by Berkeley to support the
         claim (in New Theory of Vision) that a man born blind,
         upon suddenly regaining his sight, would see distant
         objects as "in the eye" or "in the mind." Vesey adopts
         a Kantian approach to this problem, arguing that as
         immediate objects of perception, distant objects are not
         outside the mind, but that this is not to impugn their
         reality.

1359.   _____, The Embodied Mind, (London: Allen and
         Unwin, 1965).
         Attack on causal theories of experiences which can be
         construed as exhibiting interaction between mind and
         body. Such causal theories are traced to Cartesian
         dualism. Vesey defends an "embodied mind" view as an
         alternative to dualism and attempts to account for the
         crucial experiences in language that preserves the unity
         of mind and body.

1360.   _____, "Margolis on the Location of Bodily
         Sensations," A 27 (1967), 174-76.
         A reply to Margolis [#898]. Vesey argues primarily
         against Margolis' claim that non-verbal behavior is a
         criterion (especially in the case of an infant) for
         locating sensations. Vesey holds that you cannot feel
         a pain in your right foot if you don't "know about
         having" a right foot.

1361.   _____, "Being and Feeling," PAS 69 (1969),

133-48.
Discussion of the claim (advanced by Strawson and others)
that mental states are the same as felt by the subject
and as observed (via the subject's behavior) by others.

1362.   _____, Perception, (Garden City, New York:
         Anchor Doubleday, 1971).
Monograph-length book. An attack on phenomenalism,
which the author traces to a certain Cartesian tendency
to give a causal answer to a non-causal (conceptual)
question. After attacking this practice and the principles that encourage it, the author discusses (favor-
ably) the claim that the truth of the propositions
"There are physical objects" and "There are things which
can exist unperceived" are conceptual, rather than
empirical, truths; moreover if treated as empirical
claims they can be shown to be true by the same process
of justification used in showing 'There is a cat in the
room' true. Introduces the term 'epistemic appearances'
to speak of that about which one cannot make mistakes
when reporting what something appears or looks like.
Epistemic appearances are contrasted with "optical"
appearances (objectively, measurably determinable).
In the final chapters he uses the notion of an epistemic appearance in defending his thesis that philosophical questions about perception are, for the most part,
conceptual rather than causal questions.

1363.   _____, "Analysing Seeing," in F. N. Sibley,
         ed., [#1227].
A reply to Sibley.

1364. Voekel, Theodore S., "Sellars' Treatment of Sensation,"
         Personalist 54 (1973), 130-48.
Three senses of 'sensation' that author believes Sellars
uses. Discussion of Sellars' perceptual theory and how
sensations are expunged from it.

1365. von Fieandt, Kai, The World of Perception, (Homewood,
         Illinois: Dorsey Press, 1966; originally in
         Finnish, 1962).
An interesting and increasingly popular theory of perception which takes into account seeing pictures and
the active nature of the perceiver.

1366. von Senden, Marius, Space and Sight: The Perception of
         Space and Shape in congenitally blind patients,
         before and after operation. With an appendix with
         essays by A. Riesen, G. J. Warnock,. J. Z. Young.
         (translated by Peter Heath). (London: Methuen,
         1960; originally 1932).
A comprehensive study of the cases of persons born blind
who recover sight (Molyneux's problem).

1367. Vurpillot, Eliane, "The Developmental Emphasis," in
       Carterette, Edward C., and Friedman, Morton P.,
       eds., Handbook of Perception.
       Discusses Gibson, Piaget, Held and others.

1368. Waddington, C. H. Behind Appearance, (Edinburgh:
       Edinburgh University Press, 1969).

1369. Wadia, Pheroze S., "Sense-Data and the Infinite Regress
       Argument: Another Look," J Crit Anal 2 (1971), 23-
       28.
       Defense of Ryle's criticism of the sense-datum theory
       that if observing something entails a sense-datum then
       observing that sense-datum must entail another sense-
       datum and so on.

1370. _____, "Can 'The Way Things Seem to Us'
       Ever Guarantee 'The Way they Really Are'?" Phil
       Stud (Ireland) 20 (1972), 90-97.
       Because of conventions governing sense-data, a distinc-
       tion between what would make a statement true and what
       would establish the truth of a statement for someone
       cannot be drawn in the case of sense-datum statements.

1371. Wainwright, W. J., "Mysticism and Sense Perception,"
       Relig Stud 9 (1973), 257-78.
       Mystical experience and normal sense experiences are
       significantly similar.

1372. Wallach, Hans, "The Perception of Motion," Sci Amer 200
       (1959), 56-60.
       We tend to experience motion as an absolute rather than
       a relative process, even though our perception of motion
       depends upon relative displacement.

1373. Wallraff, Charles F., "On Immediacy and the Contemporary
       Dogma of Sense Certainty," JP 50 (1953), 29-39.
       Cites psychological studies by Brunswik and others to
       support a theory of unconscious inference in perception.

1374. _____, "Sense-Datum Theory and Observa-
       tional Fact: Some Contributions of Psychology to
       Epistemology," JP 55 (1958), 20-32.
       Discusses definitions of 'sense-datum' and current psy-
       chological research to discover whether psychologists
       have found any entities corresponding to definition.

1375. _____, Philosophical Theory and Psycho-
       logical Fact: An Attempted Synthesis, (Tucson:
       University of Arizona, 1961).

1376. Walsh, Dorothy, "Appearances," PQ 18 (1968), 61-65.
       On Gibson [#499].

1377. Walters, Bruce, "Basic Sentences and Incorrigibility,"
       PS 9 (1942), 239-44.
       Agrees with Russell's account of basic sentences
       according to which there are degrees of corrigibility
       and basic sentences are least corrigible of any.

1378. Walton, Kendall, "The Dispensibility of Perceptual
       Inferences," M 72 (1963), 357-68.
       Argues that any fact that can be inferred from sense
       perception could also be known directly in perception
       if the circumstances were slightly different.

1379. Ward, Andrew, "What's Not Really Wrong with Phenomenal-
       ism," AJP 51 (1973), 245-52.
       If one rejects the false assumption that an objectively
       existing external world must be the way common-sense
       dictates, then realism is seen to involve equally
       improbable assumptions, for however our sensations are
       ordered there might be an external world ordered in the
       same way. The probability of our sensations being
       ordered in the way they actually are is extremely low,
       but, the author contends, no lower than the probability
       of their being ordered in some other way. Concludes
       that phenomenalism cannot be dismissed on the grounds
       that realism is a simpler hypothesis.

1380. Ward, Keith, "The Headless Woman," A 29 (1969), 196.
       Comments on a case discussed by J. L. Austin in [#72].

1381. _____, "The Ascription of Experiences," M 79
       (1970), 415-20.
       Examines and criticizes arguments given by Strawson in
       Individuals which are designed to show that persons are
       logically primitive particulars.

1382. Warnock, G. J., "Concepts and Schematism," A 9 (1949),
       77-82.
       Given the visual criteria for having a concept, Kant's
       question in the Schematism as to how subsumption of
       intuitions under pure concepts is possible either makes
       no sense or is not answered by Kant.

1383. _____, "Empirical Propositions and Hypothetical
       Statements," M 60 (1951), 90-94.
       Discussion and extension of I. Berlin's article [#126].
       Warnock employs Strawson's distinction between a sentence
       and the use of a sentence to refine Berlin's analysis of
       material object sentences. Once these are correctly
       analyzed, phenomenalism will be successfully undermined,
       it is contended.

1384. _____, Berkeley, (London: Penguin, 1953).

Competent presentation and critical discussion of
Berkeley's views. Contains chapters on the proper
objects of vision and touch, immediate perception of
ideas, and the relation between perception and existence.

1385. _____, "Seeing," PAS 55 (1955), 201-18.
Reprinted in Swartz [#1301].
Defends a sense of 'see'--called "simple seeing"--in
which it is not necessary that one must notice, be
conscious of, or know anything about what one has seen.

1386. _____, ed., The Philosophy of Perception,
(London: Oxford University Press, 1967).
Anthology, includes articles by Bouwsma, Hirst,
Wollheim, Quinton, Grice, White and Sibley.

1387. _____, "Review of Moore's Commonplace Book and
Lectures on Philosophy," M 77 (1968), 431-46.

1388. _____, "Seeing and Knowing," M 79 (1970), 281-
87.
Review of Dretske [#357].

1389. _____, "On What Is Seen," in F. N. Sibley, ed.,
[#1227].
Detailed discussion of reasons for failure of substitutivity in seeing contexts. Even though 'A sees P' and
'P is S' may both be true there are problems that result
from uniformly accepting the inference to 'A sees S'.
Warnock argues that the cause of these problems are of
two varieties--the 'is' not being the 'is' of identity,
and the 'S' not being the proper sort of term to replace
'P' in the original sentence. A detailed discussion of
the star-speck case.

1390. Wathen-Dunn, Weiant, ed., Models for the Perception of
Speech and Visual Forms, (Cambridge, Massachusetts:
MIT Press, 1967).
A symposium with contributors from many backgrounds on
vision and speech perception and recognition.

1391. Watling, John, "The Causal Theory of Perception," M 59
(1950), 539-40.
Comment on A C. Lloyd [#824].

1392. _____, "About A. J. Ayer's The Problem of Knowledge," RIP 12 (1958), 75-85.

1393. _____, "Phenomenalism Flawed," I 6 (1963), 196-
99.
Phenomenalism cannot account for the difference between
illusions and veridical perception.

1394.   Watson, A. J., "Consciousness and Perception in Psycho-
            logy," ASSP 40 (1966), 85-100. Symposium with U.
            T. Place.
        Discusses reasons why psychologists have avoided the
        topic of consciousness. It is argued that the notion of
        perception has been too widely construed, so that an
        implicit appeal to consciousness is made in the explana-
        tion of behavior based on perception. Suggests that the
        term 'perception' might be dispensed with in theoretical
        psychology.

1395.   Watson, George, "Apparent Motion and the Mind-Body
            Problem," BJPS 2 (1950), 236-47.
        Recent evidence regarding the phenomena of apparent
        motion argued to present difficulties for several
        theories concerning the mind-body relation.

1396.   Weintraub, D. J., "Rectangle Discriminability: Percep-
            tual Relativity and the Law of ptägnanz," J Exp
            Psychol 88 (1971), 1-11.
        Percepts are reconstructions of real world objects and
        events. The perceiver is a decision making system that
        compares input with storage to make a decision about
        what is "out there".

1397.   Weiss, Paul, "The Perception of Stars," RM 6 (1952),
            233-38.
        Discussion and criticism of the time-gap argument.

1398.   Weisstein, Naomi, "What the Frog's Eye Tells the Human
            Brain: Single Cell Analyzers in the Human Visual
            System," Psych Bull 72 (1969), 157-76.
        Discussion of investigation of single units in human
        visual system discussed by behavioral and visual masking
        techniques. Includes extensive bibliography on similar
        studies involving single cell analyzers in frog's eye
        and visual masking technique.

1399.   _____, "Beyond the Yellow-Volkswagen Detector
            and the Grandmother Cell: A General Strategy for
            the Exploration of Operations in Human Pattern
            Recognition," in R. L. Solso, ed., Contemporary
            Issues in Cognitive Psychology: The Loyola Sympo-
            sium, (Washington: Winston, 1973), 17-51.
        On the use of masking to study visual processing.

1400.   Wells, Donald A., "Basic Propositions in Ayer and
            Russell," JP 51 (1954), 124-27.

1401.   Wheatley, John, "Like," PAS 62 (1962), 99-116.

1402.   White, Alan R., G. E. Moore: A Critical Exposition,
            (Oxford: Blackwell, 1958).

Section 8 deails with the sense-datum theory of perception. A critical, and often clarifying, recount of Moore's position.

1403.   _____, "Mr. Hartnack on Experience," <u>A 14</u> (1953), 26.

1404.   _____, "The Causal Theory of Perception," <u>ASSP</u> <u>35</u> (1961), 153-68. Symposium with H. P. Grice. Discusses details of Grice's argument.

1405.   _____, "Attending and Noticing," <u>PAS 63</u> (1963), 103-26.

1406.   _____, "The Alleged Ambiguity of 'See'," <u>A 24</u> (1963), 1-5.

1407.   _____, <u>Attention</u>, (Oxford: Blackwell, 1964). Analyzes the concepts of <u>attention</u>, <u>notice</u>, <u>awareness</u> and <u>consciousness</u>. The concepts are contrasted with others superficially similar to them, e.g., <u>noticing</u> and <u>attending</u>, <u>perceiving</u>, <u>feeling</u> and <u>becoming aware</u>.

1408.   _____, <u>The Philosophy of Mind</u>, (New York: Random House, 1967).
An introductory level survey of theories and topics in the philosophy of mind; includes a discussion of the concept of <u>attention</u>.

1409.   _____, "Seeing What is Not There," <u>PAS 70</u> (1969), 61-74.
Discussion of Anscombe's view that perceptual verbs are intentional. White counters this with a distinction between elliptical and non-elliptical uses of words to explain the apparent divergent senses of perceptual terms which Anscombe's thesis was introduced to explain.

1410. Whitely, C. H., "The Causal Theory of Perception," <u>PAS</u> <u>40</u> (1940), 89-102.
Defends a version of the causal theory according to which the causal relation between sense-data and physical objects is <u>felt</u> as such, and leads us to look beyond sense-data for an explanation of their occurrence.

1411.   _____, "Physical Objects," <u>P 34</u> (1959), 142-49.
Argues that the supposition that there are physical objects is a convenient, explanatory and theoretical hypothesis.

1412.   _____, "Sense-Data," <u>P 44</u> (1969), 187-92.
Includes a general characterization of the supposed differences between sense-data and material objects. Judgments about sense-data are not indubitable. To introduce sense-data <u>via</u> the argument from illusion is

to ignore the distinction between expressing tentative
beliefs and reporting sense-data with use of words like
"appears" and "looks". A more promising introduction of
sense-data would be based on unphilosophical reports of
them--e.g., in an oculist's exam.

1413. Whitemore, Charles, "Perception and Experiment," JP 54
(1957), 401-09.
Discusses significance of scientific tools that extend
sensory experience.

1414. Whyte, Lancelot Law, "Some Thoughts on Certainty in
Physical Science," BJPS 14 (1964), 32-38.
Discusses the rule relating 230 types of crystals to 230
geometrically defined infinite three-dimensional space
groups. Suggests that there may be a special branch of
physical science developed to describe the atomic con-
stitution of physical systems in terms of the three-
dimensional Euclidean character of visual space.

1415. Wieman, H. N., "Perception and Cognition," JP 40 (1943),
73-77.
Distinguishes "true" and "false" perception--allies
himself with C. I. Lewis.

1416. Wiener, Norbert, "The Role of the Observer," PS 3 (1936),
307-19.
Discussion of the generalized application of maxims taken
from development of quantum theory to all scientific
explanation.

1417. Wild, John, "The Concept of The Given in Contemporary
Philosophy: its origin and limitation," PPR 1
(1940), 70-82.

1418. _____, "Berkeley's Theories of Perception: A Phenomenological Critique," RIP 7 (1953), 134-56.
Includes extensive bibliography.

1419. _____, "An Examination of Critical Realism with
Special Reference to Mr. C. D. Broad's Theory of
Sensa," PPR 14 (1953), 143-67.

1420. Wilkerson, T. E., "Transcendental Arguments," PQ 20
(1970), 200-12.
An account of the logical status of the propositions
involved in Kant's Transcendental Deduction.

1421. _____, "Seeing-As," M 82 (1973), 481-96.
On the bases of a number of examples of 'seeing-as' and
'noticing an aspect' taken from the Investigations the
author distinguishes two senses of 'seeing-as', and then
eliminates one, leaving a set of jointly necessary

161

conditions for seeing[2] something as a Ø (the Wittgensteinian sense of 'seeing-as'). The conditions are
(1) the object I see is not Ø, or (ii) I do not see it
under the description "Here is a Ø", or (iii) Ø is not
a phenomenal or structural property (or all three).

1422. Williams Bernard, "The Temporal Ordering of Perceptions
            and Reactions," in F. N. SIbley [#1227].
        A reply to O'Shaughnessy.

1423. Williams, C. J. F., "Form and Sensation," ASSP 39
            (1964), 139-54. Symposium with R. J. Hirst.
        Discusses the problem raised by Aristotle and Plato
        whether in perception we in some sense take on the form
        of the thing sensed.

1424. _____, "Are Primary Qualities Qualities?"
            PQ 19 (1969), 319-23.
        Attempt to apply a nominalistic reduction to propositions
        in which primary quality-terms appear predicatively to
        propositions in which they occur non-predicatively. This
        sort of reduction can be used to elucidate Locke's dis-
        tinction between primary and secondary qualities.

1425. Willis, Richard, "The Phenomenalist Theory of the
            World," M 66 (1957), 210-21.
        Defense of phenomenalism as against representationalism.
        Argues we must choose one or the other.

1426. Wilson, John, "Happiness," A 28 (1968), 13-21.

1427. Winch, P. G., "The Notion of 'Suggestion' in Thomas
            Reid's Theory of Perception," PQ 3 (1953), 327-41.
        An attack on Reid's use of the term 'suggestion', as in
        "That sound suggests to me that a coach is passing by."
        Concerns the issue of direct and indirect perception.

1428. Winn, Ralph B., "Reflections on 'Causation and Percep-
            tion'," PR 55 (1946), 77-80.

1429. Wisdom, John, Other Minds, (Oxford: Blackwell, 1952).
        A sustained examination of the difference between first
        and third person psychological ascriptions by Wittgen-
        stein's most interesting student.

1430. Wisdom, J. O., "The Analysis of Sense-Data," A 2 (1934),
            78-80.

1431. _____, "The Descriptive Interpretation of
            Science," PAS 44 (1944), 91-106.

1432. _____, "Perception-Statements," PAS 49 (1949),
            47-64.

162

1433. Withers, R. F. J., "Epistemology and Scientific Stra-
tegy," <u>BJPS 10</u> (1959), 89-102.
Discussion of problems surrounding the Golgi apparatus
in biological science and the role that epistemological
assumptions play in formulating solutions to such
biological problems.

1434. Witkin, Herman A., "The Perception of the Upright," <u>Sci
Amer 200</u> (1959), 50-56.
Experiments with tilted rooms, tilted figures and perception of embedded figures suggest that ability to
orient one's body to a vertical axis in a tilted environment is correlated with the ability to perceive embedded
geometrical figures. The latter ability has been
associated with a personality type called "field
independence."

1435. _____, "Psychological differentiation and
forms of pathology," <u>Journal of Abnormal Psychology 70</u> (1965), 317-36.
Individuals exhibit certain characteristic differences
which he calls perceptual "styles" and that these are
reflected in differences in how a person experiences
objects (including his/her own body) relative to a given
field, (figure-ground differentiation).

1436. Wittgenstein, Ludwig, <u>Philosophical Investigations</u>,
(translated by G. E. M. Anscombe) (New York:
Macmillan Co., 1953, 3rd edition, 1958).
There are many references thoughout this work to
problems of or related to perception. Of special impor-
tance is the discussion of the concept of "seeing as"
that occurs in Part II, section XI.

1437. _____, <u>The Blue and Brown Books</u>, (Oxford:
Basil Blackwell, 1958).
Preliminary studies for the <u>Philosophical Investigations</u>.
Discussions throughout of color words and their uses.

1438. _____, "Notes for Lectures on "Private
Experiences" and "Sense Data"," <u>PR 77</u> (1968), 275-
320.

1439. Wittreich, Warren J., "Visual Perception and Personality," <u>Sci Amer 200</u> (1959), 56-60.
Studies involving distorted rooms (Ames rooms) show that
our perception of size and shape of other persons is
affected by our emotional relationship with them.

1440. Wodehouse, Helen, "Colour: An Alternative Statement,"
<u>P 13</u> (1938), 81-84.
Defends a realistic theory of colors.

1441. Wohlwill, Joachim F., "The Definition and Analysis of

Perceptual Learning," <u>Psych Rev 65</u> (1958), 283-95.
Evaluation of criticisms of the "specificity theory" of
perceptual learning, according to which perceptual
learning consists of progressive elaboration of features
and responding to factors of stimulation not previously
responded to. Argues that clarification of criterion of
perceptual learning needed in order to evaluate the
theory and objections to it. A criterion offered that
provides for a distinction between learning based on
perceptual functions and learning based on response
association. Includes bibliography.

1442. _____, "Developmental Studies of Percep-
    tion," <u>Psych Bull 57</u> (1970), 249-88.
    A good review of previous developmental studies.

1443. Wolf, Erik, "American Philosophy," <u>Encyclopedia of
    Philosophy</u>, Vol. 1, 88.

1444. Wolff, Robert Paul, "Hume's Theory of Mental Activity,"
    <u>PR 69</u> (1960), 289-310.

1445. Wolgast, Elizabeth H., "Perceiving and Impressions," <u>PR</u>
    <u>67</u> (1958), 226-36.
    Argues against the claim that having an illusion is just
    like seeing--the two are not comparable. Illusions are
    cases in which we are very likely to make certain sorts
    of mistakes.

1446. _____, "The Experience in Perception,"
    <u>PR 69</u> (1960), 165-82.
    Discussion and criticism of the view that there is a
    peculiar experience that is essentially involved in
    perceiving.

1447. _____, "Qualities and Illusions," <u>M 71</u>
    (1962), 458-73.

1448. _____, "A Question About Colors," <u>PR 71</u>
    (1962), 328-39.
    Raises question what 'blue' means when used to talk
    about the color of an object and when used to talk about
    the color of the sky.

1449. Wollheim, Richard, "The Difference Between Sensing and
    Observing," <u>ASSP 28</u> (1954), 219-40. Symposium with
    R. J. Hirst. Reprinted in Warnock [#1386].

1450. _____, <u>On Drawing An Object</u>, (London: H. C.
    Lewis, 1965).
    Wittgensteinian reflections.

1451. Wolman, B. B., ed., <u>Scientific Psychology: Principles</u>

and Approaches, (New York: Basic Books, 1965).
Contains articles by Abram Amsel, H. L. Ansbacher, D. M.
Armstrong, Richard C. Atkinson, Peter Bertocci, William
Bevan, R. C. Calfee, R. D. Cumming, Frederich B. Davis,
Morton Deutsch, W. H. Gantt, Jean-Blaise Grize, Mary
Henle, Otto Klineberg, Tadeusz Kotarbinski, L. S. Kubie,
B. Mandlebrot, Charles Morris, Arne Naess, Ernest Nagel,
R. S. Peters J. Piaget, K. H. Pribram, A. Rapaport,
G. Razran, B. F. Ritchie, M. Scriven, J. P. Seward, G. J.
Warnock, B. B. Wolman.

1452. Wolterstorff, Nicholas, "Qualities," PR 69 (1960), 183-
          200.
       Articulates two identity-criteria for qualities corres-
       ponding to nominalism and realism and suggests that the
       choice between them is arbitrary.

1453. Wood, Charles C., Goff, William R. and Day, Ruth S.,
          "Auditory Evoked Potentials during Speech Percep-
          tion," Science 173 (1971), 1248-51.
       Argues that different neural responses occur in the left
       hemisphere during the analysis of linguistic and non-
       linguistic parameters of the same acoustic signal.

1454. Wood, Ledger, "Inspection and Introspection," PS 7
          (1940), 220-28.
       Distinguishes inspection and introspection and suggests
       that the distinction has been misconstrued by both psy-
       chologists and epistemologists. Rightly made it affords
       a clarification of psychological methodology.

1455. _____, The Analysis of Knowledge, (Princeton:
          Princeton University Press, 1941).

1456. Woodger J. H., "Proper Objects," M 65 (1956), 510-15.
       Suggests that "views" stand to the sense of sight as
       "sounds" to the sense of hearing, though the "proper"
       objects of both senses are physical objects.

1457. Woodworth, R. S., and N. Schlosberg, Experimental Psy-
          chology, (New York: Holt, Reinhart and Winston,
          1954, earlier 1938).
       A schema theory of perception allowing for correction
       by experience.

1458. Woolhouse, Roger, "Berkeley, The Sun That I See By Day
          and That Which I Imagine By Night," P 43 (1968),
          152-60.
       Berkeley cannot by his own criteria distinguish ade-
       quately between the real, the illusory, and the fanciful.

1459. Wright, J. R. G., "Sensa," Encyclopedia of Philosophy,
          Vol. 7,   407.

1460. Wynburn, G. M., Pickford, R. W., Hirst, R. J., <u>Human Senses and Perception</u>, (Toronto: University of Toronto Press, 1964).
A study of human perception from the points of view of biology, psychology and philosophy. Book consists of three parts in which each of these areas is treated separately. In part on the physiology of each of the senses is discussed. Part two treats the psychology of perception. Topics include perception of size, shape and distance, time, movement and causality, perceptual learning and the influence of individual and social factors in perception. Part three contains discussions of alternative philosophical theories of perception. It is argued that orthodox theories of perception are based on an interactionist theory of mind, and that once this theory is rejected in favor of a "double-aspect" conception of mental activity a more adequate philosophical approach to perception is possible. A comprehensive and valuable book.

1461. Yaure, Margaret, "The Concept of Awareness," <u>J Thought 8</u> (1973), 259-67.

1462. Yilmaz, Huseyin, "Color Vision and a New Approach to General Perception," in E. E. Bernard and M. R. Kare, eds., <u>Biological Prototypes and Synthetic Systems</u>, (New York: Plenum, 1962), 126-41.
Attempts to derive the properties of human color perception from evolutionary requirements. Argues that given various physical parameters and needs for the organism, evolution will produce an optimum detection and recognition device in that organism. Presents a mathematical model for this theory of color perception, and concludes with a section of the general character of what theories of perception should be.

1463. Yolton, John W., "A Defense of Sense-Data," <u>M 57</u> (1948), 2-15.

1464. _____, "The Ontological Status of Sense-Data in Plato's Theory of Perception," <u>RM 3</u> (1949), 21-58.

1465. _____, "Linguistic and Epistemological Dualism," <u>M 62</u> (1953), 20-42.
Discussion of the dualistic presuppositions of the sense-datum theory, and the problem of justifying the influence from sense-datum claims to physical object claims.

1466. _____, "Philosophical Realism and Psychological Data," <u>PPR 19</u> (1958), 486-501.
Philosophy and psychology are both concerned with both empirical data and theory; in philosophy our metaphysics

determines the role that psychological facts will play.

1467. _____, "Broad's View on the Nature and Existence of External Objects," in P. Schilpp, ed., The Philosophy of C. D. Broad, (New York: Tudor, 1959).

1468. _____, "Seeming and Being," PQ 11 (1961), 114-22.
Argues that phenomenalists use terms in such a way that translation of statements about phenomena into statements about physical objects is impossible.

1469. _____, Thinking and Perceiving, (LaSalle, Illinois: Open Court, 1962).
Discussion of phenomenological and pragmatic theories of perception.

1470. _____, "Gibson's Realism," Synthese 19 (1968-69), 400-07.
Argues against Gibson and for a reductive theory of sensory information. Reply by Gibson, pp. 408-09.

1471. _____, "Perceptual Consciousness," in Knowledge and Necessity, Royal Institute of Philosophy Lectures, Vol. 3 (London: Macmillan, 1970), 34-50.
Argues that perceptual consciousness is our way of having a world. Cites Merleau-Ponty and Melanie Klein as support. Perceptual consciousness is a meaning response to environmental stimuli.

1472. Yost, R. M., Jr., "Professor Price on Perspectival Illusion," PR 71 (1962), 202-17.
Discussion and clarification of the notion of perspectival size as it occurs in Price [#1093].

1473. _____, "Price on Appearing and Appearances," JP 60 (1963), 328-33.

1474. Young, J. Z., Doubt and Certainty in Science, The B. B. C. Reigh Lectures, (Oxford: The Clarendon Press, 1951).
Distinguished anatomy professor's reflections on the brain and its functioning. Deals with the analogy between the brain and a calculating machine.

1475. Zemach, E. M., "Seeing, 'Seeing', and Feeling," RM 23 (1969), 3-24.
Ryle's distinction between seeing and "seeing" (imagining that one sees) is based on a misguided desire for clearly defined concepts. Yet the distinction thus made is neither clearly demarcated nor exhaustive. Ryle and the phenomenalist are operating under similar revisionist motivations.

1476. _____, "Pains and Pain-Feelings," R 13 (1971),
150-57.

1477. _____, "The Nature of Consciousness," Dialectica
27 (1973), 43-65.
Argues there is no such thing as consciousness or conscious states of anything--that perceiving is not a
conscious state of a perceiver--agrees with Malcolm and
Ryle but not with their reasons for holding such a view.

1478. Zener, Karl, "The Significance of Experience of the
Individual for the Science of Psychology," in
Feigl, H., Scriven, M., and Maxwell, G., eds.,
Minnesota Studies in the Philosophy of Science II,
(Minneapolis, University of Minnesota Press, 1958),
354-69.
Critique of behaviorism from a Gestalt point of view;
argues that direct awareness of the phenomenal field is
a crucial kind of datum for human psychology.

1479. _____, and Gaffron, Mercedes, "Perceptual Experience: An Analysis of its Relations to the External World Through Internal Processings," in S.
Koch, ed., Psychology: A Study of a Science,
(New York: McGraw-Hill, 1962), Vol. 4, 515-618.
Account of experiential aspects of a theory of perception. It is argued that traditional psychological
accounts have left out reference to experiental factors.
Neurophysiological phases of perceptual processes distinguished and described. Investigation of the concept
of behavior and its relationship to cognitive processes.
Methodological issues concerning design and executions
of perceptual experiments discussed. Perceptual organization discussed in terms of phenomenological qualities.
Interesting points made concerning light-dark and left-
right reversal and textural cues in pictures.

1480. Ziedins, R., "Conditions of Observation and States of
Observers," PR 65 (1956), 299-323.
Discusses what constitutes "standard conditions" for
observation.

1481. _____, "The Possibility of Scepticism About Perception," PQ 16 (1966), 329-40.
Scepticism about perception is possible but not inevi-
table.

1482. _____, "Knowledge, Belief and Perceptual Experience," AJP 44 (1966), 70-88.
Defends direct realism.

1483. Zinkernagel, Peter, "On the General Problem of Objective Relativity," M 71 (1962), 33-45.
Formulates three fundamental rules of language and

and argues that the attempt to explain the meanings of
physical object terms by means of sensation terms
violates these laws and so leads to linguistic nonsense.

1484. Zuckerkandl, V., Sound and Symbol, (London: Routledge
           and Kegan Paul, 1956) (translated by W. R. Trask).

1485. Zusne, Leonard, Visual Perception of Form, (New York:
           Academic Press, 1970).
      A good and thorough review of the data and theories of
      form perception.

INDEX

Abstraction: 532, 548, 1072, 1073, 1074, 1075.

Adaptation: 60, 597, 634, 635, 696, 773, 1149, 1310.

Aesthetics: 20, 49, 50, 51, 52, 108, 111, 125, 142, 253, 368,
    387, 463, 496, 508, 509, 513, 515, 538, 587, 705, 713,
    714, 804, 847, 918, 921, 939, 1040, 1041, 1079, 1113,
    1137, 1231, 1268, 1273, 1329, 1331, 1332, 1450.

After-Image: 17, 74, 224, 404, 730, 865, 891, 897.

Appearances (Appearing Statements): 8, 30. 95, 96, 258, 262,
    263, 265, 269, 314, 499, 510, 527, 612, 704, 766, 768,
    769, 770, 789, 793, 837, 844, 849, 856, 955, 958, 964,
    1019, 1058, 1097, 1108, 1161, 1312, 1331, 1368, 1376, 1473.

Aristotle: 152, 153, 576, 577, 745, 849, 1182, 1232, 1261,
    1262, 1423.

Armstrong, D. M.: 200, 288, 334, 428, 431, 458, 526, 630, 678,
    716, 849, 922, 984, 996, 1023, 1078, 1146, 1226.

Attention: 89, 198, 289, 333, 384, 736, 851, 949, 954, 987,
    1385, 1405, 1407, 1408.

Austin, John L.: 67, 83, 373, 402, 422, 594, 606, 663, 753,
    798, 858, 1032, 1103, 1283, 1347, 1380.

Awareness (see also Attention and Consciousness): 28, 133, 517,
    608, 669, 683, 726, 860, 863, 898, 988, 1113, 1148, 1156,
    1220, 1299, 1461.

Ayer, A. J.: 35, 122, 123, 352, 392, 441, 541, 829, 833, 864,
    883, 1088, 1094, 1119, 1196, 1222, 1293, 1392, 1400.

Basic Propositions: 75, 76, 79, 1067, 1106, 1191, 1377, 1400.

Behaviorism: 519, 521, 620, 926, 1052, 1165, 1170, 1216, 1308,
    1310, 1478.

Belief: 24, 46, 264, 285, 311, 351, 357, 447, 524, 596, 686,
    790, 811, 838. 839, 922, 968, 984, 1006, 1064, 1065, 1260,
    1271, 1482.

Berkeley, George: 37, 40, 61, 85, 86, 117, 118, 132, 219, 222,
    312, 318, 458, 459, 462, 501, 617, 640, 843, 844, 899,
    901, 993, 1012, 1013, 1014, 1032, 1047, 1049, 1067, 1118,
    1179, 1182, 1229, 1230, 1275, 1276, 1277, 1278, 1346,
    1356, 1358, 1384, 1418, 1458.

Boring, E. G.: 877.

Brentano, Franz: 855, 952.

Broad, C. D.: 96, 150, 474, 475, 646, 802, 889, 932, 1096, 1251, 1419, 1467.

Categories: 130, 212, 214, 250, 982, 1128, 1153, 1157, 1211.

Causal Theory: 110, 307, 311, 317, 336, 352, 401, 540, 654, 723, 763, 871, 930, 933, 951, 1006, 1025, 1038, 1090, 1120, 1138, 1145, 1202, 1218, 1284, 1314, 1362, 1391, 1404, 1410, 1428.

Certainty (see also Incorrigibility): 71, 72, 83, 90, 264, 305, 423, 424, 511, 638, 729, 767, 794, 881, 896, 946, 1110, 1132, 1228, 1280, 1311, 1373, 1414.

Chisholm, Roderick: 103, 315, 419, 421, 629, 729, 805, 822, 856, 922, 943, 1062, 1064, 1205, 1260.

Cognitive Theories: 51, 127, 131, 143, 158, 218, 476, 530, 596, 726, 792, 809, 839, 900, 912, 980, 981, 1027, 1035, 1075, 1092, 1163, 1185, 1186, 1187, 1226, 1353, 1362, 1365, 1378, 1415.

Color: 23, 47, 53, 59, 68, 134, 135, 136, 137, 138, 176, 234, 251, 319, 335, 348, 397, 506, 580, 598, 602, 603, 659, 694, 716, 741, 806, 825, 878, 935, 936, 1003, 1006, 1021, 1029, 1041, 1063, 1070, 1101, 1142, 1181, 1225, 1236, 1239, 1288, 1302, 1323, 1440, 1448, 1462.

Computers: 159, 244, 468, 472, 476, 480, 522, 569, 949, 1183, 1184, 1336, 1337.

Concepts (see also Categories): 228, 473, 811, 976, 1092, 1382.

Consciousness (see also Awareness): 98, 149, 165, 332, 372, 396, 410, 546, 782, 971, 1054, 1075, 1184, 1190, 1394, 1471, 1477.

Depth (Distance) Perception: 40, 186, 481, 482, 504, 711, 742, 846, 932, 1047, 1071.

Descartes: 171, 911, 1014, 1109, 1143.

Developmental (see also Infant Perception): 145, 146, 173, 174, 175, 213, 440, 749, 841, 857, 1033, 1034, 1139, 1140, 1158, 1259, 1367, 1442.

Dewey, John: 204, 373, 1324.

Direct Perception (see also Immediate): 296, 490, 492, 494, 498, 553, 860, 880, 1050, 1108, 1117, 1147, 1167, 1240, 1330, 1427.

171

Direct Realism (see also Direct Perception): 7, 39, 41, 106, 524, 662, 922.

Discrimination: 101, 121, 409, 742, 801, 830, 905, 1037, 1070, 1076, 1129, 1141, 1236, 1285, 1328, 1396.

Dreams: 61, 695, 738, 833, 882, 1020, 1274.

Drug Perception: 698, 909, 1247, 1249.

Empiricism: 116, 158, 162, 257, 269, 418, 517, 542, 599, 611, 681, 682, 722, 761, 803, 821, 823, 834, 868, 1057, 1135, 1202, 1207.

Esthetics (see Aesthetics)

Flesh: 446

Form Perception: 65, 347, 403, 487, 507, 641, 665, 672, 722, 1037, 1235, 1336, 1390, 1423, 1485.

Frogs: 816, 1398.

Functionalism: 48, 216, 217, 332, 480, 787, 1077.

Gestalt Theories: 49, 247, 389, 471, 497, 570, 572, 772, 774, 775, 842, 1014, 1026, 1101, 1133, 1478.

Gibson, J. J.: 178, 393, 502, 553, 554, 573, 619, 719, 853, 1076, 1328, 1470.

Given (The): 102, 652, 655, 809, 821, 823, 910, 1036, 1162, 1213, 1417.

Hallucination: 39, 72, 183, 252, 375, 495, 524, 627, 828, 905, 1038, 1117, 1247, 1253.

Hearing: 32, 98, 278, 885, 892, 959, 980, 1001, 1002, 1043, 1044, 1160, 1224, 1295, 1484.

Hume, David: 40, 271, 287, 429, 432, 790, 969, 1019, 1297, 1444.

Idealism: 148, 151, 280, 910.

Identification: 66, 71, 489, 492, 581, 582, 657, 658, 1294, 1353.

Illusion: 31, 39, 41, 55, 56, 57, 72, 203, 422, 454, 457, 504, 530, 531, 532, 534, 535, 561, 588, 621, 633, 658, 660, 664, 679, 708, 709, 710, 711, 712, 743, 745, 751, 754, 764, 777, 799, 808, 828, 833, 845, 864, 908, 994, 1005, 1034, 1038, 1058, 1093, 1108, 1124, 1194, 1196, 1228, 1282, 1343, 1393, 1395, 1412, 1445, 1447, 1472.

Image: 18, 307, 321, 327, 328, 347, 432, 460, 525, 583, 585, 586, 627, 750, 781, 797, 1252, 1253.

Image, Retinal: 120, 341, 342, 343, 395, 449, 458, 609, 610, 628, 850, 867, 992, 1014, 1101, 1149, 1341.

Imagining: 19, 61, 91, 240, 338, 339, 706, 1059, 1137, 1272, 1297.

Immediate Perception: 41, 42, 46, 179, 241, 301, 374, 556, 653, 703, 735.

Incorrigibility (see Certainty): 41, 67, 179, 250, 408, 694, 703, 834, 924, 1156, 1217, 1225, 1315, 1333, 1377.

Induction: 759, 982, 1019, 1031.

Infant Perception: 173, 174, 175, 403, 409, 478, 482, 484, 736, 749, 898, 1021.

Information: 44, 64, 173, 175, 178, 197, 205, 468, 484, 533, 536, 556, 558, 559, 934, 939, 949, 980, 981, 987, 1060, 1124, 1183.

Intentionality: 34, 159, 160, 168, 265, 266, 270, 275, 332, 354, 415, 544, 549, 784, 818, 855, 943, 952, 1078, 1147, 1205, 1308, 1409.

Introspection: 43, 363, 464, 671, 761, 974, 975, 1454.

Judgment (see also Knowledge): 229, 285, 732, 953, 1159, 1246.

Kant, I.: 95, 306, 789, 1210, 1296, 1420.

Knowledge: 71, 102, 116, 118, 565, 568, 579, 596, 599, 608, 611, 648, 649, 650, 651, 652, 697, 720, 787, 817, 852, 903, 919, 997, 1006, 1007, 1027, 1061, 1062, 1063, 1064, 1065, 1100, 1108, 1110, 1111, 1112, 1116, 1117, 1134, 1162, 1163, 1164, 1169, 1219, 1260, 1263, 1293, 1296, 1298, 1311, 1338, 1454, 1482.

Learning, Perceptual: 394, 450, 484, 661, 796, 808, 1033, 1034, 1035, 1076, 1129, 1141, 1144, 1259, 1328, 1337, 1352, 1353, 1441.

Lenin, V. I.: 1017.

Locke, John: 45, 85, 86, 429, 759, 760, 886, 901, 915, 1013, 1014, 1179, 1215.

Looks: 71, 540, 1063, 1222, 1269, 1302, 1315, 1319, 1456.

Mach, E.: 26, 1122.

Malebranche, N.: 124, 915, 1014.

Martians (and other extraterrestrial beings): 282, 539, 542, 1320.

Materialism: 45, 46, 48, 129, 288, 292, 293, 405, 433, 480, 630, 678, 717, 840, 917, 923, 1054, 1055, 1153, 1207, 1237, 1240, 1323.

Meaning: 79, 205, 647, 705, 924, 1165.

Memory: 4, 99, 313, 456, 457, 493, 555, 556, 627, 729, 987, 995, 1073, 1074, 1075, 1086, 1178, 127·4, 1341, 1353.

Merleau-Ponty, Maurice: 94, 303, 362, 446, 538, 783, 859, 926, 927, 928, 929, 1189, 1307, 1324, 1471.

Moore, G. E.: 77, 79, 170, 172, 595, 727, 829, 880, 884, 906, 944, 945, 946, 947, 948, 1080, 1114, 1269, 1387, 1402.

Motion Perception: 337, 431, 481, 488, 489, 776, 777, 1009, 1138, 1195, 1243, 1266, 1372, 1460.

Music Perception: 1043, 1044, 1136.

Naive Realism: 55, 56, 57, 59, 304, 806, 827, 869, 1080, 1306, 1344.

Neurophysiology: 60, 63, 145, 146, 165, 180, 181, 182, 225, 233, 253, 376, 377, 378, 406, 525, 553, 566, 624, 625, 626, 658, 687, 688, 689, 690, 691, 692, 778, 782, 816, 851, 857, 862, 888, 909, 970, 971, 1005, 1008, 1060, 1081, 1082, 1083, 1084, 1085, 1122, 1158, 1248, 1326, 1345, 1398, 1399, 1453, 1460, 1474, 1479.

Non-epistemic Seeing: 351, 357, 863, 1214, 1226, 1385, 1388.

Observation (terms): 18, 25, 36, 236, 239, 259, 292, 295, 355, 390, 411, 443, 588, 590, 591, 631, 632, 637, 642, 643, 779, 813, 814, 812, 854, 874, 875, 916, 1067, 1104, 1106, 1131, 1174, 1182, 1185, 1191, 1206, 1233, 1238, 1264, 1317, 1416, 1449, 1480.

Operationism: 464, 520, 877.

Optics: 14, 112, 448, 449, 832, 1152, 1175.

Pain: 87, 245, 319, 408, 675, 676, 677, 730, 738, 820, 866, 897, 925, 1048, 1197, 1333, 1476.

Parapsychology: 194, 326, 940, 1087, 1192, 1371.

Peirce, C. S.: 518, 953, 1159.

Phenomenalism: 1, 10, 41, 69, 78, 82, 126, 139, 297, 336,
    420, 593, 662, 824, 868, 870, 876, 907, 942, 965, 1010,
    1119, 1132, 1165, 1169, 1182, 1193, 1202, 1208, 1237,
    1238, 1279, 1290, 1362, 1379, 1383, 1393, 1425, 1468,
    1475.

Phenomenology: 125, 169, 195, 220, 303, 368, 372, 379, 546,
    547, 548, 549, 550, 699, 700, 701, 702, 724, 739, 781,
    783, 831, 927, 928, 929, 950, 963, 1043, 1044, 1267,
    1292, 1298, 1324, 1325, 1326, 1350, 1469.

Picture Perception: 111, 142, 154, 371, 496, 508, 509, 532,
    584, 744, 1028, 1137, 1231, 1365.

Plato: 827, 849, 972, 973, 1020, 1423, 1464.

Price, H. H.: 77, 96, 157, 223, 430, 562, 932, 989, 1135,
    1260, 1472, 1473.

Primary Qualities: 41, 85, 118, 189, 455, 837, 901, 958, 1234,
    1235, 1424.

Privacy: 97, 98, 183, 190, 200, 301, 571, 589, 613, 697, 757,
    784, 810, 826, 828, 895, 936, 1011, 1153, 1270, 1436,
    1438.

Psychoanalysis: 756, 1121, 1248, 1350, 1471.

Psychophysics: 64, 88, 121, 155, 215, 217, 299, 393, 519, 520,
    521, 670, 671, 718, 733, 778, 796, 1000, 1009, 1011, 1130,
    1140, 1149, 1180.

Realism: 45, 280, 388, 401, 411, 468, 494, 824, 910, 998,
    1057, 1126, 1127, 1199, 1200, 1201, 1202, 1203, 1204,
    1208, 1237, 1342, 1379, 1419, 1452, 1466, 1482.

Recognition: 231, 244, 290, 346, 383, 427, 445, 795, 1092,
    1128, 1183, 1281, 1336, 1337, 1339, 1462.

Reid, Thomas: 202, 369, 370, 1014, 1427.

Representation: 64, 111, 142, 213, 509, 544, 587, 662, 673,
    915, 918, 1017, 1046, 1231, 1250, 1256, 1258, 1273,
    1332, 1342, 1425, 1450.

Russell, Bertrand: 256, 385, 791, 869, 1164, 1165, 1166, 1167,
    1168, 1169, 1230, 1325, 1344, 1377, 1400.

Ryle, Gilbert: 98, 432, 469, 592, 693, 850, 883, 890, 1011,
    1102, 1170, 1171, 1172, 1173, 1174, 1224, 1260, 1272,
    1283, 1369, 1475.

Scepticism: 171, 836, 882, 886, 936, 946, 1069, 1289, 1338,
    1481.

Schema: 66, 380, 381, 398, 399, 509, 624, 736, 995, 1037, 1073, 1457.

Secondary Quality: 42, 45, 118, 506, 826, 837, 901, 958, 996, 1234, 1239.

Seeing As: 19, 20, 427, 686, 839, 847, 1281, 1355, 1421, 1436.

Seeming (Seems): 8, 81, 191, 308, 353, 654, 656, 1091, 1107, 1468.

Sensation: 12, 14, 16, 26, 34, 42, 97, 105, 106, 115, 166, 167, 224, 227, 229, 276, 291, 310, 314, 319, 363, 364, 370, 405, 452, 500, 511, 520, 521, 528, 539, 574, 580, 588, 589, 590, 614, 615, 620, 647, 665, 668, 676, 677, 684, 716, 717, 726, 759, 760, 809, 818, 820, 821, 859, 889, 890, 894, 895, 896, 898, 904, 905, 912, 917, 918, 981, 988, 990, 998, 1025, 1030, 1042, 1055, 1102, 1105, 1115, 1153, 1163, 1170, 1180, 1193, 1197, 1198, 1203, 1208, 1210, 1212, 1223, 1285, 1286, 1287, 1291, 1292, 1304, 1318, 1323, 1340, 1360, 1364, 1423, 1449, 1459, 1470, 1483.

Sense Datum: 7, 10, 15, 17, 30, 67, 72, 75, 76, 77, 81, 82, 83, 96, 122, 140, 170, 180, 183, 193, 206, 229, 241, 257, 269, 302, 308, 322, 375, 392, 417, 441, 453, 470, 474, 475, 515, 516, 562, 567, 582, 595, 612, 645, 646, 653, 662, 674, 720, 727, 728, 757, 765, 809, 829, 834, 874, 879, 906, 913, 932, 944, 945, 947, 948, 961, 964, 983, 1015, 1016, 1024, 1052, 1067, 1079, 1096, 1097, 1099, 1109, 1142, 1146, 1161, 1164, 1165, 1166, 1167, 1168, 1169, 1170, 1188, 1196, 1216, 1242, 1245, 1254, 1256, 1269, 1271, 1282, 1316, 1321, 1369, 1370, 1374, 1402, 1410, 1412, 1429, 1463, 1464, 1465.

Set: 209, 210, 212, 380, 381, 555, 795, 830, 968, 1265, 1304, 1352, 1353, 1439.

Smell: 941.

Speech Perception: 198, 284, 830, 1390, 1453.

Stimulus: 4, 54, 166, 167, 175, 317, 434, 435, 436, 467, 468, 485, 486, 490, 491, 492, 493, 498, 521, 647, 758, 796, 1129, 1141, 1286, 1287.

Structure: 29, 247, 465, 468.

Subliminal Perception: 133, 344.

Taste: 985.

Time-Lag Argument: 177, 242, 243, 320, 639, 967, 1282, 1300, 1397.